Dance Anima

Dance Anima

Techniques of Vitality

HILARY BERGEN

OXFORD
UNIVERSITY PRESS

OXFORD
UNIVERSITY PRESS

Oxford University Press is a department of the University of Oxford.
It furthers the University's objective of excellence in research, scholarship,
and education by publishing worldwide. Oxford is a registered trade mark of
Oxford University Press in the UK and in certain other countries.

Published in the United States of America by Oxford University Press
198 Madison Avenue, New York, NY 10016, United States of America.

Library of Congress Cataloging-in-Publication Data
Names: Bergen, Hilary author
Title: Dance anima : techniques of vitality / Hilary Bergen.
Description: New York, NY : Oxford University Press, [2026] |
Includes bibliographical references. |
Identifiers: LCCN 2025049444 (print) | LCCN 2025049445 (ebook) |
ISBN 9780197786642 paperback | ISBN 9780197786635 hardback |
ISBN 9780197786673 | ISBN 9780197786666 epub
Subjects: LCSH: Dance—Philosophy
Classification: LCC GV1588 .B47 2025 (print) | LCC GV1588 (ebook) |
DDC 792.8—dc23/eng/20260217
LC record available at https://lccn.loc.gov/2025049444
LC ebook record available at https://lccn.loc.gov/2025049445

DOI: 10.1093/9780197786673.001.0001

Paperback printed by Marquis Book Printing, Canada
Hardback printed by Lightning Source, Inc., United States of America

The manufacturer's authorized representative in the EU for product safety is
Oxford University Press España S.A. of Parque Empresarial San Fernando de Henares,
Avenida de Castilla, 2 – 28830 Madrid (www.oup.es/en or product.safety@oup.com).
OUP España S.A. also acts as importer into Spain of products made by the manufacturer.

For my parents,
Mary and David

Epigraph

After Beau Travail—
Olivia Wood

Self sends a branch to whither before another comes to bloom.

You made your body a glorious machine
and now joy clangs free in utter seriousness.

Wholly of that room and air
and generous generous music and

what internal pulley shudders
ribbed through what grace to yank you, by
your animated center, from the floor?

Repetition gave you glamor and command
and now at the disco by the river's edge
you bash and bash and turn.
Brilliant master-servant you're no longer
metering your ecstasy but

gazing, moving, lunging in the air and as
love-able now as a leaping vein and a
not-death in the morning.

Contents

Preface: Dancing with Miku and Kate

I am standing in a production suite at Concordia University's Milieux Institute, in front of a large computer screen propped up on a low desk, performing the choreography for Kate Bush's iconic song, "Wuthering Heights." The cement floor is cold and hard underfoot—not ideal for dancing—and a white scrim behind me curves where it meets the floor, to give the appearance of a non-background: a vacuum-like space. I am wearing black tights and a leotard so that the Microsoft Xbox 360 Kinect, which is balanced precariously next to the computer monitor, can better recognize my body and read my movements.

The room fills with a deep, powerful humming sound as the heavy Alienware computer—the only one I could find that was outfitted with Windows 7, which is required to run a Microsoft Kinect—powers on. Black aeration flaps that resemble aquatic gills along the top of the computer flare open as the hum gets louder, funneling hot machine breath into the room. The computer is huge and heavy, and, in order to transport it to the production suite, my collaborator Michael Li and I had to heft it onto a metal dolly and steer it carefully through hallways and in and out of elevators. The monitor displays a two-dimensional cartoon girl in a bright red kimono, standing on a grid behind which recedes a black void. Her joints and facial features are marked by dots which are tethered by neon lines to various points on the grid beneath her (see Figure 1). Like a reverse marionette, her body—which is a product of MikuMikuDance (MMD), a freeware choreographic program[1]— is controlled not from above, but from below. Next to the monitor, my Mac laptop rests open on a plastic office chair. It shows a YouTube choreography tutorial for Kate Bush's song "Wuthering Heights" (see Figure 2).[2] This video is paused, suspending the dancer on screen in mid-twirl.

That dancer on screen is also me.

I am a part of this gathering of screens and apparatuses as I begin to dance Bush's choreography in the production suite. I glance often at the YouTube video to execute the moves as accurately as possible. Acting as a mimetic interface between Bush's music video and MMD, the idea is to use my dancing body to feed the choreography to the animated dancer on the Alienware

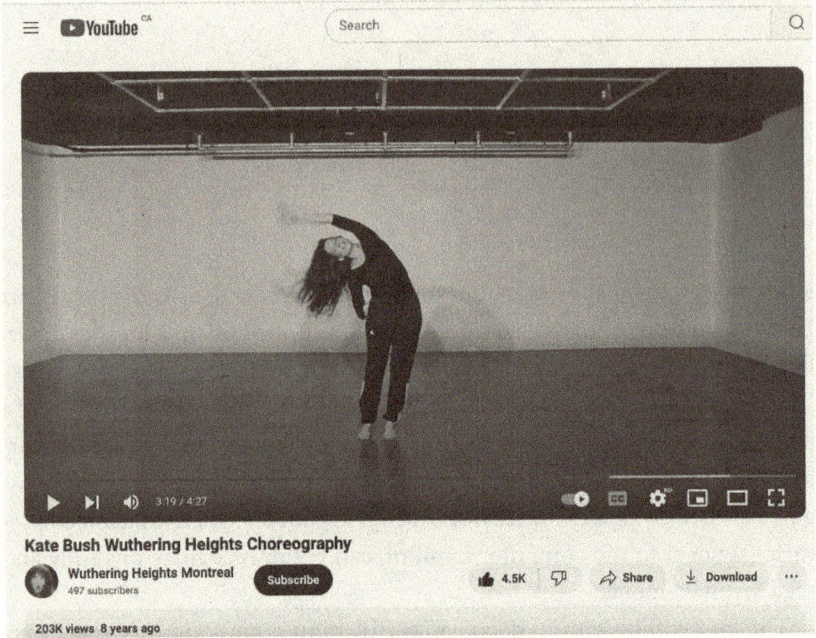

Figure 1 The computer monitor displays the software for MikuMikuDance (MMD), with Miku's avatar (in a red kimono, to emulate Kate Bush), tied down to the grid. The Kinect sits on the table in front. (Photo by Darren Wershler, Concordia University, 2016.)

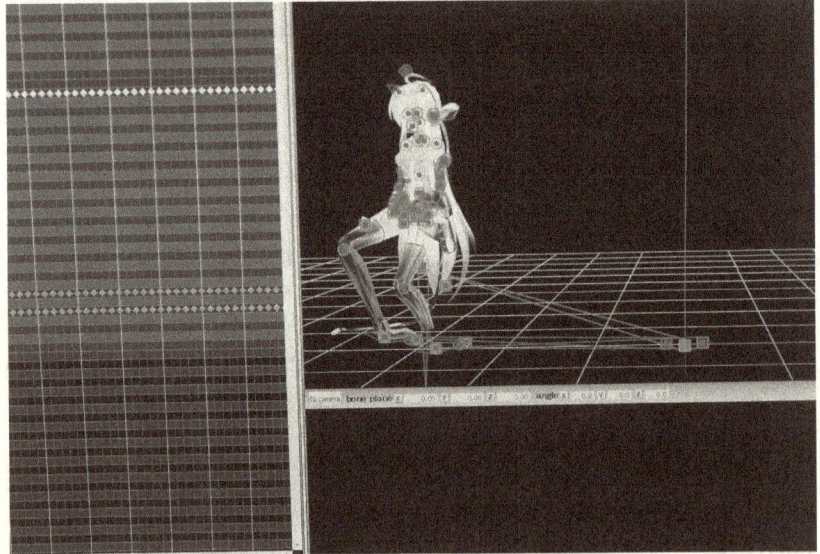

Figure 2 I am the dancer in a video tutorial for Kate Bush's "Wuthering Heights" choreography, filmed in the same production suite I describe at the start of the Preface. (Screenshot from YouTube, Video uploaded June 30, 2016, filmed at Concordia University's Milieux Centre, Videographer: Emilie St. Hilaire. https://www.youtube.com/watch?v=IziOMwBu7ws)

computer screen. To do this, I am using a "Kinect," a now-discontinued motion-sensing device designed by Microsoft, which reads my body and transmits my gestures to the body of my little avatar. She responds immediately to my dancing, but only by jerking spasmodically. The cartoon girl cannot mirror me, and it seems as though her limbs are tied down to the grid beneath her. I find myself performing Bush's dance moves more "loudly" than is correct to have the Kinect read me accurately. I throw my arms up into an exaggerated V, and instead of letting my limbs swing and fall with gravity, I resist, holding the shape of Bush's signature side kick one second longer. My body is being shaped, mechanized even, by the assemblage I am dancing within (see Figure 3).

I am but one of the many "bodies" involved in this dance experiment, which also includes:

- The IRL body of Kate Bush, who was eighteen when she wrote "Wuthering Heights," and contributed to the choreography for her accompanying music video.[3]

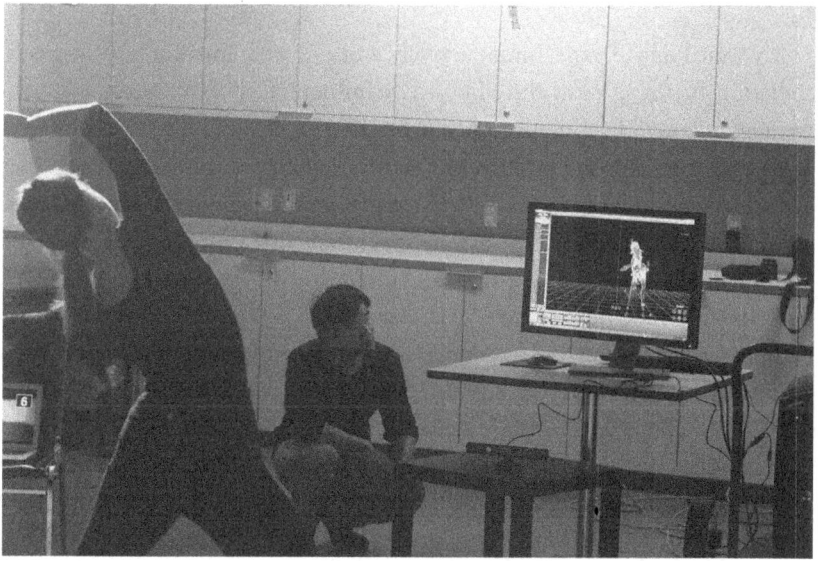

Figure 3 I dance the choreography for Kate Bush's "Wuthering Heights," facing the Alienware computer, the Microsoft Xbox 360 Kinect, and the YouTube tutorial video. Technician Michael Li watches. (Photo by Darren Wershler, Concordia University, 2016.)

- The on-screen body of Kate Bush, whose music video for "Wuthering Heights" I have watched repeatedly, to learn her dance.[4]
- My own filmic body in the YouTube tutorial, which, as of July 2025, has been viewed over 208,000 times (see Figure 2).[5]
- The manipulatable digital avatar body displayed on the computer monitor against the grid in MMD.
- The "hologrammatic" body of Hatsune Miku—a Japanese pop star who tours the world performing a live stage show, and whose videos and stage choreographies can be created using MMD.[6]
- The bodies of the fans at Miku's show, many of whom help create her choreography.
- The clunky, loud body of the Alienware computer.
- The sensing body of the Kinect.
- The helpful body of Michael: my technician and collaborator/MMD expert.
- The many other bodies that have inhabited and will inhabit Kate Bush's choreography, in particular at the international yearly event, the "Most Wuthering Heights Day Ever," where thousands of fans come together to dance in red dresses *en masse* in city parks all over the world.[7]

My weird dance experiment actively engages with this multibodied constellation, bringing Bush and Miku—two influential yet disparate pop stars—to meet my own dancing presence in a web of techniques and technologies. Even with this expanded notion of "body," my list does not encapsulate all the agents, or active processes, that contribute to this assemblage. In an exchange of gesture that travels across space and time via screens, code, algorithmic media, technical training, and biometric data, the point is to explore how dance movement passes between bodies, both virtual and organic, dispersing agency often attributed to the human body alone. I allow my datafied gestures—borrowed from Bush's iconic dance in a misty field—to move through and *with* Miku's avatar, thereby relinquishing mere puppetry or mimetic realism in favor of the machine's lively, glitchy performance. This project, titled "Let me in Through Your Window," which I have written about previously in much greater length, introduces some of the key arguments I will make in this book.[8] It demonstrates that dance (and the dancer) always carries ghost-like traces of other bodies. And it follows the wandering passage of what I call dance *anima*: the energetic life force that both drives and is produced by dance. Dancing puts multiple bodies and gestures into relation with each other, and this relation co-produces *anima*: a distributed energy with a life of its own.

I chose the choreography for Kate Bush's "Wuthering Heights" as my input for the MikuMiku project precisely because it has already passed through so many bodies over time and space. Written by Bush at just eighteen years of age, "Wuthering Heights" was her breakout single on her debut album, *The Kick Inside* (EMI Records),[9] which went on to top the UK charts for four weeks. It remains her most successful song. Every summer for the last five years, an international event called *The Most Wuthering Heights Day Ever* brings together thousands of international participants to reproduce the choreography of "Wuthering Heights" as a group number, in their respective cities. As an organizer of the Montreal edition of this event in 2016, I danced in the instructional video posted to YouTube—a video which thousands of participants have learned the dance, using my body as a guide, mirroring my movements with theirs, just as I learned by watching Kate Bush on my laptop screen. Bush's song is a kind of collaborative hub—a center for communal activity that occurs across screens and bodies. My dance translation project adds another layer to this collectivity, asking Hatsune Miku (herself a hub for collective digital participation) and Kate Bush to dance together, with me.

We three dancers meet in the gridded digital space of MMD, a Japanese freeware animation program originally created by HiguchiM (Garnek) that enables users to create music videos for Hatsune Miku by maneuvering, posing, and choreographing 3D models—many of them resembling Miku herself. MMD users can customize backgrounds, add sound and music with the VOCALOID voice bank, and manipulate every one of the thirty or more "bones" in the figure's body in what is essentially digital puppetry. Given that her movements and songs are user-generated by a large collective of fans using the choreographic program MMD, Miku can be seen as a "nonorganic embodiment of an organic subjectivity."[10] Yes, Miku is a collectively made, digital assemblage, but she is also a nexus of human fantasies about ownership, control, and the pliable body. Her digital avatar's placement on the grid invites what Bernhard Siegart calls operations of "governance."[11] In MMD, the grid serves a diagrammatic and choreographic function, as well as enacts boundaries of space where there are none. Hatsune Miku's avatar stands against the vacuum of digital space, waiting to be danced, and the grid marks coordinate potentialities for her body positions and gestures, delineating the very possibility of her movement. However, because I am "dancing" Miku's avatar via the Kinect's capture of my own body movements, I do not feel I am using the grid to control her dance *anima*. Rather, there is a sense of feedback in my duet with her—I am affected—demarcated, even, by her dancing too.[12]

After recording the motion data, Mike and I drag the computer and equipment back upstairs and return to the lab, where he aids in adding a background for our video and experiments with costuming.[13] Even with the approximate details in place, the video does not look the way it is "supposed to," according to the unspoken performance codes of MMD.[14] It is glitchy and lacks the polished aesthetic that other MMD users achieve through long hours of editing. My unedited dancer, on the other hand, looks as though she has lost control of her body and is just realizing this. *The dance moves through her like a river.* It pushes and pulls her and her sickled ankles drag behind (see Figure 4). Witnessing this spectacle, I do not have the urge to manipulate her into pretty positions. Instead, I turn toward my own dancing body. I wonder about my own level of control over my limbs, my gestures. After all, dance is about toeing the line between doing and being done, between moving and being moved along the current.

The glitch, which Dutch artist Rosa Menkman calls an "unstable process" of "shock," is the moment where the assemblage asserts its nonhuman agency.[15] The glitches in the dance are, for me, cracks in the "window" or screen behind which Miku dances—fissures in the seamless ideology of

Figure 4 A still from the final product of my MMD dance translation project, "Let Me in at Your Window" (2016), depicts my Kate-Miku hybrid avatar mid-choreography, in a glitchy pose.

control that MMD proposes; the "unruly edges" of my little dancer are crucial to her liveliness and potential for relation. The vulnerability of my avatar's precarious digital body becomes exaggerated in my dance translation. My dancing avatar is propelled by biometrics mined from my human body, mapped onto gestures programmed into MMD, and therefore my bodily labor is transformed into data coordinates, opening up new possibilities for what constitutes a "body" when it comes out the other end of the interface. To allow my tiny dancer to flounder is also to allow her to express *anima*. In her uncanny gestures, she carries traces of other bodies, of other relations and power dynamics which neither of us can control.

***

I begin with this preface—a brief excerpt of my Miku–Bush project, "Let Me in Through Your Window"—to enter the book from an embodied perspective. By doing the awkward, repetitive work of dancing with technologies— what Kiri Miller imperatively describes as *"do it yourself, and do it again"*—I wanted to traverse the "window" between the virtual and the real in order to learn something new about the limits and affordances of my human dancing form.[16] The opportunity to dance with Hatsune Miku and Kate Bush was not just a fleeting experience; it has informed my critical analysis of case studies throughout the book and shaped the way I write about dance. It is my hope that readers will feel this in my exploration of dance as *anima*.

Acknowledgments

I thank all those who have read and offered feedback on parts of this book in its various stages, including Darren Wershler, Alanna Thain, Charles Acland, Angelique Willkie, Carrie Rentschler, the late, great, Jonathan Sterne, Priscilla Guy, Anthea Kraut, and Deborah Levitt. Their comments and suggestions have given me the confidence to move between disciplines and find my own voice. A special thanks to Darren for starting me down the path by encouraging me to see technique as a place where dance and media studies intersect. I am grateful to Darren for his mind, which is a deep well of knowledge that I have been lucky to draw from, and for his incisive edits (especially his obsession with the active voice, which I am trying to absorb as an aspirational philosophy for life). A special thanks also to Alanna, for the opportunities she has given me, and for her generous support. Her kindness, intelligence, and prolific inventiveness within the space of academia inspires me daily to forge my own identity as a scholar. Thanks to Angelique for her incredible warmth and integrity, and for modeling for me what embodied research really means. Thank you to Deborah for her supervision during my postdoc at The New School, and for letting me sleep in her daughter's room when I was pregnant and hobbling around NYC doing research. Thanks to Bernhard Siegert, whose mentorship at the 2019 Princeton-Weimar Summer School for Media Studies shaped several key sections of the book. And my two fantastic editors—Holly Vestad and Emily Doucet—whose indispensable feedback corralled the unruly form of this manuscript into something I am proud of. Thank you to my choreorobotics group, Sydney Skybetter, Eric Mullis, and Benny Simon: our collaboration and monthly chats have invigorated my thoughts. Thanks, too, to the brilliant participants of my 2024 *Dance and/as Technology* Conference (co-organized with my colleague Philippe Bédard), whose research and creative work has influenced this book deeply.

I owe so much of my thinking to my friends, who have "studied" with me through our ongoing dialogues. Thanks to the brilliant Sarah Burgoyne for her wise and sensitive insights, and for her dear friendship; to my bosom friend Nikaela Peters, for knowing me fully and helping me see myself more clearly; to Sandra Huber for the magical solidarity; and to my favorite person to dance with, Christie Peters, for the phone calls and for her patience as I articulate my ideas. Thanks to Kathryn Jezer-Morton for the book-writing dates and mountain-ski meetings, and for bringing levity. Thank you to Bernice Sorge and Yvon Geoffroy for their curiosity and exchange around my project. Thanks also to Mara Eagle, Philippe Bédard, Olivia Wood, Eileen Holowka, Cody Lee Walker, Kasia Van Schaik, Robert Regier, Emily Bergsma, and Jeff Noh for talking me through many of the ideas I explore in these pages—I feel lucky to be in conversation with each of them.

I wish to thank those who have fostered a love of dance throughout my life: among others, my dance teachers at Winnipeg's School of Contemporary Dancers, especially Odette Heyn, Faye Thomson, Gaile Petursson-Hiley, and (the late, wonderful) Stephanie Ballard; Kathy Casey for giving me the rich experience of co-facilitating Montréal Danse's choreographic workshop; Philip Szporer for his mentorship in teaching and sharing dance research; and Ming Hon and Freya Bjorg Olafson for expanding my understanding of what dance can be. Thank you also to my students at Concordia University and Dawson College, whose curiosity and openness motivate me, and who teach me so much about the world as it is today.

I am very grateful to both the Social Sciences and Humanities Research Council of Canada and the Fonds de Recherche du Québec for supporting my research and granting me scholarships that have given me precious time to write and think. My gratitude, also, to the anonymous peer reviewers who offered suggestions along the way, and of course to Norm Hirschy, for believing in this book and giving me the opportunity to publish with Oxford.

Lastly, I thank my family: my amazing parents for their endless support and for nurturing my love of both dance and writing; my three younger brothers, Nick, Luke, and Levi, for their kinship and laughter; my dear little dancing daughters, Ingrid and Ramona, for inspiring me every day; and my sweetheart, Yann, for believing in me.

Introduction

Paris, 1911: Michel Fokine's ballet *Petrouchka* premieres to a packed house. It is the third season of Sergei Diaghilev's Ballets Russes: Igor Stravinsky has composed a brilliant score, and Vaslav Nijinsky is dancing the titular role—Petrouchka, the puppet with a human soul.[17] Nijinsky's wife, Romola, watching her husband perform as the marionette, finds his first stiff and jolting movements "convulsive" and "charged with electricity"—he has successfully emulated a puppet whose dancing brings it to life.[18] As the ballet progresses, all of the puppet characters begin to move less erratically and their limbs start to follow the guidance of their torsos (or centers); through dance, they exhibit their own will, enacted without the input of the magician who previously controlled them. Over the course of the performance, Nijinsky (the human dancer) uses dance to transform himself into a puppet, who in turn uses dance to transform himself into a human. The ballet's cyclical process, in which dance can produce both a mechanistic and a human subjectivity, displays the continuities between automata and human beings, positioning dance as a central animating force in concepts of human agency and subjecthood. Simply put, *Petrouchka* shows us that dance animates life. Dance's driving energy—what I term "dance *anima*"— a kinetic and collective force produced by dancers, choreographies, technologies, and the imagination of the audience, is therefore a valuable resource for engineering life and ensouling bodies beyond the human. This book explores the contradictions inherent to thinking about dance: a force which cannot be fully controlled or contained but which is also an extractable energetic capital with humanist value.

Because it combines thinking, feeling, and action, dance acts as a perceived expression of selfhood that moves beyond the Cartesian "cogito, ergo sum," to an embodied articulation of human concerns: I *dance* therefore I am (human).[19] The idea that dance expresses something innately human has been articulated across multiple centuries: as historian Judith Hanna asserts in 1979, "to dance is human, and humanity almost universally expresses itself

Dance Anima. Hilary Bergen, Oxford University Press. © Oxford University Press 2026.
DOI: 10.1093/9780197786673.003.0001

in dance."[20] This is a position in keeping with Anthea Kraut's 2016 observation that early modern dance was "bound up with theories of the expressivity and individuality of the [human] body," where "bodies "externalized what was internal and proper to the self."[21] Earlier, in the 1700s, choreographer Jean-Georges Noverre proclaimed that the "dancer's technique" does not just express their human interiority, but "the highest things of the soul."[22] Choreographer Merce Cunningham's statement that dance is a "spiritual activity in physical form"[23] echoes this sentiment, as does Susan Sontag's suggestion that "no art lends itself so aptly as dance does to metaphors borrowed from spiritual life" (words like "grace" and "elevation" are often close at hand when describing it).[24]

These writers clearly see dance as a way to express human selfhood and as a mode for engaging with a "larger rhetoric about human possibility,"[25] demonstrating the almost religious humanizing power that dance holds in our cultural imagination. There is therefore a kind of ensouling force to dance, the presence of which can anthropomorphize all types of nonhuman entities, such as in *Petrouchka*, where dance affords the puppet a human soul. Dancers and choreographers articulate something profound about dance and humanity when they explore the boundaries of the human as it intersects with the mechanical. This exploration—of the relationship between humans and machines—allows dance to interrogate itself and by extension, the human.

Dance Anima argues that the practice of dance holds a paradox at its core: we view dance as a *human* thing, and yet, the acquisition of choreography and technique, not to mention the use of tools and technologies such as pointe shoes, stage lighting, or the camera, to name a few, produces the dancer as a kind of mechanized body and networked cyborg: one whose porousness of boundaries mark the more-than-human condition of our present. Yes, dance "interweaves with all aspects of human life, such as communication and learning, belief systems, social relations and political dynamics, loving and fighting, and urbanization and change," asserting what Judith Hanna names "the essence of humanity."[26] And yet, dance does not merely spring from innate human impulse but is also, as Norman Bryson argues, "the most blatant and unarguable instance of the disciplined body."[27] What can dance tell us, then, about the relationship between technique and what it means to be thinking, feeling humans? What new knowledge can dance reveal about our interactions with technologies, and the qualities we uphold as integral to humanity? On the one hand, we use dance to humanize

machines (or give them the appearance of cognition, sensation, and emotion) and, on the other hand, we use machines to *dehumanize* dance (to
abstract bodies and turn them into dancing images). However, here is the
twist: *dance itself can already be understood as a kind of machine*, a technical
assemblage that produces a valuable energy or *anima*.

To articulate the nature of these assemblages and define this simultaneously human and machinic energy, *Dance Anima* takes up a media-historical
approach—examining both the various cultural techniques that stem
from the practice of dance (e.g., notation systems, mocap animation, and
chronophotography) and the idea that dance itself is a cultural technique
that can animate mechanical beings, cartoons, or robots to ensoul them or
bring them to "life." Because they carry energetic movement and a sense of
liveliness, dancing bodies have been instrumental in the development of
emergent media, from photography and film to VR. Dance tests and reveals
the capacity of these tools to capture, reproduce, and even create human
kinetic life. Technologies like motion capture, for example, which distill
human motion into data, have often been characterized as merely extractive or, as Harmony Bench writes, "inherently nostalgic" in their connection
to the "archive" and a "rhetoric of loss."[28] But these types of technologies do
not only look backwards—they also throw movement forwards, replicating
a dancer into a series of externalized images and making dance gesture necessarily plural and transferrable between bodies. This plurality of transfer
makes dance *anima* a relational energy. In her work on screendance, Alanna
Thain writes that animation is "neither representational nor simply indexical
in nature"; it is "fundamentally the art of the in-between" in that it "activates
in its relation to other art forms . . . a vivid sense of their potential," and in
particular, the "body's potential for relation."[29] Like Thain, I look to animation, along with other forms of dancing media, to propose *relation* as a mode
of being (human) and as a model for imagining what the future might be.

Commonly understood as ephemera, dance lives in the body and yet it
also exceeds that body's material boundaries, making it a viral renewable energy to be shared or distributed across multiple bodies and forms. A kind
of effervescence or heat, stirred up through gesture, dance can transfer between entities, enlivening other bodies (including those of an audience),
calling them to participate, act, and feel—to be filled up and *moved* by the
fluid of dance—what I am calling dance *anima*. Because dancing produces
an energy that can be lifted from the bodies and technologies that make it,
it can become like a floating "soul," unmoored from the moving, sweating,

aching human, yet paradoxically grounding whatever body it lands in with a perceived sense of authentic human expression. This "lifting off" of dance from bodies is often assisted through various forms of technological mediation that we might again understand as cultural techniques—many of which I address in this book, from puppetry to animation tools like rotoscoping and digital motion capture, to choreorobotics. The dancer, and dance more generally, are therefore instruments of exploration between two realms that seem to be at odds and yet are deeply imbricated: the concept of the human and that of emergent media.

Anima/Soul

Dance and soul have an interwoven relationship throughout history. No matter if the dancer's body is mechanical, hand-drawn, or digitally rendered—the presence of dance, like that of the kinetic *anima*, enlivens that body as it resides there for whomever is watching it. Furthermore, because dance is a cultural technique that can be passed (and is even viral or contagious) between bodies, including nonhuman (robotic, animated, digital) bodies, it makes the boundaries of the individual human dancer porous. There is a mystical quality to this line of thinking about dance that can be traced back to the etymology of the term *anima*. The word *anima*, Latin for "soul" or "breath," connects movement with life. Aristotle's *De Anima*, Gottfried Wilhelm Leibniz's *Monadology*, and the animistic theories of the seventeenth-century medical philosopher G. E. Stahl all contribute to definition of the soul as a "travelling substance" or one defined first and foremost by movement.[30] In these conceptions, as Spyros Papapetros explains, the soul is characterized by its "endless promiscuity, its inability to be permanently attached to any person, thing, or concept:" "Three-dimensional bodies are mere containers of this mobile entity that is either invisible or flashing, intermittently, and at the very threshold of the visible," and which presents "kinesis [as] the fixed core of [its] animation."[31] Notably, for the notion of *anima*, it does not matter whether the body housing the soul is an organism or "an automated mechanism whose movement is without consciousness" because "anima is a mobile energy that is independent from the bodies it infuses."[32] Similarly, Aristotle characterizes the soul in *De Anima* (350 BCE) as a kind of "strange, invisible 'air'" that "suffuse[s] everything with an enigmatic buoyancy," making "words and things move when they

[are] not supposed to be swaying."[33] As this book argues, the bodies that produce and are propelled by dance *anima* do not have to be human; indeed, they do not have to be bodies at all.[34]

Anima, then, is just as deeply connected to philosophical concepts of agency or selfhood as it is to Christian theology or other religious understandings of the word.[35] This is not to neglect the spiritual energy that dance *anima* carries, but to track the ways in which embodied and situated techniques, as well as structures of power, can shape, corral, and produce *anima*.[36] This is an idea that comes from Michel Foucault, for whom power is not just oppressive but productive and who sees the soul, in fact, as "the prison of the body."[37] Following Foucault, who views the soul as "the effect and the instrument of a political anatomy" that is "born out of methods of [...] supervision and constraint,"[38] I am interested in the relationship between the concept of humanist selfhood, the production of agency or liveness via dance, and the maintenance of power implemented through techniques of the body and visual technologies. Dance *anima* is similar to Foucault's soul insofar as it is often produced under techniques of "supervision," and acquired through constrained repetition (often painful, often scrutinized) of body movement. Dance *anima* can temporarily possess a body, and we might even imagine this is a kind of imprisonment. On the other hand, dance *anima* is overflowing, shared, and dynamic—it can evade governance—making it quite different from Foucault's soul, which is forged from punishment and carries that control forward, foreclosing the possibility of freedom.[39]

To think dance and soul together is to re-imagine the concept of soul as something kinetic, relational, and ongoing, rather than singular, innate, or deterministic. Whether in the Judeo-Christian tradition, where the separation of body from soul primarily occurs in the event of the body's death, in a Western secular philosophical articulation, where "soul" is much more abstract, or in an Eastern, animistic conception where nonhuman objects and parts of the natural world each possess a distinct spiritual essence, the soul is a thing full of a special vitality. It is driven by movement across all these definitions. This is evident in Aristotle's description of the soul as a "travelling substance" and in the nineteenth-century concept of the soul as a "sort of vapour, film, or shadow" or a "phantasm separate from the body," as Anthropologist Edward Burnett Tylor writes in 1871. In a similar vein, dance can be separated from the body that produced it, both as a thought experiment and in material, mediatized ways, as in the movement data retrieved from dancers using mocap systems. Even after this separation, dance carries traces of the body's labor—"possessing the personal consciousness and volition of its corporeal owner, past or present."[40] In the following chapters, I demonstrate the viral or contagious nature of dancing and the ways in which corporeal movement can transfer between dancers (human- or non-), carrying spectral evidence of gestural energy.

The word "anima" in the title of this book may lead readers to mistakenly believe that the topic is Jungian psychology. Swiss psychiatrist Carl Jung (1875–1961) used the term "anima" in his work to refer to the archetypal, animistic parts within the Self, in particular the unconscious "feminine" qualities within a man. Jung's psychological theory adheres to a limiting gender binary and ascribes stereotypical qualities associated with femaleness to *anima* and maleness to *animus*—the flip of *anima*, *animus* comprises the masculine qualities that dwell within a woman, according to Jung. However, I do find Jung's theory helpful in qualifying dance *anima* as something necessarily plural, rather than rooted in the singular human form. Just as Jung's *anima* entertains the idea of body as vessel inhabited by other bodies, personalities, or specific energies, dance can also allow access to this type of temporary possession; when we dance, we invite the energy of dancing, and the traces of other bodies and practices that that energy holds, to inhabit us and drive our gesture.

Like Tylor's definition of soul, and the Platonic concept of *anima* as a kinetic soul force, dance *anima* can "[continue] to exist and appear to men after the death of that body" and be "able to enter into, possess, and act in the bodies of other men, of animals, and even of things."[41] Tylor's definition can act as a jumping off place for thinking about the shadowy nature of dance as an animating force that carries memories of other bodies and volitions and manifests "physical power" even in its impalpability.[42] However, Tylor's writing about animism, which he regarded as the first (and most "unevolved") phase in the development of religion, betrays his presumption of his own superiority to those he termed "primitive" peoples, or "rude races." Tylor's colonial approach, while foundational for anthropology, illustrates a power imbalance between the white anthropologist and the nonwhite subjects of his studies—one that perserveres and is evident in several of the examples I examine in this book, especially where dance *anima* presents as an extractable soul force.

To this point, the book puts forward a new, interdisciplinary framework for understanding the more-than-human history of dance *anima* as thoroughly imbricated with the extraction of movement and work from human bodies through apparatuses of capture such as the camera, the rotoscope, dance notation, and robotics interfaces.[43] In tracking dance *anima's* material traces and networks across screens, assembly lines, and machines of war, questions of race are crucial. Dance is widely understood as ephemeral—a concept which is inherently political, as per Diana Taylor's question: "whose memories, traditions, and claims to history disappear if performance practices lack the staying power to transmit vital knowledge?"[44] Or, to put it another way, what happens when memories, traditions, and claims to history (as embedded in the material, gestural traces of dance *anima*) are cleaved from the dancing bodies that produced them? Modern and postmodern visions of the disembodied or datafied human form in dance, for example, can sometimes reveal uneasy fantasies of post-racial abstraction. Such aesthetic visions nevertheless often rely on the *labor* of nonwhite bodies and/or the fetishized racial semiotics of costumes, objects, or gestural vocabulary to produce a sense of vitality, soul, and *anima* in the dance, whether in the appropriated orientalist skirt dances of Loïe Fuller and Ruth St. Denis which I address in Chapter 1, in Max Fleischer's early animated works which use technologically extracted movement from dancers of color like jazz bandleader Cab Calloway covered in Chapter 3, or in the reliance on Black social dance in the staging of Boston Dynamics' choreorobotic spectacles, as seen in Chapter 4.

Many previous studies of these kinds of technologized dance detrimentally ignore questions of race.[45] One intention of this book is to show how the writing of critical race theorists can and should inform the way we think about the intersection of dance and technology. Anne Anlin Cheng's research on the ornamental surface, for instance, draws together urban architectural technologies, modernist fantasies, and epidermal inscription—a perspective that can offer a much-needed material-racial analysis to dancing bodies in 1920s America, and Sianne Ngai's writing on aesthetic categories such as the "zany"—though she does not study dance outright—can helpfully frame popular depictions of factory work within the concept of choreography, or the organization of a bodily energy which is also, in Ngai's view, racialized.

Meanwhile, Brenda Dixon Gottschild's work on dance gets to the heart of the issue of technological extraction and the depersonalization of Black social dance gesture without mentioning media or technology; her contributions can nonetheless productively extend to an analysis of the cultural techniques and technologies of dance *anima*. Gottschild explores the Africanist influence on American and European concert dance, arguing that because Africanist

dance styles (with their polycentric, polyrhythmic, ephebic quality of movement) propel a concept of "vital aliveness," they historically hold cultural
capital for Western dance aesthetics.[46] By contrast, Gottschild writes that the
"Europeanist" dancing body, "as assessed by Africanist aesthetic criteria […]
is rigid, aloof, cold, and one-dimensional."[47] The Africanist dancing presence
therefore often stands in as what Gottschild calls "soul force" and an "aesthetic
of cool," making it attractive to white American and Eurocentric dancemakers
wanting to imbue their work with the same.[48] Gottschild's "Africanist presence" bears similarities to what R. A. Royston calls "Soulcraft": "the meta-
physical and material assemblage of Black techne."[49] Tracking the history of
soul music, DJing, and African viral dance to Black liberation and the Civil
Rights Era, Royston demonstrates how technological processes have been integral to concepts of "soul" and Black emancipation in the African diaspora.
Although they do not focus on dance specifically, Afrofuturists like Alondra
Nelson, Alexander Weheliye, and Kodwo Eshun likewise highlight the creative, speculative projects of Black artists, writers, and musicians working
across technoculture and art. These thinkers inform my approach to thinking
about dance *anima* as an energetic force with capital—a force that may appear
to be deracialized by virtue of its disembodiment, but which in fact carries
traces of bodies with culturally specific ways of moving.

The biopolitics of dance as animating force, and its relationship to the
extracted and abstracted labor of material, human bodies, are main concerns
in my book.[50] How might dance (and especially dance technique and choreography) complicate humanist values such as free will, individual agency,
and self-sovereignty? What are the procedures, technologies, and techniques
that produce and control dance *anima*, historically and today, and how do
these processes affect our understanding of human agency and experience?
Who owns the dance of the dancing body, and the soul-effects of that dance?

Dance as Cultural Technique

In addition to being an expressive body, the figure of the dancer can be seen
as a trained instrument, constructed by various outside forces rather than
merely at the helm of their self-expressive form; the dance *anima* they produce is therefore not only a result of their intentional and individual emotion or intention, but also of the unseen, subconscious body knowledge of
the dancer: learned habits, codified routines, and gestures acquired from

other bodies. This is what Pierre Bourdieu calls "habitus," or the way our movements and behaviors are shaped through social processes and repeated patterns of reward or punishment: a "subjective but not individual system of internalized structures."[51] This is also what Marcel Mauss calls "techniques of the body," as explored in his 1934 study of various human activities such as swimming, running, and eating. Mauss writes that people have different ways of moving, and that these "are not simply a product of some purely individual, almost completely psychical arrangements and mechanisms" but are rather produced and encouraged by different types of education and reward: "These 'habits' do not just vary with individuals [. . .] they vary especially between societies, educations, proprieties and fashions, prestige."[52] In this way, dance is particular to the dancer, but not because of a solely conscious expression of unique individuality; using technique, dancers draw (consciously or subconsciously) from their embodied storehouse of movement vocabulary, banked through rigorous kinetic repetition.

Oftentimes, this results in the appearance of spontaneous and free movement—an aesthetic quality we might associate with emotional interiority or ensoulment. Elsewhere, as in group and social dance scenarios, dance is mimicked from other bodies, either in real time or from memory. Thomas DeFrantz has an anecdote about a family dance party where he observed party-goers gathering in the communal space of the living room, prompting an intergenerational dance circle where many different styles of dancing, including voguing, the cha-cha slide, the electric slide, and the Dougie were on display. DeFrantz writes about the "call to dance" in this scenario (where individuals are summoned into the circle by the other participants) as a "challenge; a reminder to participate in the social capacity of black creativity through public-private dance within the circle."[53] He writes: "A cheer rose up, and we sent celebratory energy toward him, crossing into the circle, enjoying a surprise visit of engaged physicality and identity-laden dance. He danced, and we all knew him differently because of it."[54] This anecdote demonstrates the relational quality of dance *anima*, which is produced at the intersection of audience and dancer. At some point, DeFrantz notes, the younger party-attendees pulled out a laptop to look up the music video for the 1990s hit "Poison" by Bell, Biv, DeVoe to remind them of the exact steps of the dance. This shift to the "music video as authoritative document of authentic gesture" reveals the changing social relationship to technologies of dance, which increasingly play a formative role in producing the identity or soul of the dancer.[55]

If dancing is a way to communicate something human and ensouled, and dance is made from acquired technique and engagement with technologies, the "soul" of the dancer therefore emerges out of a process that is both relational and, perhaps controversially, artificial, or fabricated (in the non-pejorative sense of these terms). This idea—of dance as a technique for expression (or performance) of humanness and interiority—fascinated Francois Delsarte, whose Paris lectures in 1840 tied a system of gestures to the expression of soul, writing, "to each spiritual function responds a function of the body; to each grand function of the body corresponds a spiritual act."[56] Delsarte aimed to create a rigorous science of the embodied expression of emotions in dance, acting, and singing using charts, diagrams, and strict technique, and his research fed directly into the physical culture movement of the late nineteenth century.[57] Ted Shawn, a pioneer of American modern dance, described Delsartean technique as one that aimed to "train and discipline the body that it would become a responsible and expressive instrument through which fluid movement could pass without the obstacles of stiff and unyielding joints and muscles."[58] Key to Delsartean and nascent modern dance technique was the idea that all movements originated from the trunk of the body, or the "region of the heart," as this would produce an expression of ensoulment and inner feeling in the movement.[59] This new style of dance freed the body from the rigid confines of upright ballet technique, but was nonetheless a technique of its own, and one that often prized torsion, or the image of the spiral, drawing connections to the emergent machine culture of the time. The practice of dance technique therefore produces the dancer (*as* dancer) and the dance—or dance *anima*—with its particularities of mood, rhythm, and shape.

Dancers often have a complicated relationship with technique. As Judith Hamera writes:

> Technique is both the animating aesthetic principle and the core ambivalence housed in every dance studio and manipulated by every teacher, every choreographer, every performer. It is both taskmaster and mastered, both warden and liberator. It demands to be replicated even as it asks to be exceeded.[60]

Indeed, technique can seem rigid and militaristic—it was after all Marcel Mauss's experience as a soldier doing group drills that led him to write *Les techniques du corps* (1934), and to declare the human body as the "first and most natural instrument."[61] Ben Spatz argues that "when Mauss's idea of bodily technique is inflected by Foucault's analysis of power—that is, the way that structures of power are produced by institutionally-sanctioned procedures and methods—we may begin to grasp how the training we each receive reflects not only a variable knowledge of technique but also the social hierarchies that determine how this knowledge is distributed."[62] In German media theory, "cultural techniques" names a wide swathe of practices such as farming, counting, eating, and mapping, all of which have produced certain habits, customs, and media (e.g., the plow, the abacus, the fork, the grid) that shape how humans interact with and make sense of the world. To think dance as a cultural technique can help make sense of it as a practice comprised of its own history, aims, and techniques—all of which formulate the figure of the dancer as we know it (in the words of Cornelia Vismann, "the operation itself produces the subject").[63] Additionally, there is a second way in which dance can be seen as a cultural technique: as a strategy implemented by filmmakers, roboticists, animators, and storytellers to imbue bodies with the appearance of vitality.

Dance operates as a cultural technique of vitality because of the strong association between dance movement and the perceived expression of human emotion. But dancers are not always dancing what they feel; they are using technique to express things with their body and produce the sense of an emotion that they need not truly feel within themselves. As Susanne K. Langer writes, "the most widely accepted view is that the essence of dance is musical: the dancer expresses in gesture what he feels as the emotional content of the music which is the efficient and supporting cause of his dance. He reacts as we all would if we were not inhibited; his dance is self-expression, and is beautiful because the stimulus is beautiful."[64] The reason people believe the dancer is always expressing what they feel, Langer explains, is because "all dance motion is gesture" and "gesture is *vital movement* (emphasis mine)," indicative of lively human emotion and will.[65] Following Langer, I argue that it is this dual association, between dance as embodied gesture and gesture as a symbol of vitality, that facilitates dancing as a technique for the production of soul in nonhuman bodies as well. Langer continues:

> Gesture is vital movement; to the one who performs it, it is known very precisely as a kinetic experience, i.e. as action, and somewhat more vaguely by sight, as an effect. To others it appears as a visible motion, but not a motion of things, sliding or waving or rolling around—it is seen and understood

as vital movement. So it is always at once subjective and objective, personal and public, willed (or evoked) and perceived. In actual life gestures function as signals or symptoms of our desires, intentions, expectations, demands and feelings. [...] Gesticulation, as part of our actual behaviour, is not art. It is simply vital movement. [...] It is not dancing.[66]

When we see someone dance, we immediately see the body of the dancer as a "center of vital force" whose "expressive movements" are "signals of its will."[67] This is what dance gives us. But this, Langer, explains, is also the *trick* of dance. Because "the primary illusion of dance is a virtual realm of Power—not actual, physically exerted power, but appearances of influence and agency created by virtual gesture."[68] She elaborates that in dance, "the actual and virtual aspects of gesture are mingled in complex ways, sometimes in ways not even comprehended by dancers themselves."[69] The dancer's movements, "of course, are actual; they spring from an intention and are in this sense actual gestures; but they are not the gestures they seem to be, because they seem to spring from feeling, as indeed they [often] do not."[70] In this way, "the dancer's actual gestures are used to create a semblance of self-expression, and are thereby transformed into virtual spontaneous movement, or virtual gesture."[71]

In other words, every human dancer is already a bit like the dancing robot, using gesture to express, rather than self-express, a *symbol* of vitality or vital will, understood as soul. This is not to say that the dancer's "virtual" gestures cannot spring from real feeling or stimulate actual emotion in the audience of dance (or even in the dancer themselves), or that dancing robots, for example, who lack central nervous systems, could ever improvise, or move with the passion of a seasoned human dancer. It stands, however, that dance is an affective exchange—a kind of contagious body movement or "metakinesis" (to quote John Martin)—regardless of whether the dancer's interior emotions, as communicated through gesture, are authentic, so to speak. What I am suggesting here may cause some dance scholars, dancers, or choreographers to bristle—of course there is no match for the experience of watching live, ephemeral dance happen (and disappear) in the moment of its making. One feels things—poetic things—watching human bodies dance live that one might not feel watching a dancing automaton or an image of a dancer on screen. However, it remains true that what the audience feels (regardless of the type of dancer they are watching) is not synonymous with what (or whether) the *dancer* feels. A dancing avatar or robot can produce feeling in an audience, even if it does not in fact feel anything. It is the presence of dance *anima* that produces the feeling, regardless of what kind of body it inhabits.

The various techniques and technological assemblages that comprise and produce dance as *anima*, engineering new bodies and life forms in the process, necessitate a methodology informed by media history. Historically, this book covers ground from the early nineteenth century to the present day. The practice of using dance to animate or ensoul nonhuman bodies can be traced back further, to the automaton fairs of the Renaissance, or even earlier to the moving tripods created by Hephaestus in Homer's *Iliad* and to the first-century CE descriptions by an Alexandrian engineer, Heron, of a dancing automaton figure of the god Pan.[72] However, I have chosen the case studies of this book to illustrate an intensifying relationship between dance and the concepts of "human" and "soul" as articulated from the early 1800s through modernism, postmodernism, and to our current digital era, which Anna Kornbluh also calls "too-late capitalism."[73] Some of the shifts that occur over the course of these changing periods are a move from the lone, genius figure of the Romantic, and early-modern-era choreographer or dancer to representations of the mass or swarm of moving bodies, including, for example, Busby Berkeley's large group choreographies shot from above for the cinema, and the choreography of labor on the assembly line under Taylorism. This shift away from the singular body also extends to the rising cultural technique of dance notation, in particular Labanotation of the 1920s, which tended to abstract the dancer's body—and therefore their potential *anima*—into disembodied shapes and lines.

Even before filmmakers like Edison were enchanted by the potential of dance on screen, nineteenth-century English photographer Eadweard Muybridge and French physiologist Étienne-Jules Marey devised photographic apparatuses to observe the mechanics of the human body in motion, often using dancers as models. Because the material image of the moving body in these cases could be "reified and remobilized as a *res extensa*," "movement was no longer located in the lived-in object . . . but in the machine devised . . . to project the image."[74] I follow this photographic history (which is also a history of work science and choreographed productivity) forward to the current-day use of motion capture, or mocap, which gained popularity after its implementation in video game design in the late 1980s. Like the older (modernist) animation technique of rotoscoping, mocap is often used to preserve the lively gesture of the human body, or the feeling of *essence* (as produced by techniques), which is hard to achieve with animation alone. If the dancing body is understood as an interface for the human soul, then the notion of biometric intervention seems particularly invasive in that it seeks to turn not just the body but the *soul* into a string of numbers, which in turn becomes an animated body—with a morphing, nascent quality that seems to be "an-ontological" (Levitt 2018) or without being.

The material figure of the dancing human and the an-ontological force of dance or soul are in a sense triangulated through the image of the dancing machine, which can be seen dually as a technologized human, or a humanized technology. Much of *Dance Anima's* argument is deeply indebted to Felicia McCarren's book *Dancing Machines*, which explores the rise of capitalism as informed by abstract and anonymous moving bodies, across work science and the development of cinema and other modernist technologies. McCarren takes up the Taylorist principles of minimum gesture and productivity in relation to the "dancing machine," which she describes as "both an idealization of the body's performative prowess and a critique of its mechanization, the coordinated precision of rhythmic ensembles and the fragmented but functional isolated gesture of industrial production." McCarren's book was published in 2003, and while she provides a thorough overview of early modernist examples of the mechanized dancer, she was too early to analyze some of today's most compelling "dancing machines," including those born of mocap data explored in Chapter 3 and Boston Dynamic's dancing robots which appear in Chapter 4. These dancing robots uncannily embody McCarren's dancing machine—a distilment of the worker as a kind of dehumanized instrument of a capitalist choreography. McCarren also looks at dance technique more specifically to argue that "the perfectly autonomous, self-creating, liberated body of the modern dancer *is itself a technological fantasy* [emphasis mine]"[75]—a fantasy that obscures dance as work, or a product of the laboring body.

Many of the examples given in this book, from the contagious phenomenon of Kate Bush's "Wuthering Heights" dance to Busby Berkeley's unison group dances and the repetitive daily sequences of assembly line workers, interrogate the idea of dance *anima* as it relates to choreography. As Andre Lepecki has written, "'choreography' names a very specific masculinist, fatherly, Stately, judicial, theological, and disciplinary project—a project that, moreover, removed from dance from its social terrain (the communal yard) and placed it in a private (courtly) chamber."[76] As a mode for organization of bodies (and their *anima*) in space, choreography is an attempt to own and delimit dance, and it is a cultural technique used to produce dance as repeatable object or experience.

At contrast, some of the case studies in this book, including the animated dance performances of Cab Calloway, Savion Glover, and Bill T. Jones, are rooted in the improvisational vernacular mode rather than a clearly choreographed sequence. These case studies are important because of the way they assert Black social dance (or more generally dance that does not emerge from the European, concert-balletic tradition) as ante-choreographic, in the sense that it both challenges and precedes what we understand as the choreographic. These ideas are explored further in a conversation between Afrofuturist poet and dancer Jaamil Olawale Kosoko and dance theorist Rizvana Bradley, at her 2018 CUNY studio visit. In her response to Kosoko's work "Chameleon," Bradley notes that in centering relationality, Kosoko dismantles notions of authorship and intention and poses an answer to the question of "how to move in excess of and in imminent relation to a world that conveniently forgets history."[77] If dance itself is, to quote Bradley, a "rhythmic act of preserving memory"—a "besideness" or "horizontal intimacy between ancestral time and our time"—then it has the power to exceed apparatuses that wish to archive, capture, and extract it for gains.[78] Dance *anima* can resist capture not through virtuosity or sheer force, but through what Bradley calls the "minor grammar of the body's trace as an aesthetic event"—the subtle and intimate gestural echoes that dance holds and which complicate the choreographic as a mode of standardization or precise synchronicity.[79] The tension between choreography and improvised dance is something I pick up on again in the conclusion to this book, especially in relation to the idea of the trace.

I often use the term "trace" in this book. My use of the word is influenced by French poststructuralist Jacques Derrida, who believed that meaning is derived not from a concrete, self-present source, but from a series of deferrals or traces—also described by Derrida as a process of haunting or "hauntology"—which destabilize fixed truth and produce a multiplicity of meanings and ways of being.[80] For Derrida, the trace is the mark, track, or impression left in the mind by a word's absence; like a ghost, which "haunts by inhabiting a place without occupying it," the trace lingers like a "promise that will be fulfilled in the future."[81] The word (or concept) haunts future instances where it is not present, but could be, and so there is a constant return to or accumulation of past iterations of that haunting presence. Similar to Derrida, I use "trace" to move away from the search for origins—dance can rarely be tracked back to one singular inventor (something I explore in my chapter on Loïe Fuller) and dance gesture can haunt other bodies across large swathes of time. Using Derrida as a jumping off place, my conception of dance *anima* as trace is less about absence or difference—for Derrida every sign must also contain a trace of what it does *not* mean—than about a shared sense of embodiment and relation: an undeniable gestural (and relational) presence that persists.

Diana Taylor's theory of "repertoire" is also influential for my use of the term "trace." Taylor argues that performance, and all embodied "acts usually thought of as ephemeral, nonreproducible knowledge," do, of course, transmit knowledge.[82] She writes that such embodied practices—acting, singing, dancing, etc.—destabilize the archive because "the actions that [comprise] the repertoire do not remain the same. The repertoire both keeps and transforms choreographies of meaning."[83] Taylor's theory of repertoire suggests that performance "persist[s] [...] through a nonarchival" and "vital [...] system of transfer."[84] Rather than reject the archive outright, Taylor expands it to the transmission of "social knowledge, memory, and a sense of identity."[85] Relatedly, Joseph Roach writes that "performance genealogies draw on the idea of expressive movements as mnemonic reserves, including patterned movements made and remembered by bodies, residual movements retained implicitly in images or words" and that such remembered movements function as both "quotation and invention."[86] Many of the case studies across this book, especially Loïe Fuller's Serpentine Dance, Cab Calloway's rotoscoped performance, and Bill T. Jones's autobiographical improvised solo, *Ghostcatching*, demonstrate dance *anima* as a complementary concept to that of Taylor's repertoire and Roach's performance genealogies. Dance *anima* operates as a force that troubles the archive (and archival media or technologies of capture), consists of embodied experience and residual gestures, and likewise mediates and carries forth important memory and knowledge.

Like Taylor's repertoire, which is not bound to the narrative form, but can be understood as a series of transposable "scenarios," dance *anima* can be dispossessed from the particular history or story—even the particular body that produced it, yet retain traces of bodies and their cultural memories. While Taylor focuses on embodied performance more broadly, my specific focus in this book is on dance, or a set of kinetic gestures of the body (choreographed, rehearsed, or improvised), and the vitality that dance produces. Dance *anima* possesses an energy inherent to itself, and it need not be attached to the organic human form. Its driving force animates and propels life forms across various media. This further complicates the notion of the archive, as it would seem that dance *anima* is valuable not so much for its contribution to any kind of heritage, legacy, or history-based repository (it cannot cement anyone person in the role of genius dancer or choreographer), but is valuable instead as a renewable and distributed resource that is at once superhuman and carries traces of the human as ontological category (it acts as proof of the human where there may not be a human present).

In the postmodern dance tradition, the ephemerality of dance is again countered by its conception as a living archive—an idea bolstered by methods like Labanotation or film preservation. The transfer of dance *anima* between bodies often involves tools such as choreography, notation, or technological mediation, situating dance within various mechanics of reproducibility and "apparatuses of capture."[87] And yet, dance *anima* tends to multiply and resist such capture as well—a proliferation that makes it a renewable resource. From early dancing automata in fiction and film to today's dancing computer-generated imagery (CGI), video game avatars, robots, and AI-generated bodies, dance *anima* is increasingly recognized as a valuable resource for engineering life beyond the human. In our current world, where mechanical reproducibility has given way to a thoroughly mediated experience of life, and the real and the artificial are virtually indistinguishable, dance still harkens back to the expressive soul of the human subject, regardless of whether a human is actually there, dancing.

The history of dance, then, has often been a history of attempts to delineate the distinction between dancer and technique, pinpointing just where the *anima* comes from. Certain forms of dance (especially traditional Western forms such as classical ballet, jazz, and certain contemporary styles) champion virtuosity, in which impressive bodily feats allow dancers to briefly exceed traditional human limits and the impression of bounded form. This virtuosity is not inherent in dance or proof of "natural" human potential, but rather is the product of painstaking practice. Dancers, "like athletes [...] are often read as moving unconsciously, or naturally, with a kind of animal speed or grace—as if their movements were driven by instinct. Their use of movement for expression connects dancers to the realms of pre-linguistic or pre-technological, the animal or the 'primitive' that is the obverse, but not the opposite, of the machine."[88] In this way, dancers represent "both the capabilities of a highly mechanized body and the pre-technological body whose powerful naturalness is imitated by machinery."[89]

American modern dance pioneers such as Isadora Duncan and Ruth St. Denis rejected the rigid mechanization of ballet at the turn of the century, trading pointe shoes for bare feet and emphasizing the spiritual, organic, and "earthbound" qualities of human movement. This resistance to machine culture and technology is one of the prevailing conceptions about American modern dance in the 1930s. However, modern dance technique and choreography is nonetheless learned by rigorous repetition that produces the dancing body as an *instrument* of soul-infused movement, so that human expression is not merely autonomous, free, or born of innate emotional response, but also somewhat machinic at least in ethos. And this machinic habitus of dance, which is never perfect and holds within it the potential for what Rizvana Bradley names the "disruption" of "gestural failure," can also act "as an access point for everyday desire and as a point of transfer for the cultural exchange of knowledge."[90] In its articulation to both the technical mechanics of the body as a tool for expression *and* the overflow of human expression, dance *anima* is always vacillating between being a motor of agency and a vaporous substance. Does this animatic energy propel dance gesture, or does dance gesture harness and propel *anima*? Both, it seems, and simultaneously.

One facet of this historical shift is that as dance *anima* becomes digital (and therefore more slippery and harder to own), it becomes increasingly possible to be multiply iterations of that digital *anima*, and to use it widely (often without legal penalty). A recent example of this is choreographer Kyle Hanagami's lawsuit against Epic Games for their video game Fortnite which uses "emotes" (dance moves performed by digital avatars in the game) that he claims are inspired by his signature choreographies.[91] The lawsuit was originally rejected because the court decided that the dance moves that resembled Hanagami's were actually poses, which are not subject to copyright, but the emotes bear a strong resemblance to Hanagami's work and because they are made of digital data, they are infinitely repeatable in the game across characters.

Due to both its reproducibility (or rehearsability) and its ephemeral nature, the embodied practice of dance calls up similar anxieties around the concept of aura as described by Walter Benjamin in his essay "The Work of Art in the Age of Mechanical Reproduction." In Benjamin's concept, the painting or sculpture with aura is that which contains traces of the artist's body—evidence of their hand movements in the brushstroke or a fingerprint in the side of a vase. Although dance has been generally neglected in studies of Benjamin's writing, it presents a special case of aura because the trace of past-embodied technique—the metaphoric thumbprint in the vase—is seen and felt through the body of the dancer as they move. Dance carries aura (evidence of its embodied craft) even if that body is not an organic, human figure moving in real time. Dance's aura (which I am calling *anima*) does not track back to a singular dancer as artisanal craftsperson or author so much as a genealogy of bodies through which the technique has passed. Because its aura is literally produced through repeated or copied movement, which can be seen as a mechanicity of the body, and because the *anima* of a body can persist outside of the organic human form (e.g., in rotoscoped animation), dance complicates Benjamin's thesis that aura dies or becomes devalued in the age of mechanical reproduction. Dance *anima*, like aura, is produced by technique in the moment of its making (dancing). Unlike Benjaminian aura, dance *anima* does not wither as it is reproduced (or produced outside of the human), but rather flourishes, precisely because it is no longer limited to the singular body but can still energize a feeling of ensoulment. Dance, when performed live, is fleeting, but offers a slippery chance at an immediate spatiotemporal encounter with the specific aura of the dancer, along with their embodied expression (of musicality, rhythm, technique, emotion, etc.). With the development of photography and film, and the potential to animate and choreograph digital avatars and material automatons using machine learning, mocap, and other technological developments, the question of dance's "aura" is no longer limited to its original "presence in time and space" in which the (human) dancer originally danced, and furthermore can be externalized, mediated, replicated, reproduced, and standardized.[92]

***

What inspired American modern dance pioneer Isadora Duncan, famously sentimental and technology-averse, to claim that, in order to dance, "I must place a motor in my soul"? Why does Loïe Fuller's Serpentine Dance at the turn of the century—described by symbolist poet Stéphane Mallarmé as "the dizziness of soul made visible by an artifice"—become even dizzier within today's algorithmic suck of YouTube, where it gathers up countless dancing bodies under Fuller's name? Why are the Boston Dynamics robots, designed to be soulless and unfeeling on the battlefield, doing the twist to Black soul music in viral videos online? How is the persistent association between dance and soul in fact a bid for power and control over vital kinetic energy—or life—as an extractable resource? And how does that vital resource also escape capture? This book follows these and other questions to explore dance as both an apparatus of vitality—one that plays a role in the engineering of life beyond the human—and a renewable energetic force that can multiply.

The experience of dancing is always the experience of being multiple, but as my Preface demonstrates, there is a special kind of multiplication that emerges when dancing within a technological assemblage. My Preface, which briefly describes a research creation project I did involving the choreography for Kate Bush's "Wuthering Heights," performed *en masse* with hundreds of others and the avatar body of Japanese CGI pop star Hatsune Miku, opens the book with an embodied experience of dance *anima*. The awkwardness of the glitch, the power and control of the grid, and the various technologies of capture that inform and produce the *anima* of my research creation project set up some of the stakes of my book, which I have detailed in this introduction—namely, the relationship between dance technique, technology, and soul. The Preface introduces the impossibility of owning one's own dance *anima* (which is always multiply embodied), an idea I examine more closely in Chapter 1. Chapter 1 turns to *fin de siècle* performer Loïe Fuller's popular "Serpentine Dance"—a stage show performed by Fuller as well as countless imitators in late nineteenth-century France and America—as a contagious form of *anima* that moves across various bodies and screens. Fuller herself was never filmed, in large part because she was so paranoid about having her dance stolen. But a search for the "Serpentine Dance" on YouTube today turns up numerous videos that claim (erroneously) to feature Fuller. Following Walter Benjamin's arguments about mechanical reproducibility and the multiplying force of film, the Serpentine not only "substitutes a plurality of copies for a unique existence" but positions plurality as a condition inherent to its ontology. In other words, its aura (or *anima*) is plurality.

The Serpentine Dance was ultimately a choreography of nonhuman bodies, as its success depended not just on the dancer's choreographed gesture, but on her enormous silk costume, her hooked wooden canes, and the luminescent salt gels used to color the stage lights—what Stéphane Mallarmé called a "fearsome bath of materials." While Chapter 1 takes interest in the choreography of these non-anthropocentric materials into something vitally alive—a concept that also ultimately facilitates questions about what choreography really is—Chapter 2 tracks dance as a cultural technique for engineering vitality in humanoid (or human-appearing) bodies, this time through the example of the "dancing machine," a term I borrow from Felicia McCarren. I offer four case studies to illustrate a brief history of the dancing machine from film, literature, and social media: Olympia, the automaton from E. T. A. Hoffmann's 1817 German-Romantic short story "The Sandman"; Maria, the *maschinenmensch* from Fritz Lang's German-Expressionist film *Metropolis* (1927); Kyoko, the artificially intelligent cyborg from Alex Garland's *Ex Machina* (2014); and Lil Miquela (2025), a digital Instagram influencer who sings and dances, animated by motion capture technology. All four of these artificial women are brought to life through dance, and all four navigate the plight of their choreographed existence by blurring the line between puppet and agent of their own desire. This chapter underscores the crucial role of the screen (from cinema to the iPhone) in the transmission of narratives and fantasies about the dancing machine whose *anima* (or soul) is produced through the technique and technology of dance.

Chapter 3 historically situates the abstraction of dance movement as a fantasy of disembodiment that occurs across modernism, postmodernism, and advanced capitalism. I focus on the techniques and technologies of extraction that prey on dance *anima*, from dance notation to animation techniques such as rotoscoping and motion capture (mocap). These animation tools, which reconfigure the organic or human dancer into an "impossible body, unencumbered by gravity, technique, time or death" (Rosenberg), presenting the fantasy of a plastic body that cannot die, often depend on the extracted and uncredited labor of dancers of color. I follow this phenomenon through several case studies involving Black dancers, including the Fleischer Brothers' rotoscoped animations of American jazz bandleader Cab Calloway, and Mumble the animated penguin from *Happy Feet* (whose motion was provided via mocap by American tap dancer Savion Glover). Such animated works rely on the tangible capital of Black vernacular dance *anima* while simultaneously erasing the actual bodies that did the dancing, demonstrating a particular kind of racial capitalism that intensifies in our era of metamorphic animated characters and viral digital media. Brenda Dixon Gottschild describes this as the rendering invisible of the Africanist presence to frame it as a kind of "vitality" inherent to America.[93] The chapter also looks at Bill T. Jones's 1999 screendance work *Ghostcatching*, a collaboration with digital media artists Paul Kaiser and Shelley Eshkar. *Ghostcatching* actively engages with these questions from the perspective of Jones, an African American dancer-choreographer, making it an important, situated, counterpoint to the other case studies in this chapter.

Chapter 4 is about the choreography of labor and dance as capital. Drawing on examples from the human motion studies of Eadweard Muybridge and Etienne-Jules Marey in the late 1800s, Taylorism and the standardized body labor of the assembly line, as well as the spectacle of American Engineering firm Boston Dynamics' dancing military robots, I explore the role of choreography in the organization, exploitation, and weaponization of bodies throughout history—the forced mechanization of the human body. This chapter is attentive to the camera as an agent in the procedures that govern bodies in space, filmic technologies of science and work, and the distillation of the human worker into their role as standardized, dehumanized performer. I look especially at the use of soul music and social dance in the Boston Dynamics videos to think about the cultural capital that Black labor (and dance) provides to the process of humanizing and ensouling machines of war. This final chapter also marks a shift in scale, from the singular dancer who carries the traces of others, to the many-bodied, depersonalized dance of the military–industrial complex. My conclusion draws back to my personal, embodied experience through the choreographies of new motherhood under the regulations of the global pandemic. Through this and a close reading of Claire Denis's experimental military film *Beau Travail* referenced in the poem that serves as epigraph, I explore the power of repetition as a means for improvisation, and the potential for dance *anima* to erupt (and disrupt) in explosive, glitchy, embodied joy.

1

The Dizzy Soul of the Serpentine

> ... all the magic of Merlin, the sorcery of light, colour, flowing form
> ... She transformed herself into a thousand [...] images before the
> eyes of her audience. Unbelievable. Not to be repeated or described.
> —Isadora Duncan writes about the Serpentine Dance

Repeating the Unrepeatable

Type the term "Loie Fuller Serpentine Dance" into the search bar on
YouTube, and you will find a string of uploaded videos, all of which mistakenly credit the American dancer Loïe Fuller as performer (see Figure 5). Each
of these videos features a single female dancer using hidden rods to manipulate large swathes of silk fabric, creating a perpetual transformation of shapes
and abstract images. Most of the dancers in these videos perform on a wooden
stage for a front-facing camera as a stand-in for a live audience. Many of the
films are hand-tinted in rose, violet, and green hues to emulate Fuller's signature stage lights, which she outfitted with colored gels and projected onto her
voluminous costume in both her "Serpentine" and "Fire" dances.[94]

Although they are labeled with her name, it is likely that *none of these videos
feature Loïe Fuller.* Instead, they present a variety of different dancers—
many of them contemporaries of Fuller such as Crissie Sheridan, Annabelle
Whitford-Moore, Maud Madison, and Maybelle Stuart—with obviously different body shapes, facial features, costumes, and kinetic styles, who perform
the choreography with slight variations. The comments underneath these
videos run the gamut from wonder (*Nono le vieux crabe* writes, "She was an
extraordinary artist!") to critique of the dancer's appearance (*ytcarol*: "her
little face is all grimace and frown—how lovely would a smile be ... "), but
the most common occurrence in the comment section is a dispute about the
identity of the performer in the video. For example, the comments under a
video titled "Loïe Fuller (1905) [silent short film]," which features Fuller's

Dance Anima. Hilary Bergen, Oxford University Press. © Oxford University Press 2026.
DOI: 10.1093/9780197786673.003.0002

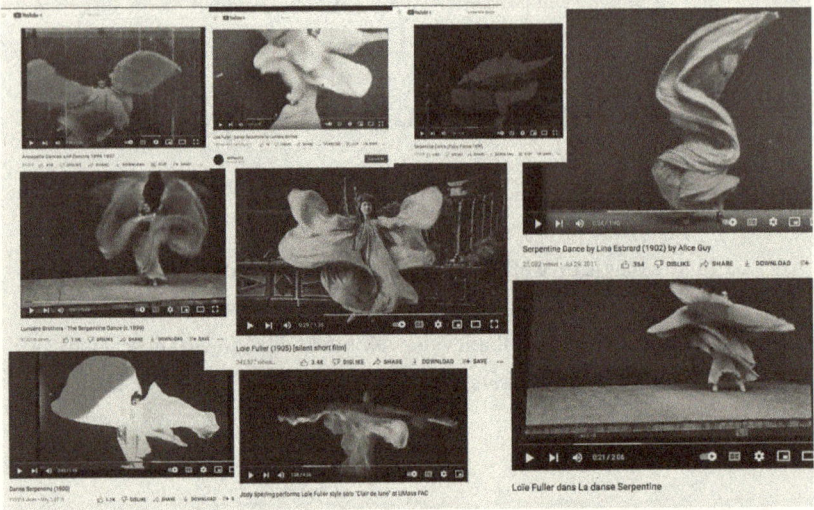

Figure 5 A collection of the Serpentine videos found on YouTube, many of which are erroneously credited with Loïe Fuller's name. (Screenshots taken by Hilary Bergen.)

name in the opening credits and was posted on December 27, 2014, by YouTube user *Social Deception*, and boasting 439,000 views read as such:

> @*littleoldlady523* (5 years ago): "This is not Loïe Fuller. There are no extant films of her dancing. The Lumière Brothers hired someone else, now unknown, to perform the dance: she seems to ahve [sic] been a thorn in Fuller's side thereafter."
>
> @*Yorkshiresoul* (5 years ago): "MOMA links to this and says it is her, is there definite evidence either way?"
>
> @*08pixiedust* (3 years ago): If you mean Minnie Redwood, this doesn't look like her. It does look like other pictures of Loie, though.
>
> @*GiselaHere* (2 years ago): @Yorshiresoul: There were plenty of Loie imitations, and those even used her name [sic]. None of the footage is actually Loie. Check the evidence in her autobiography, published in 1908.
>
> @*RealPreCinema* (1 year ago): This is Loie. The woman you're thinking of is her compatriot Isadora Duncan, who also revolutionized the practice of dance with her great freedom of expression.
>
> @*Leslie Stevens*: "I believe she was never filmed. This is just a follower copycat."[95]

These comments are written casually by individuals who do not announce themselves as historians or dance scholars, making them exterior to the recognized institutions of history-making. Sometimes commenting years apart, and from various unknown locations, these YouTube users enact a conversation that traverses space and time to actively construct and deconstruct Fuller's mythology in the present. The Serpentine dance has always mystified its audience, whether viewed on stage, in the early filmic form, or on a laptop screen. Distributed across many "bodies," including performative nonhuman materials such as emergent electric light and billowing silk, the Serpentine exists as a contagious phenomenon that elides origins and refuses to reside in any one, singular dancer while at the same time carrying Loïe Fuller's name with it wherever it goes. In 2018, for example, American pop star Taylor Swift paid tribute to Loïe Fuller in her Reputation tour, featuring Serpentine dancers in her live show and announcing that Fuller "fought for artists to own their own work"—a battle near and dear to Swift, who recently re-recorded her own songs to control their licensing for commercial use.[96] The Serpentine is therefore an example of dance *anima* that stretches across the historical continuum of this book, from early modernism to advanced capitalism. The viral distribution of the dance across other bodies reveals that, despite Fuller's righteous insistence otherwise, dance (and its *anima*) is not something that anyone can own or control.

It was over 130 years ago, in 1892, that Loïe Fuller first captivated audiences at the Folies Bergère in Paris, where she performed the legendary "Serpentine Dance" to a packed house. At a time when theaters were just beginning to convert gas to electricity, Fuller's experiments with fabric and colored lights stunned audiences and transformed her body into what the *London Standard*, in 1900, called a "kaleidoscopic vision."[97] Fuller was part of the rapid changes of modernity in *fin de siècle* North America and Europe, predicting future cinema spectatorship by turning herself into an animated screen for the audience to gaze upon and expanding the notion of what constitutes a dancing body.[98] According to the posters advertising the show, Fuller's costume was made of 500 yards of heavy white silk, which she manipulated invisibly by hooked bamboo canes from within, in spirals and loops.[99] Fuller used embodied technique to disappear into a fluid spectacle of abstract and symbolic forms (described as a flame, butterfly, flower, or even a uterus), but her bodily labor was just one component of this dance assemblage, which redistributed authorship (and therefore agency and ownership) from Fuller to the many other material and ideological components that construct the dance: yards upon yards of silk, electricity, the poems of Stéphane

Mallarmé, academic discourses of feminism and technology, Fuller's autobiography, the chemical element radium, the unidentifiable Serpentine dancer
on advertisements for the stage show, Marie Curie, YouTube algorithms,
the movie camera, Maybelle Stewart, Crissie Sheridan, and so on. The
Serpentine demonstrates the force that dance *anima* can gather and propel,
and the anxious relationship between ego, spectacle, and disembodied personhood that results.

Despite her proto-cinematic stage show, there is no proof that Fuller was
ever actually filmed performing the Serpentine dance.[100] In the quote that
opens this chapter, Isadora Duncan proclaims that the Serpentine Dance was
not to be "repeated or described." And yet it was repeated, and often, by other
dancers, so that its "signature" force was necessarily distributed across various bodies and screens, technological and organic agents. Dance and film
scholars (see McCarren 2003; Garelick 2009; Gunning 2003) often credit
Fuller as the inventor of the Serpentine, and her name has become tightly
fastened to the dance, both in academic and popular discourse.[101] However,
the origins of the piece are unclear, in spite of the fact that Fuller's technique
does bear resemblances to Hindu Nautch Dancing,[102] and that she admitted
that her silk costume was gifted to her by a British soldier who had spent time
in India, details that often get lost in the telling of Fuller's mythic "invention"
and which I will explore in greater depth later in this chapter.

Fuller's own account of arriving in Paris for the first time to discover an
"imitator" named Maybelle Stewart performing her choreography positions
the Serpentine as property stolen from Fuller herself: "Imagine my astonish-
ment," she writes in her autobiography, "when, in getting out of the carriage
in front of the *Folies*, I found myself face to face with a 'serpentine dancer'
reproduced in violent tones on some huge placards. This dancer was not Loïe
Fuller."[103] Upon seeing posters advertising her show with a different dancer
at the helm, Fuller went to see her "rival" and "robber," dance on stage, and
was relieved to discover that Stewart's version of the Serpentine paled greatly
in comparison to her own. "My imitator was so ordinary," Fuller writes,
"that, sure of my own superiority, I no longer dreaded her."[104] Crucially,
Fuller's anxious bid for ownership over the dance did not prevent her from
agreeing—since the publicity for Stewart's Serpentine Dance had already
been circulated—to replace Stewart and dance under her name for the first
two nights of the show."[105] However, Fuller seems to include this anecdote in
her autobiography to secure her position as "inventor"—and thereby most
skilled performer—of the Serpentine Dance. There are several reasons why

Fuller might see herself as an inventor rather than a creator or choreographer; certainly, Fuller's friendship with scientist Marie Curie and her interest in lighting technologies and radium point to a scientific approach aligned with invention. The word inventor also gestures toward an assemblage of media that forms the Serpentine (lighting, props, costuming) as opposed to choreographer, which implies the creator of a sequence of movements. It seems Fuller wanted to assert possession over the *entire* aesthetic experience of the work, rather than merely the steps or figure-eight gestures of her arms while dancing it. Fuller's vigorous pursuit here reveals that dance *anima* is produced by an assemblage of techniques and technologies that includes but is not limited to choreography (or the singular dancer moving through space with a sequence of gestures).

The Serpentine's disembodying technique transferred *anima* to the swirl of fabric and colored light, evoking various forms as if from thin air—an effect described by poet Stéphane Mallarmé as "the dizziness of soul made visible by an artifice."[106] This "soul"—the dizzy dance *anima* of the Serpentine—is conjured by assemblage, in which the circulation of posters and print media, along with the tangle of electricity, costuming, and props onstage, work together to efface Fuller's identity as an original and singular creator and interrogate the mythology of Loïe Fuller as "the" Serpentine Dancer. It is precisely in this gap, between the Serpentine as an illusion of disembodiment and Fuller's (impossible) wish to tie the dance to her unique and singular body, that I locate three main tensions at play in a theory of dance *anima*:

First, the Serpentine exemplifies the dancer (and dance *anima*) as an instrument of exploration between two realms: the concept of the human and the emergence of new media. The Serpentine, with its techniques and technologies—canes, swirling silks, and colored lights—takes on its own agency, one that expands beyond the human bodies operating the dance and threatens to erase the human altogether. This more-than-human vitality is further driven by the emergence of film as an apparatus of capture and distribution, a process accelerated by video-sharing sites like YouTube, where dancers' identities are not verified and captions are not fact-checked. Under the spell of the Serpentine, it seems all dancers are Loïe Fuller. And yet, secondly, the Serpentine represents dance *anima* as unpossessable, even by Fuller. Fuller was so preoccupied with the originality of her work precisely because there was something characteristically evasive about the Serpentine Dance—due to a combination of emerging modernist values, the relationship between the Serpentine and early cinema, the rise of what Walter Benjamin named techniques of "mechanical reproduction," and the fact that it was danced by a woman—that made it antithetical to the notion of ownership. Ironically, it is Fuller's claim to invention and originality that reveals dance as an always already mediated assemblage. Fuller's patented stage materials and props, and her "signature" techniques all ascertain the reproducibility and virality of the Serpentine. Third, the Serpentine, all the rage at the turn of the century and at the dawning of the film era, acts as a pseudo starting point for the media history explored in this book. Because its popularity endures to the present day, the Serpentine demonstrates that the questions surrounding technologized dance about authorship and authenticity predate postmodernism, illustrating the historical continuum of dance *anima* as one punctuated by various emergent media, apparatuses, and energies that can propel and corral vitality outside of the live human body.

"Movement Uncomplicated by Persona"

One reason why dancers in the Serpentine videos on YouTube are so often mistaken for Fuller is because their faces and bodies are barely visible, revealed only in flashes from behind the whirling silks. The Serpentine dance itself effectively erases the personhood of the dancer—a tendency that flourished in the decade following Fuller's stage shows via an early modernist aesthetics of abstraction. The quest for depersonalized, "pure" form (or a turning away from the primacy of the human subject) was more prevalent in the realms of visual art and literature than in dance at the turn of the century, yet traditional Western conceptions of dance, and in particular ballet, often align with some similar fantasies of transcendence. American dance historian Deborah Jowitt writes of the weightless, supernatural quality prized by classical dance in the Romantic era leading up to the turn of the century, where "insubstantiality [was] close to godliness."[107] Dancers were praised not so much for their physical prowess as for their ability to look and move in an angelic fashion. Jowitt remarks that the female dancer in particular was something of a paradox in that she was seen as both a poetic image and a "panting perspiring body," and dancing was seen as a way to release or *free* said poetic image from the body.[108]

The frequent use of the word "freedom" in descriptions of dance's aim is striking, and points to the misogynistic impulse to wish away the abject corporeality of the (often) female dancer. Susanne Langer argues that "the most important [force], from the balletic standpoint, is . . . the sense of freedom from gravity,"[109] as does Paul Valéry, who writes that in dance, the body seems to have "broken free from its usual states of balance. It seems to be trying to outwit—I should say outrace—its own weight, at every moment evading its pull, not to say its sanction."[110] Although Fuller's dancing can be placed more accurately within a genre of early modern dance than one of ballet, the Serpentine is nonetheless concerned with this idea of freeing the *anima* of the moving images from the body producing them. Whereas ballet is often associated with a series of technical poses and body positions, the Serpentine dance, praised for its flow and rejection of stasis, reflects modernism's (and early modern dance's) obsession with fluidity and transformation.[111] Deleuzian media scholar Stamatia Portanova writes that Loïe Fuller's performance of the Serpentine highlights "the nature of movement as an infinitely decomposable continuity, [. . .] one in which the form has not fully determined its own difference, its "presence and precision," from the continuities of matter."[112] In other words, the Serpentine illustrates "a continuous process of formation, rather than a form" or a particular body: a description that likewise characterizes dance *anima*.[113]

The Serpentine is often associated with Symbolism, the late nineteenth-century European arts movement which rejected realism in favor of spirituality, imagination, and dreams. Fuller's gender, or rather, her ability to transcend her gender, was also key to her role as the Symbolist's muse. In "Ballets" (1886), Mallarmé writes:

> the ballerina is *not a girl dancing* . . . she is *not a girl*, but rather a metaphor which symbolizes some elemental aspect of earthly form: sword, cup, flower, etc., and that *she does not dance* but rather, with miraculous lunges and abbreviations, writing with her body, she suggests things which the written work could express only in several paragraphs of dialogue or descriptive prose. Her poem is written without the writer's tools.[114]

In his aesthetic abstraction of the dancer, Mallarmé demonstrates that in his view, the dancer's body is also prosthetic/subservient to the imagery she is capable of evoking. As Amy Kortiz writes, "[t]he dancer's agency has at best a precarious place in [Mallarmé's] formulation, since she is text, writing implement and meaning all at once, while at the same time *not* being a subject, who could write [emphasis mine]."[115] If according to Mallarmé, the dancer's "poem" is "written without the writer's tools," it refuses her the status of writer/author and the autonomy associated with such a subject position. Mallarmé's commentary on dance and his praise of the Serpentine reveals that in early modernist discourse the unownable quality of dance *anima* is crucially tied to a process of disembodiment: an almost imperative disownment of dance from the body (or author) that produced it, and a transfer of that dance *anima* into a series of metaphors and metamorphic images.

Perhaps counter-intuitively, Mallarmé *emphasizes* the dancer's gender through negation, when he writes that she is "not a girl dancing." Despite her obvious success in various male-dominated fields such as chemistry and electrical engineering, Fuller was similarly unable to escape gendered projections and assumptions about her work. Ted Merwin, for example, writes that Fuller used technology to "wed" her organic, womanly body with the masculine force of electricity on stage, thus "marrying" dance (female) and science (male).[116] Here, Fuller's use of electricity is framed as a foray into a man's world through the patriarchal metaphor of marriage, reinforcing a Cartesian binary that delegates the dancing body as feminine, and the scientific mind as male. While many scholars have interpreted Fuller's work through feminism, it is worth noting also that claims for Fuller as a distinctly feminist artist are largely speculative (and generalizing), drawing from Fuller's stereotypically masculine expertise where electricity and science were concerned, and from her lesbian identity.[117] There is a temptation, in historical writing, to equate women working in scientific fields with feminist politics. I do not mean to suggest that Fuller cannot stand as a powerful representation of women's engagement with male-dominated areas. However, I find it curious that in the writings about Fuller's performance, her body is often configured as an impediment to freedom, so that on the one hand she is called a feminist and on the other she is applauded for making her female body disappear. This is because feminist analyses of Fuller's work often cite her transformative potential—the *erasure* of her fixed female form—as a means of liberation from the increased commodification of women's bodies in the industrial age. Ironically, her metamorphosis into a dehumanized spectacle, much like the "vanishing woman" in stage magician acts, hinges on the "commodified visibility" of the very thing it is erasing: the female body.[118] The erasure of the dancing body in favor of dance as an energy (*anima*) to be engineered, exchanged, and multiplied as valuable resource merely commodifies that *anima* instead of the body involved in making it, and furthermore risks reframing dancers' bodies as impediments to these processes, or as mere vessels that temporarily contain, but cannot own, dance *anima*.

Figure 6 A photograph of Loïe Fuller dancing outdoors, her body hidden within her voluminous Serpentine costume. (Photograph by Samuel Joshua Beckett, circa 1900 (MET, 2005.100.950), WIKICOMMONS.)

In fact, Fuller's gendered image was a draw for audiences, as demonstrated by the posters for her shows which misleadingly feature drawings of a scantily clad female dancer in a coquettish pose, as seen in Figure 7. These posters often rendered Fuller so unrecognizable that it was unclear whether they depicted her or one of the many other Serpentine dancers. This ambiguous portrayal of the Serpentine dancer's body again speaks to the interchangeable nature of the dancer in the dance or the way the *anima* of the Serpentine powerfully gathered many bodies under one name, and the role of media and fantasy in this consolidation. At times, the posters erroneously implied that the performer would be dancing nude beneath her costume, when in reality the audience of the piece would experience a kind of reverse striptease in which the dancer's body became increasingly covered up and obscured. Given that Fuller came to exemplify such an array of abstract and philosophical conceptions, and that she is often described in inhuman, even immaterial, terms, it is easy to forget that she was also just a woman, dancing in front of an audience.

Figure 7 A poster for Fuller's stage show depicting a sexualized dancer who looks like nothing Fuller. (*Folies Berger: La Loïe Fuller*, 1893, poster by Jules Chéret. WIKICOMMONS.)

Many of Fuller's fans were surprised by the shape and size of her body when they saw her offstage, in normal lighting, and there she was: a "rather plain-looking girl from Illinois."[119] Garelick writes that Fuller's 1895 performance of *Salome* was "met with critical failure—largely because it failed to keep a plump and visibly sweating Fuller under wraps or at a suitable distance from the audience . . . but so long as Fuller kept her somewhat graceless self out of sight and centered her performance on her technological genius, she dazzled her crowds."[120] There was a contrast between the "highly eroticized body" portrayed on Fuller's publicity posters, not to mention the otherworldly butterflies and orchids she evoked on stage, and her mundane organic body, which critics have described using various derogatory terms like "pudgy," "stocky," "heavy," "shapeless," and "unglamorous."[121] The misogyny of these descriptions—to Jean Cocteau, for example, Fuller was merely a "fat, ugly American woman with glasses" who managed to create "the phantom of an era"[122]—is striking. As Garelick writes, "Fuller made a career out of staging her own immateriality,"[123] leaning into the tension between the fantasy image of the disappearing female body, and the material reality of the dancer's embodied labor and skill. The Serpentine Dance, which re-embodies the dancer into a swathe of media, navigates between the categories of human and technology to reveal dance *anima* as a transcendent, de-anthropomorphic, fantasy form.

The detachment of dance *anima* from the singular human body—its disembodiment, whether discursive or material—contributes to the concept of dance as an unownable thing. Anthea Kraut has written at length about Fuller's attempts to copyright the *Serpentine*, including her 1892 lawsuit against performer Minnie Renwood Bemis on the grounds that she had stolen Fuller's dance. The court judge ultimately rejected this suit because "the *Serpentine Dance* told no story and was therefore not eligible for copyright protection."[124] In other words, the Serpentine was "too abstract" to be copyrighted.[125] Kraut demonstrates that "for Fuller, the lack of power to control the circulation of her commodity-image stripped her ability to derive value from it."[126] However, Fuller did not stop trying, and in the case of the Serpentine in particular, there are multiple points of erasure that serve to uphold Fuller as rightful owner. For example, Kraut and others have pointed out that for all of Fuller's anxieties about being recognized as the *true* creator of the dance, the origins of the Serpentine likely stretch back further, to vaudeville skirt dancing, in which the dancer's legs were revealed seductively with every twirl of the fabric. Skirt dancing in turn evolves out of "Nautch dancing, the generic, colonialist term for Indian dance in the nineteenth and twentieth centuries."[127] The Serpentine is indebted to Nautch dancing both in terms of technique but in the static body poses that Fuller used to begin and end the piece—poses very similar to those seen in the cabinet cards of nautch dancers.[128]

The material of Fuller's silk skirts also hold within them a lineage that draws back to nautch: in a chapter of her autobiography titled "How I Invented the Serpentine Dance," Fuller explains that her costume was a "Hindu skirt . . . sent [to her from India] by two young officers" who she describes in colonial terms as "essentially and purely English."[129] Even while she mentions the "Hindu skirt"—the material that literally *dances* in her stage show—Fuller fails to recognize the Hindu Nautch dancers as an influence on the Serpentine, instead naming the British officers as stewards of the fabric and active contributors to her invention. Fuller's narrative, bolstered by humanist values of divine inspiration and individual creation, reflects Kraut's observation that "the history of dance in the United States is also the history of white 'borrowing' from racially subjugated communities, almost always without credit or compensation."[130] Fuller's refusal to acknowledge Nautch dancing as influence is unsurprising, given early white modernism's socially accepted Orientalist aesthetics and appropriations.[131] A theory of dance *anima* reveals how this type of borrowing without attribution appears to be justified or made inevitable by the slippery, viral, ephemeral properties of dance. Considering the Serpentine's nautch dance origins therefore does not isolate it as an instance of mere cultural appropriation, but rather allows us to interrogate the authenticity and cultural specificity of *all* dance.

Yet even as the dance slips between bodies and Fuller attempts to pin it down using patents and autobiographies, the Serpentine carries traces of its Nautch origins in a material way; the important and yet depersonalized role of the Hindu skirt in the Serpentine's mythology reflects Anne Anlin Cheng's theory of "Ornamentalism," which extends Edward Said's foundational work on Orientalism toward a theory of the "yellow woman" focused not on skin, but on the ornamental surface. Cheng's "yellow woman," a figure that is "present/absent, organic/synthetic, a figure of civilizational value and a disposable object of decadence," can be seen in Fuller's appropriated dancing silk costume, which becomes *the* dancing body in the Serpentine.[132] Fuller's silks, which become ornamental in movement (taking on folds and swirls), gaining a sense of *anima* through animation, demonstrate what Cheng describes as "a different historiography of raced bodies: one constructed through fabrics, ornaments, and 'skins' that never enjoyed the fantasy of organicity; one populated by nonsubjects who endure as ornamental appendages."[133] Cheng's work shows how decentering the human (e.g., in the fetishization of the modernist surface or in a theory of dance *anima*) can in fact re-center race in the conversation. She writes that if we "think through, rather than shy away from, that intractable intimacy between being a person and being a thing" we can examine the substitution of "*ornament* for *flesh* as the germinal matter for the making of racialized gender."[134] The Serpentine illustrates the slippery embodiment of dance *anima* because it presents both abstract movement and instructions for a material ornamental form (in patents and props), carrying vestiges of Indian Nautch dancing forward into an unofficial European-American archive, yet erasing those remnants of the "ornamental" Other through Fuller's quest for genius-status.

Techniques of Ownership

Even at the time of its creation, Fuller's deep wish to be seen as the inventor of the piece betrays her awareness of the ways in which the Serpentine evades bids for ownership. During her first tour of the dance in New York in February of 1892, prior to her Paris show, she was dismayed at the fact that even as critics praised the Serpentine, her "name was nowhere mentioned," remarking, "They had stolen my dance."[135] I mentioned earlier that Fuller considered herself the "inventor" of the Serpentine. We might consider, also, Fuller's description of the Serpentine Dance as both her creation and as a "great discovery," from her 1908 autobiography titled *Quinze ans de ma vie* (translated to English in 1913):

> Golden reflections played in the folds of the sparkling silk, and in this light my body was vaguely revealed in shadowy contour. This was a moment of intense emotion. Unconsciously I realised that I was in the presence of a great discovery, one which was destined to open the path which I have since followed. Gently, almost religiously, I set the silk in motion, and I saw that I had obtained undulations of a character heretofore unknown. I had created a new dance.[136]

Fuller frames this experience as religious, emotional, and predestined, and the dance becomes a conduit for spiritual experience. Throughout her autobiography, Fuller employs proprietary language to lay claim to the dance and all elements of her stage show. Of her "chemically composed colours, heretofore unknown," which she used to tint her stage lights, Fuller writes: "I stand before them like a miner who has discovered a vein of gold,"[137] presenting herself as a laborer whose discovery, like gold, has tangible monetary effects for her as an artist. Likewise, the fabric's "undulations," which Fuller characterizes as "heretofore unknown," frame the Serpentine as a kind of mystical river flowing past, which Fuller dips into and uses in her creation.

Similarly, while the descriptions of Fuller's Serpentine by those who saw it performed live evoke an undeniable sense of aura,[138] the capture and distribution of that dance on film stretch its aura away from the singular body, encompassing many different (oftentimes unnamed) dancers. The dance was a major source of inspiration for film pioneers like Edison and the Lumière Brothers, whose Serpentine films at the turn of the century illustrate the proliferating effect of what Walter Benjamin names techniques of "mechanical reproduction." Interestingly, the mechanical reproduction of the Serpentine made it resistant to notions of authorship and ownership, but not to possession of Benjaminian aura, which seemed to multiply and gain power along the viral path of the Serpentine's *anima*. In his widely cited 1936 essay, Walter Benjamin argues that with the rise of technologies of mass production, which can unmoor images from their unique spatial and temporal locations (the "fabric of tradition"), the art object loses its "aura" or authentic character.[139] As Benjamin writes: "The presence of the original is the prerequisite to the concept of authenticity," an authenticity which, when copied, becomes more and more difficult to verify, and marked by an "aura" that dissolves as copies of the original are made. The most "powerful agent" of such reproducibility, Benjamin argues, is the film.[140] Framed within Benjamin's observations about mechanical reproducibility and the multiplying force of film, the Serpentine does not only "substitute a plurality of copies for a unique existence," but positions plurality as a condition integral to its ontology. In other words, its aura (or *anima*) *is and always has been plurality*.[141]

It is notable that the different Serpentine dancers on film are not identical or standardized like commodities on an assembly line, but they have a visible sameness that makes telling them apart difficult: the multiple Serpentine Dancers present plurality not as a string of exact copies but as a conglomerate of bodies that approximate sameness through likeness in dance *anima*. As Anthea Kraut writes, "Fuller's image . . . was thus an embodied one but also capable of being dis-embodied (or re-embodied by another)" and "this duality raised the stakes and amplified the complexities of trying to control the traffic in her image, and thus protect her subject status, by controlling the circulation of her choreography."[142] The measures Fuller took to prevent others from doing her dance, such as claiming authorship in her autobiography, filing lawsuits, and publishing patents of the set designs and costumes speak once again to her anxiety over ownership.

Because dance is ephemeral, and "leaves no object behind after its performance," as André Lepecki notes, its ephemeral nature is also its "afterlife," in that it "haunts every second of the present with its potential return."[143] Fuller's patents for her stage design and costuming were intended as safeguards against the ephemerality of the Serpentine, as a means of ascertaining control over the profits of the dance, and to protest the "loss of control over her bodily labour."[144] Anthea Kraut argues that copyright historically allowed choreographers to "position themselves as possessive individuals and rights-bearing subjects rather than as [. . .] objects of exchange."[145] To that end, however, the patents were unsuccessful or perhaps even counter-productive in their instructive nature: they rendered the Serpentine *repro-ducible* as a cultural technique and therefore as a commodity. Kraut points out that the Fuller's written description in the copyright actually "reads like instructions for re-creating the solo dance."[146] And indeed, between the years of 1895 and 1905, there was a sudden influx of "Serpentine" dancers in Europe, prompting Fuller to believe her choreography was being copied by performers like Ameta, Chrissie Sheridan, Annabelle, Ruth St. Denis, Émilienne d'Alençon, Lina Esbrard, and the "flame dancer" Papinta (who some have suggested as another possible inventor of the Serpentine and Fire dances to which Fuller laid claim).[147]

Faced with this quandary about ownership, Fuller could not patent her choreography, but she could patent the tools used to produce it (see Figure 8). These patents illustrated in great detail the techniques, props, and technologies used to produce the dance, from the skirt "formed of several triangular pieces" and "affixed to a suitable crown [made of a] light material such as aluminum" in order to achieve a "radial latitude" as the skirts swirled, to the "hook-shaped wands" held by the dancer and used to propel the silk "wings" of the costume.[148] It seems important to note that when Fuller's lawsuit against Minnie Redwood Bemis was rejected, it was done so on the grounds that "the merely mechanical movements by which effects are produced on the stage are not subjects of copyright where they convey no ideas whose arrangement makes up a dramatic composition."[149] The "mechanical movements" as described in the legal document, Mallarmé's use of the word "artifice" and Fuller's various techniques, costumes, and stage tools come together to show that perhaps the Serpentine was too technologized a dance—too mediated, with too hidden a human body—to protect under copyright or own. It was not, however, too technologized to produce a feeling of soul. In fact, it was precisely the "artifice" that Mallarmé describes that produced the "dizzy soul" of the Serpentine.

With her lawsuit against her imitator, Kraut explains, Fuller appealed to "the Romantic notion of originary authorship [which] constructs the artist as a singular visionary whose work is by definition new and unique rather than imitative or derivative."[150] Given the way that Fuller's name persistently attaches itself even to videos of the Serpentine dance which do not feature her in any way, it seems she still does achieve credit for "originary author-ship," regardless of who is dancing the dance. Yet, the multiplying effect of the Serpentine's reproduction also points to a core of uncertainty or confusion (or transformative potential) that lies at the heart of the dance. In *Valuing Dance: Commodities and Gifts in Motion*, Susan Leigh Foster explains the relationship between dance and commodification as such:

> For dance movement to be salable, it must be given firmer borders and boundaries, and clearer shapes and patterning. The ephemeral messiness of movement must be sorted out and regularized, replacing its indecipher-able blurriness, uncontainable wiggling, endless flow, or unpredictably sequenced bursts of action with individuated moves, steps, and sequences that are precisely shaped and metrically timed. This augmentation in movement's concreteness makes it more identifiable and consequently repeatable.[151]

Foster's definition of salable movement is at odds with the Serpentine Dance, which was defined by its "indecipherable blurriness" and "endless flow" and nonetheless was highly "repeatable," thanks to Fuller's descriptions in her patents of the methods and techniques of producing such effects (e.g., the patent specifies that the hooked wooden canes be manipulated in figure eights and that the silk costume be attached to the dancer's head). The patents give the Serpentine "firmer borders and boundaries," in the words of Foster—borders which reflect Fuller's attempts to make dance concrete in her desire to "own" the Serpentine. Her failure to fully own the dance reveals both that dance is always already a technical assemblage, and that *anima* (something produced via technique between and amongst bodies) exceeds the saleable movement of a dance.

Fuller's patents (e.g., see Figure 8) display the technical wizardry neces-sary to produce such an unstable and imaginative image. They also set up technique as the ground of ethereality in dance, and therefore, technique as a *technology* for imagination/freedom, in the sense that freedom is an aes-thetic that can be artificially produced by rigid discipline. It is the technique/technology of the Serpentine Dance that propagates itself across bodies, and that technique is visible not in the obscured and abstracted dancer's body, but in the materials manipulated by that (highly disciplined) body, as well as in the space traversed, the duration of the performance, and, perhaps most

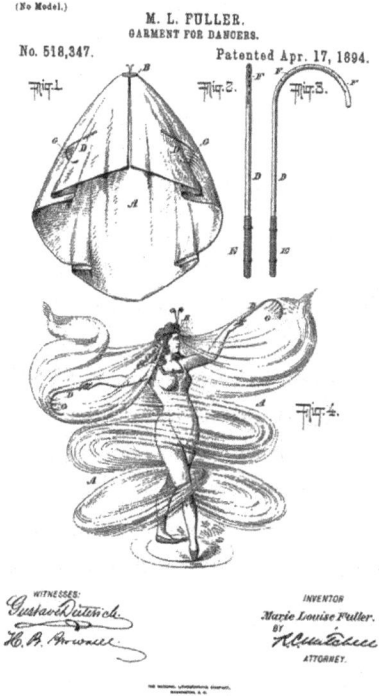

Figure 8 The patent for Fuller's stage costume includes a human figure, mid-Serpentine, to illustrate the technique required to manipulate the silks in figure eights. (Marie Louise Fuller, "Garment for Dancers," No. 518347. Patented April 17, 1894, United States Patent Office, https://patents.google.com/patent/US518 347?oq = 518347).

distinctly, in the affect it produces in the audience. While dance technique can be understood as the repetitive standardization of the body, there is also something about the Serpentine dance that resists such standardization, as is obvious from the different styles or approaches to the dance in the videos drawn together under the umbrella of Serpentine, preventing the dance from being categorized as commodity, which, in the words of Mark Seltzer, "stands still," "waiting to be sold."[152] Yet Fuller did profit off of the Serpentine during her time as a performer, and even if she is disputed as its creator, her name continues to accrue what Pierre Bourdieu calls "institutionalized cultural capital," in which her esteem increases with every academic citation or YouTube comment that links her to the dance.

The Viral Echo

Fuller is but one body of the Serpentine's multiple bodies, each of which are in complex relation with each other via the *anima* of the dance. The Serpentine presents the act of copying, not just as reproduction of a set of cultural techniques, but as an unintentional symptom of the relational aura of the work: one that might be qualified through the image of the echo. For an echo to be produced, sound ricochets off surfaces and is re-doubled, to be sensed again and again. An echo is both a natural phenomenon and a tool or technology. Animals such as bats, whales, and dolphins use echolocation to sense the world around them in great detail. Before the invention of radar, the military also used large stone monoliths as acoustic mirrors (or sound mirrors) to reflect ambient noise off their concave surfaces and discern far away sounds such as an airplane's engine. In an echo, sound waves actually take the shape of the objects they bounce off of, meaning that the echo is simultaneously a machine of mimesis and transformation. In her memoir, Fuller attempts to connect each "echo" of the Serpentine back to herself as inventor, but it dances away from her.

In a chapter titled "The Value of a Name," Fuller writes of the uncanny experience of watching one of her imitator's dance the Serpentine, an experience that allowed her to "see with [her] own eyes 'la Loïe Fuller' dance before [her] face."[153] This image, of Fuller facing "Fuller"—twin dancers doubled by the repetition of technique—demonstrates the ability of the dance to multiply the subject in uncanny fashion and confront Fuller with dance *anima* that is both hers and shared. This experience that no doubt registered in Fuller's body, and also calls up what John Martin calls "metakinesis," or the transference of energy between dancer and spectator, where, "because of the inherent contagion of bodily movement," the "onlooker [feels] sympathetically in his own musculature."[154] Like metakinesis in dance, an echo is a process of relation, putting bodies (human and non-) into mutually affecting networks. The Serpentine Dance is therefore an illustration of dance *anima* because it transforms and exceeds the dancer's body with motion, fabric, and electricity and because it predicted cinema and the proliferating quality of filmic media.

Much of the scholarship on Fuller frames the messy trajectory of her contribution, not through the echo, but through the figure of the trace. In her book on Fuller, titled *Traces of Light*, Anne Cooper Albright frames dance as a practice of "tracing" histories: an embodied experience of all the "material artifacts that constitute the stuff of historical inquiry, the bits and pieces of a life that scholars follow, gather up and survey."[155] Albright inhabits Fuller's choreography, dancing the Serpentine herself to better understand the traces it carries—"the actual imprint of a figure that has passed, the footprint, mark or impression of a person or event"—of her work.[156] Albright's project is a postmodern one, but there are many modernist examples of this obsession with tracing human movement. Muybridge and Marey's chronophotographic motion studies at the turn of the century (which I address in Chapter 3) and Marcel Duchamp's cinematic painting, "Nude Descending a Staircase" (1912) are good examples. The bodily residue of the dancer, extracted and animated through the technique of rotoscoping in early Disney films, is another example, and one that paves the way for today's experiments with motion capture technologies and computer-generated animations—I explore this in greater detail in Chapter 3 as well. Albright's forensic endeavor, to recover something of Fuller's original presence in the face of her double erasure (the ephemerality of live dance compounded by Fuller's refusal to be filmed), in fact emphasizes the impossibility of finding an origin for the Serpentine or for any dance. As Derrida writes, "There are only, everywhere, differences and traces of traces."[157]

Fuller's preoccupation with being seen as the one who created, discovered, or invented the Serpentine is most likely due, as I have argued, to its slippery nature: the impossibility of owning the abstract, depersonalized dance (championed in modernist aesthetics), and Fuller's simultaneous barring from the status of modernist genius, a label mainly reserved for male artists at the time. The aura of enchantment that Fuller's Serpentine bestowed upon her audiences is evident in the accounts of many viewers, journalists, and poets who attempted to write about her live show, but it seems that to see Fuller dance was to witness a unique and extraordinary event, one that was always in excess of any kind of archival impulse. Duncan's assessment, that Fuller's performance could not be "repeated or described," not only characterizes the Serpentine Dance as resistant to a historical repository, thereby enhancing the holy aura that seemed to hover about the performance, but also reads as predictive, given the constant repetition of the Serpentine dance by other bodies, both on stage and on film, for Edison and the Lumiere Brothers several years later. It is not surprising that this particular choreography would be so popular for early pioneers of film, given that there was something uniquely filmic about the Serpentine Dance. Dancing just prior to the birth of cinema, Fuller's silk costume acted like a screen that caught projected light and re-doubled the spectacle of her dancing body.[158]

Jody Sperling—historian, dancer, and renowned re-constructor of Fuller's choreography (making her, like Albright, another *echo* of Fuller)—notes the specific quality of Fuller's stage dance which made her like a precursor to the cinematic screen: rather than using shin lights, which spill past the dancer's body to illuminate the whole stage, Fuller used a series of follow spot lights, each operated by a human technician, who would "follow" her body with the light, ensuring it stayed within the parameters of her silk costume. In this way, the "screen" of her body contained the light, lit-up against a black background, predicting not just cinematic viewing practices but the magic-lantern slide projections that became popular with skirt dancers in the early 1900s.[159] Sperling also notes that Fuller was one of the first dancers to turn off the lights on the audience during the performance, allowing them to direct their collective vision at her own body/screen. Fuller traveled with a crew of technicians who "danced" with her as they operated the lights. Felicia McCarren argues that "the smooth transition between movements" of Fuller's dance presented "motion rather than pose" and therefore introduced the fluid seriality, or the "appearance of uninterrupted motion [. . .] that early cinema addressed."[160] Renowned film theorist Tom Gunning even announced in a 2000 conference presentation that Loïe Fuller "invented the cinema." However, as I have stated, it seems that Fuller herself was never actually captured on film performing the dance, and she was famously wary of the camera's intervention into the ephemerality of live dance performance, remarking in her memoir, "[s]o unliving a thing is [dance] that it exists only in itself and can no more be copied than wind and storm are copied in the camera."[161] Nevertheless, the Serpentine Dance *was* filmed, and many of these films exist on the Internet today.

While a few of them can be found through the Library of Congress and several other archives, the most abundant repository for these videos is YouTube. While Fuller was likely never captured on film, despite the 1906 film that credits her as dancer, many other dancers performed the Serpentine for the new medium of cinema, inscribing their bodies within the filmic archive (and attaching their dances incorrectly to Fuller's name).[162] Given Fuller's anxieties about choreographic reproduction and loss of ownership, it seems a cruel irony that the Serpentine videos should end up on a networked digital media platform like YouTube, where content is uploaded and circulated endlessly and without official verification. Yet, Fuller is the name most commonly associated with the dance, regardless of the fact that none of the dancers in the videos are her—and her enshrinement in this archive is thanks to her cumulative attempts (as illustrated through her patents and lawsuits) to lay claim to the dance.

Edison's 1897 un-tinted film version of the Serpentine Dance (viewable on the Library of Congress) is the recording that is most often credited with Fuller's name on YouTube, but in fact the film features dancer Crissie Sheridan, who quite resembles Fuller in her strong stature, stern face, and grounded gestures, as well as her manipulation of the silks to fully obscure her body. Some of the uploads have been overlaid with contemporary music, such as one that features a song by the Icelandic band Sigur Ros as soundtrack, and also erroneously lists the dancer as Loïe Fuller. In a Serpentine film from Pathé, directed by Spanish cinematographer Segundo de Chomon and released in 1902, the dancer performs on a stage with a hand-drawn set behind her and has the steely facial expression Fuller was known for. The video is again hand-tinted, and the dancer is in pointe shoes. The use of a fade out gives the appearance that the dancer is evaporating off the screen. The IMDB entry for the film claims that the dancer is Loïe Fuller, and her name appears in the opening credits, but from my research it is unclear whether the dancer is actually her.

Other search results include Edison's 1895 "Annabelle Serpentine Dance," starring Annabelle Whitford-Moore and "Annabelle Dances and Dances" featuring both Annabelle and Sheridan. Anabelle's style of dance is airier and more sprite-like than Sheridan's, and the rods she uses to propel her silk veil are much shorter. By moving these instruments in an S-shape under the veil, however, she achieves an approximation of the Serpentine dance that Fuller and Sheridan perform. In these videos, her body is clearly visible, her legs extending below the costume, and her bare arms reaching out to grasp the rods. Fuller, by comparison, rarely revealed her limbs or body from beneath her costume in her live show. Costumed in a corseted burlesque dress with fairy wings and a headdress, Annabelle smiles coyly as she performs, engaging with the camera. Alice Guy-Blaché's version of the Serpentine Dance (1902) features dancer Lina Esbrard, who is taller than Sheridan, and less slender than Anabelle. She also smiles at the camera. Like Sheridan, she reveals more of her legs as she twirls and appears to be wearing pointe shoes, although she never rises to her toes. She ends her dance by separating herself from the Serpentine "persona," dropping her rods and costume, and taking a bow, blowing kisses to the camera. In another video directed by Alice

Guy-Blaché (with the same music as the video described just previous), a dancer named Mme. Bob Walter performs the Serpentine with recognizable technical skills; her *relevés, tendus* and back arches clearly visible from behind the swirling fabric. A viewer of many of these videos may catch glimpses of an ankle, a thigh, or the dancer's smiling face.[163]

The names of the Serpentine dancers are not always appended to the videos posted on YouTube; sometimes they are buried within the credits of the video, other times they are not credited at all, speaking to a general erasure of not only the labor of dancers, but women's labor more generally. Wendy Haslem expands on this type of historical erasure, noting that the Edison film "Annabelle Dances and Dances" (1894–1897), which features several other unnamed dancers in addition to Annabelle Whitford-Moore and was hand-tinted by the "unnamed wife of an Edison employee," illustrates the "larger agenda of history to gloss over the impact of individual women."[164] In contrast with the often unacknowledged identities of these dancers however, Loïe Fuller's name appears in almost all search results for the Serpentine Dance on YouTube, if not in the video description, then in the comments beneath the video itself.

The videos on YouTube are not linear. They show up in my feed without a traditional historical sequencing, and are prompted to play algorithmically, based on views. "Over four hundred hours of video content are uploaded to YouTube every minute," writes Arnesh Koul. "YouTube analyzes viewer behavior on videos watched, click through rates, average time spent, engagement—likes, dislikes, comments—and explicit feedback submissions among hundreds of data points."[165] Content and form are here mutually influential in that the circulation of the Serpentine Dance on YouTube, an unreliable archive which is constantly in flux, matches the aesthetics of the dance, which presents an "unreliable body" in nonstop movement. The experience of watching the Serpentine Dance, like its muddied origin story, is resistant to notions of progress or linearity, even historicity. Unlike narrative ballet, which relies upon the symbolic movement from past to future, or traditional modern dance, which calls upon a series of gestures that begin and end, the perpetual motion of the Serpentine embodies the shock of modernity *and* the immersive experience of the digital-era present.

It strikes me as interesting that a dance emblematic of the birth of cinema (an event crucial to the modern age) should end up circulating in the unstable archive of YouTube—a platform that embodies the ethos of our digital-algorithmic present. This aleatory stream of anachronistic videos is the ideal home for the Serpentine Dance because of the dance's uncertain author-function and also because, long out of copyright, films of the dance can also be monetized and exploited with little fear of reprisal. When it was first gaining popularity, YouTube was sometimes described as the new "cinema of attractions"—Tom Gunning's term for such as the first Edison Kinetoscope films that play "within shallow spaces, often shot against a darkened background that forces us to focus intently on the movement of the human figures," with the "scrutiny of scientific observation."[166] Cinema of attractions films intended to "harness visibility" in an effort to "show something."[167] Like the early "trick films" of Méliès and the Lumière brothers, the Serpentine dance films lack narrative and characterization; they are free of "diegesis" and instead place emphasis on "direct stimulation;" they are therefore an excellent example of the cinema of attractions.[168] Early YouTube videos were similarly short and not narrative-driven, instead "created to illicit a reaction from the viewer, whether it be shock, surprise, laughter, or excitement."[169] Because YouTube videos promote community engagement through commenting, they engage a "communal process that compares with the advertising techniques of vaudeville and sideshows, and contrasts the rigidly corporate advertising of narrative cinema."[170] Both audiences—the early viewership of the Serpentine and the viewers of Serpentine videos on YouTube—possess agency in the conjuring of the Serpentine's aura as *anima*.

YouTube, with its algorithmic behavior, is well suited as a viewing platform for the Serpentine dance, which itself seems to be powered by a more-than-human drive, as if the endless motion of the silks transfers to the auto-play setting on YouTube, prompting Crissie Sheridan's body to blend with Annabelle's and Lina Esbrard's and the many other dancers who twirl across the screen of my laptop. On the one hand, this phenomenon illustrates the common erasure of actual dancing bodies throughout history but on the other, it reveals the inevitable *anima-tic* quality of dance, whereby gesture is always in excess of any one body, initiating collectivity while negating ownership. The Serpentine Dance, like a sonic echo, is both *of* the material bodies that work and move to produce it, and an invisible signal, felt in the body where it resonates.

The Serpentine serves as a case study—a choreographic and technological phenomenon—that demonstrates how the questions and anxieties about technologized dance (anxieties about the impossibility of owning dance *anima*) historically predate postmodernism. Through her inventive use of stage lighting and costuming and the patents she filed to protect these innovations, Fuller can be seen as the author of a set of cultural techniques that propel the *anima* of the Serpentine into the future.[171] Fuller's claims of invention and originality paradoxically reveal dance as an always already mediated assemblage, as demonstrated through the way that emergent media, from electricity to film to the unstable archive of YouTube, unmoor dance *anima* from the singular human performer. I have been arguing in this chapter that the aura of the Serpentine does not diminish as it is mechanically reproduced; rather, the soul, *anima*, or aura of the Serpentine is its multiplicity: its ability to contain multitudes (of bodies, abstract ideas, forms, media, etc.).

Although the Serpentine is multiple and distributed, it is, however, still recognizable—we know it when we see it. A Serpentine dancer need not move the canes in precisely the manner Fuller laid out in her legal description of the dance, nor does the video need to be hand-tinted or in color. From the sprightly nymph-like steps of Annabelle in Dickson's 1894 and 1896 films with American Mutoscope to the grounded and voluptuous dancing of Crissie Sheridan in Edison's 1897 black and white Serpentine film, to Jody Sperling's pristine stage recreation at the Saban Theater in Beverly Hills in 2017, all versions of the dance contribute to the perseverance of its *anima* as a discernable thing. I cannot help but think of the viral dances that move across TikTok, Instagram, and other video-based social media platforms today: as a particular choreography moves from body to body, there are changes in elements such as the gender, age, size, color, costuming, and shape of the bodies performing the dance, but an overall consistency in *anima*—one can perceive the dance on its own, lifted off and traveling between dancers, coming to land in the next algorithmic opening.

And yet, even though it holds a recognizable form, the dance *anima* of the Serpentine, in its symbolic rejection of stasis, also resists commodification or ownership, thus contesting processes of capitalism that seek to define it. In its embrace of fluid motion without beginning or end, the Serpentine (itself a kind of subject, body, or soul) moves against notions of linear history and the inscriptive tools of power (writing, choreography) that work to uphold teleological views. Yet this same boundlessness, this aura that is distinctly anti-auratic and therefore anti-indexical, also performs a kind of erasure of the distinct bodies, in particular female bodies, that have inhabited the dance over time. In both academic and popular writing, the Serpentine Dance has come to stand for the subject-less abstract of Symbolism, the depersonalized visions of Futurism (via the manifestos of F. T. Marinetti), and even the dispersed cyborg of posthumanism (see Karpenko, Haslem), making it particularly amenable to a fantasy of disembodiment. The Serpentine Dance calls the sovereign self, embodied in the individual dancer, into question, offering instead a many-bodied dancer, a cyborg dance in which the distribution of movement (and therefore agency) across material and technological actors mirrors the dispersal of truth (or historical fact) across written memoirs, academic articles, and YouTube comments sections.

In examining the repository of "Serpentine Dance" videos posted to YouTube today—many of which mistakenly list Fuller as performer—I argue that the Serpentine's *dance anima* resides precisely in the fact that it was *both hers and not hers*, bringing multiple bodies (human and non) into relation across time and space. Against the concept of the *singular* body of the dancer as a mimetic tool used to extract the power of other forms returns us to the idea of the sovereign self at the helm of an instrumentalized corporeality, where the multiple other "bodies" evoked by the dance are subordinated to the will and power of the singular body that dances, the Serpentine gives us a vocabulary for what dance—perhaps more than any other art form—has already shown us: that we are never singular beings with complete control over our bodies and surroundings. The Serpentine serves as a starting point for my theory of dance *anima* because it illustrates a transhistorical relationship between the imagination of the audience and *anima*, which cannot exist without a gaze to fantasize it into reality.

2

The Dancing Machine

The "line of gravity" that the marionette follows is "nothing other
than the path of the dancer's soul."

—Heinrich von Kleist (1810)[172]

In his 1810 essay titled "On the Marionette Theatre," Heinrich von Kleist
recalls a conversation with an old friend—a principal dancer for the local
ballet company—who tells Kleist of his fascination with the "mute gestures"
of the puppets he has seen at the marionette theater. Kleist's friend explains
that the marionette's limbs are not moved individually, but rather, "each
movement [. . .] will have a center of gravity" that, if controlled, will cause
the limbs to follow mechanically "without anyone's aid."[173] The marionette's
limbs, he explains, function as "nothing more than a pendulum, swinging
freely," and that "when simply shaken in an arbitrary manner, the whole
figure assume[s] a kind of rhythmic movement that [is] identical to dance."[174]
The line of gravity that Kleist's dancer friend names, when "viewed in another way," can present as "something very mysterious"; as Kleist's friend
declares, "It is nothing other than the path to the *soul* of the dancer" (emphasis mine).[175] These puppets are, as Kleist's friend says, "lifeless, pure
pendulums," and yet he also declares them in possession of life and soul:
dance *anima* produced by the law of gravity.[176] From here, the conversation between Kleist and his friend shifts to the ways in which human consciousness, as a kind of "lost innocence," interferes with "natural grace."[177]
Humans, Kleist explains, are cursed with self-consciousness, an "invisible
force" which "restrict[s] the free play of [their] gestures like an iron net."[178]
The innocence of the marionettes therefore can also be read as a kind of
neutrality—an empty screen onto which fantasies of soul can be projected.

Dance plays a unique role in the narrative of engineered life. Kleist's
friend is certain that the weightlessness of the puppets, along with their
blank-slate-bodies, which move without the distraction of *habitus*, makes
them in some way superior to human dancers, especially when it comes to

Dance Anima. Hilary Bergen, Oxford University Press. © Oxford University Press 2026.
DOI: 10.1093/9780197786673.003.0003

conveying a sense of *soul*. This idea, of the material human body as an impediment to the expressive capacity of dance, will be familiar to formally trained dancers who often feel this "discrepancy between what they want to do and what they can do."[179] As Susan Leigh Foster explains, in acquiring dance technique and choreography, there is often a "prevailing experience" of "loss, of failing to regulate a miragelike substance" because "one never has confidence in the body's reliability."[180] There is something crucially human in this fraught relationship to the body as instrument, and it is therefore ironic that Kleist's friend declares that the dancing of the marionettes expresses humanness better than the dancing of human dancers. What kind of "soul" is at stake here? And could it be that even as dance acts as proof of the human, the human body as interface somehow prevents dance from reaching its ultimate, unfettered soul-energy, at least in the estimation of Kleist's friend? It strikes me that Kleist's friend uses the word "soul" to describe a kind of depersonalized force that moves without the distractions of the awkward, earthbound human body. Certainly, some kind of "body" is needed to perform dance. But Kleist's story conveys that these bodies need not be human, and better yet should have access to a kind of weightless virtuosity and plasticity human dancers can only dream of. Gravity, however, seems essential to the perception of the marionettes as human and therefore ensouled.

Von Kleist's essay reflects early modernist anxieties about the concept of selfhood and the limits of the expressive human form. As Jessica D. Brier writes:

> Von Kleist used the marionette to work through what he saw as a problem inherent to Enlightenment thinking, which privileged rational individualism as a framework for understanding the world. The role of a moveable but insensate object in his text seems no accident in an age that saw the constant invention and proliferation of artificial but kinetic objects that acted as extensions of the human body.[181]

Like Loïe Fuller's silks, which she propelled with her wooden canes, the marionettes von Kleist describes are extensions of the puppeteer's dancerly movements, *and* they are also in possession of their own agency and *anima*. Von Kleist's essay suggests that the soul can be simulated or choreographed, and that that simulation might be more graceful, emotional, even more *human*-seeming than the real thing.

The marionettes Kleist refers to are a form of "dancing machine," a figure that Felicia McCarren explores in depth in her 2003 book of the same name. McCarren names two types of dancing machine: a dance that looks machinic or mechanical, and "dancing that works like a machine, producing the image of a force of nature, a superhuman functioning" or an "indefatigable" machine logic.[182] The figures described in this chapter borrow from both of McCarren's categories to suggest a new description of the dancing machine: one whose dance transforms the machine into something ensouled. Dancing machines not only dance to perform mechanical prowess, but that they also obscure their machine-ness through dance, which humanizes them. A theory of dance *anima* helps show how the energy dance produces is a valuable resource for inventors and storytellers who want to give their machines liveliness and the appearance of energetic interiority. The strategic ensoulment of the machine through dance is a process we see in the development of real-world technologies (as I explore in Chapter 4 on Boston Dynamics), but it is also a tool of mythology: a parable designed to communicate the powers and dangers of human attempts to create synthetic life. The stories we tell ourselves about the ensouled dancing machine are influential myths that reveal our changing relationship with technology, and which engage the various audiences and gazes that make this transformation possible. The examples in this chapter demonstrate not only that the trope of the dancing machine is pervasive in our world, but the way in which this figure is multiply mediated, first by a mechanical body which simulates the human form, and next, by whichever storytelling media it inhabits (fiction, film, screen-based social media, etc.).

Chapter 1 was an exploration of the ultimate impossibility of owning dance and its viral *anima*, as explored through Loïe Fuller's "Serpentine Dance," an assemblage of electricity, fabric, and embodied labor. In Fuller's case, her human body somewhat disappeared beneath the swirl of fabric and lights, passing agency to the nonhuman performance of objects. The dancing machines described in this chapter enact a kind of reverse process. Whereas Fuller's human agency was complicated by the nonhuman agents in her performances, the dancing machines I present in this chapter—comprised of nonhuman components like gears, clockwork, computer-generated images, kinetic motion data, and (fictionalized) algorithmic gesture sequences— stir up an illusion of human agency with their kinetic bodies. I present four different examples of the dancing machine: Olympia, the dancing automaton made with clockwork from E. T. A. Hoffmann's 1816 short story, "The

Sandman"; the dancing "*maschinenmensch*" Maria, the first on-screen robot, from Fritz Lang's *Metropolis* (1927); Kyoko, the disco dancing robo-servant from the film *Ex Machina* (2014); and Lil Miquela, the present-day CGI Instagram influencer and pop star who dances in her own music videos. These four examples, all of whom are coded female, come from literature, film, and animation-based social media feeds.

Although conceptually there is no human body hiding within the machine, there are human creators at the helm in each of my case studies for this chapter. The puppet is controlled by the human puppeteer; the dancing robot or automaton is created and manipulated by its human inventor. The CGI dancer is choreographed by an animator. In part, these inventors make their creations dance to demonstrate the supremacy of machines, which are ultimately are a human creation; they get accolades for the skill of their mechanical dancers. Yet dance remains a slippery thing and something difficult to control—and it is this perception of dancing as a demonstration of free will, or a harnessing of an energy that is alive and layered with feeling, that really imparts a sense of humanness in the machine.

The activation of this fantasy by (human) audiences is a key piece of the puzzle. In a world that wants to test the capacity for machines to behave in human ways, dance acts as proof of human interiority and agency in large part because we as viewers wish it so. I approach this line of analysis in my chapter through a psychoanalytical framework that affords Lacanian and Freudian concepts, such as the gaze, the Real, the imaginary, and the uncanny, that are key to the idea of a relational audience.[183] Thinking about the dancing machine as uncanny also introduces the importance of the gaze to a theory of dance *anima*. Concepts of the uncanny draw together the dancer as a body overflowing with liveliness, and the *eye* of the spectator as both engine and hypnotized receptacle for this animacy. In his essay on the uncanny (which is also an essay on Hoffmann's "The Sandman"), Freud spends a good deal of time analyzing the fear of harm coming to one's eyes, connecting it to his theory of "castration," or, symbolically, the death of the father, or a general loss of power.[184] While I am not so interested in getting into the weeds of Freud's castration theory, each of my case studies in this chapter specifically appeal to the motif of the eye—where the gaze of the spectator is both arrested by the kinetics of the dancing body *and* propels that body to dance.[185] Following Lacan, I propose that the *gaze* here is different than the look because it refers to the sense that the object we are gazing at is looking back at us out of its own volition. This is what makes the dancing machine uncanny, or discomforting: it meets our gaze with its own agency. The power of the (dual-direction) gaze therefore plays an important role in the ensoulment of the dancing machine.

Additionally, this chapter accounts for the feminized bodies of dancing machines as fetishized spectacles that draw the gaze with their often sexualized (and certainly commodified) physiques. In contrast with the perceived genderless, abstract fluid of dance *anima*, the fictional machines that contain and propel it in this chapter are explicitly feminized and (in the case of Kyoko and Miquela) constructed as Asian and mixed-race, conditions which contribute to their objectification. Why is the dancing machine so often gendered female? The longevity of the Pygmalion myth in literature, theater, and visual art means that the project of engineering life becomes a paradigm for the enduring male desire to create a fantasy woman.[186] This fantasy is also one of power and control, connecting with the trope of a female mechanical body that bears scrutiny to determine its inner-workings, or "trick." In his 2011 history of the automaton in the European imagination, Minsoo Kang explains that while the Medieval and Renaissance conception of the automaton was linked to magic and occult forces, where automatons were considered trans-categorical shape-shifters that possessed special powers, with the heightened focus on mechanical craft that came about during the Enlightenment, the automaton became a model of mechanistic science and "pure rationality."[187] As such, automata in this time were subject to invasive tests and examinations to uncover their impetus for movement. Their bodies were scrutinized in the name of science. This is true of all the cyborg figures I refer to in this chapter—from Olympia, whose body is put on display at the ball and dissected by alchemists and inventors, to Miquela, whose social media posts host endless comments about her appearance, her body, and whether she is "real."

There is a general mistrust around the technologized female body. Kang writes that the introduction of vitalism in the late-enlightenment brought about the fear that vital humans might be turned into machines, and as explanations for the magical became secular, powerful ambiguous emotions were transferred to machines, especially automatons, which were anthropomorphic.[188] The attribution of stereotypically feminine qualities to technological objects is an old trick that works to unite woman and machine as unpredictable entities and then contain that threat through their objectification. This narrative can also help explain why female cyborgs are so often conceptualized as "soulless"—or without the power that soul affords.

In Villiers de l'Isle-Adam's 1886 novel *L'Eve future* (*Tomorrow's Eve*), an artificial woman named Hadaly (a word the author believed was Persian for "ideal") is created and said to have a magnificent and mechanically perfect body, yet she lacks a soul. Hadaly's body is therefore configured—like Olympia's—as an empty container, or one waiting to be filled by soul, but Hadaly does not dance in l'Isle-Adam's novel, whereas Olympia, Maria, Kyoko, and Miquela are all dancing machines. They illustrate the mechanical body's commodity potential as a specimen of engineered life—a potential that is realized through dance and the power of dance *anima* to evoke soul.

Each of these feminized dancing machines, which will be given chronologically, illustrates a shift in the "stage" upon which the story is told: from Olympia's appearance on the social dance floor at an aristocratic ball as told in the pages of a story, to the space of the darkened theater (Maria) and living room (Kyoko) as depicted on the film screen, to Lil Miquela's residence in the digital platform of social media, held in the palm of the viewer's hand. As the story of the ensouled dancing machine becomes increasingly more mediated and visually focused, it also draws nearer to the body of the audience, heightening intimacy. This shift illustrates a transformation in the nature of the relationship between humans and technology—the "threat" of the enlivened machine is no longer something separate or far away but has fully penetrated the private domestic sphere of the human. In addition, the chronological presentation of my four case studies reveals historical continuity between the first three examples—mechanical dancers who want to be taken as human—and a historical shift with the arrival of Lil Miquela, my last example. Miquela is a digital influencer who identifies as a "robot," but whose presence is nonetheless ensouled. Aligned with late capitalist, postpandemic *human* subjectivity, dancing for us in a proliferation of screens and digital effects, Miquela thereby introducing the question of what it means to be human (or even "real") today.

Olympia (1816)

One of the first literary depictions of the dancing machine is Olympia, the automaton from E. T. A. Hoffmann's German-Romantic short fiction, *Der Sandmann* (The Sandman). Olympia's portrayal illustrates the anxieties that attended the development of real automata (or moving mechanical devices) in late eighteenth-century Europe. Hoffmann's satirical tale follows a fragile, sensitive man named Nathanael as he deals with childhood trauma around the nightmarish death of his father. Nathanael meets a professor named Spalanzani who keeps his "daughter" Olympia shut away in a glass cabinet. In true Pygmalion form, this daughter is actually the creation of Spalanzani—a mechanical, wooden, glass-eyed doll who can sing, play instruments, exclaim "Ah!," and, importantly, *dance*.[189] Nathanael spies on Olympia from across the street with a telescope, noticing her "angelic countenance" and "unvarying gaze," and remarking that there is "something fixed about her eyes as if [. . .] she [has] no power of sight."[190] At first, Nathanael recognizes her as somewhat mechanical, but this shifts after he attends Spalanzani's party, observes Olympia playing the harpsichord and singing, and invites her to dance. At the party, Nathanael becomes certain that Olympia not only has agency but romantic desire for him which quickly becomes reciprocal: "Ah! then he saw with what a longing glance she gazed towards him, and how every note of her song plainly sprang from that loving glance, whose fire penetrated his inmost soul."[191] Once Olympia is attached to the performance assemblage of the harpsichord and the audience—as well as the desiring force of Nathanael's imagination—she begins to seem full of life, so much so that she throws Nathanael's own (human) agency into question. When she begins to dance, Olympia, who moves with an alluring yet "peculiarly steady rhythm," becomes even more enlivened, causing Nathanael to view his own sense of time as "most defective," as if it is he who is an automaton and not Olympia.[192]

Hoffman's work has a close relationship with dance (or more specifically, mechanical dancers): "The Sandman" was later adapted into a ballet titled *Coppelius*, and Tchaikovsky's ballet *The Nutcracker* is based on Hoffmann's novella, *The Nutcracker and the Mouse King*, a story that also features a dancing doll who comes to life. Hoffmann seems fascinated with dance as a litmus test for whether an inanimate or mechanized body can perform the role of "human" in a convincing manner. Spalanzani hosts his ball expressly to debut his invention and have his guests marvel at his handiwork, but also to have them question whether Olympia is indeed a real, human, woman. Olympia's rigid, militant dancing, in which "every movement seems to depend on some wound-up clockwork," in fact betrays her as potentially "soulless" to everyone but Nathanael.[193] Evidently, the presence of dance alone is not a guarantee of ensoulment in the dancing machine. Dance requires the desiring gaze of the audience—what Thomas DeFrantz qualifies as "the channeling of scrutiny into wonder"—to activate soul.[194] Nathanael's insecurities cause him to push past feelings of uncanny discomfort about Olympia's automatism, projecting an organic fantasy onto her cold exterior. As he looks "into her eyes, which [beam back] full of love and desire," Nathanael also feels Olympia's "pulse [begin] to beat and the stream of life to glow in [her] cold hand."[195] He "clasp[s] the beautiful Olympia, and with her [flies] through the dance," and Nathanael wills away Olympia's uncanny clocklike rhythm to allow "the joy of love" to rise in his "soul."[196] Olympia's interiority is linked with Nathanael's. As he dances with her, and gazes into her eyes, he feels something in himself come alive, and believes that she, too, is living. Olympia's dancing alone does not prove her as human; it must be attended by Nathanael's gaze and his projections of fantasy in order to prevail.

Laura Mulvey's psychoanalytic theory of scopophilia—or the pleasure of looking at other's bodies as objects—can help us understand how Olympia (an object) becomes a screen of pleasure for Nathanael in the story, and in fact how that "pleasure of looking" interweaves itself with the concept of dance *anima* (as energy with agency), thus ensouling the dancing machine through endless feedback between the two. Mulvey's analysis is of the cinema, and Hoffmann's story takes place on the page, but there may be something proto-cinematic about Hoffmann's depiction of Olympia at the ball scene. Mulvey writes that the cinema satisfies a "primordial wish for pleasurable looking" that also "goes further, developing scopophilia in its narcissistic aspect:" "Here, curiosity and the wish to look intermingle with a fascination with likeness and recognition: the human face, the human body, the relationship between the human form and its surroundings, the visible presence of the person in the world."[197] Nathanael's gaze is a narcissistic one that projects his own fantasies and even self-recognition onto Olympia (he becomes automaton-like, "defective," upon dancing with her).

It is not just that Olympia provides a screen for Nathanael's ideal ego, however. Olympia is not a static image or merely an object. It is important that Nathanael dances with her, because in dancing, he feels the animatic motor of her clockwork-compelled dancing and contributes to it with his own human movement across the dance floor—together they make an assemblage that produces dance *anima* and ensouls Olympia. The kinetic movement of Olympia joins with the fantasy gaze of the audience (in this case Nathanael) to heighten Hoffmann's use of dramatic irony in which the reader knows that Olympia is a mechanical woman but suspends their disbelief to experience Nathanael's pleasure.

Hoffmann's tale invites a psychoanalytic interpretation and is perhaps best known as the case study in Sigmund Freud's widely read essay, "The Uncanny" (1919). Unlike Ernst Jentsch's earlier analysis of the story, Freud does not pay much attention to Olympia's dancing. When Freud mentions Olympia, he focuses mainly on her eyes, which fall out of her head at the end of the story, horrifying Nathanael and forcing him to accept that she is a wooden doll and not the human woman he fell in love with. Freud refuses to see Olympia as the locus of the uncanny in the story; that place, he argues, belongs to the "figure of the Sand-Man, that is, to the idea of being robbed of one's eyes"—an idea he connects to the fear of castration.[198] To me, however, Olympia is the most interesting thing about Hoffmann's story. She is an early example of the dancing machine who illustrates pre-modernist anxieties about human agency. We see this when, dancing with Olympia, Nathanael starts to question his own impulses and human selfhood, wondering if he himself might be a mechanical doll. This scene is foreshadowed earlier in the novella, when Nathanael recalls his father's colleague Coppelius (one incarnation of the Sandman in the text) "unscrewing" the "mechanism" of the boy's hands and feet.[199] This traumatic interaction casts a shadow over Nathanael's future, cursing him with Freud's death drive, or compulsion to repeat, and bringing Nathanael and Olympia together as mirrored in a kind of existential anxiety about free will and the human.

Readers of Hoffmann's 1816 story would have been familiar both with these anxieties and with the debut of automata in a public venue, as during this time it was a popular activity to attend automata exhibitions, which showcased mechanical self-movers such as those made by inventor Jacques de Vaucanson. Automata such as the harpsichord player and the dulcimer player (made between 1730 and 1810) could play their musical instruments with realistic motions of arms, hands, and fingers, and even breathe, blink, and bow their heads. Clockwork mechanisms hidden within their bodies enabled them to move this way.[200] Onlookers scrutinized these automata, marveling at their ability to move unmanipulated, as if alive. There are limited real-world instances of *dancing* automata from this time, likely because it was quite difficult to build a mechanical dancer with smooth, life-like gestures, as we see in Hoffmann's fictionalized account, but most automata did have some sort of performative aspect, and it is not a stretch to imagine that a dancing automaton would be a fascinating specimen in such a display.

The *anima* produced by these automata held intrigue for many who witnessed them. The so-called father of the computer, English mathematician and inventor Charles Babbage (1791–1891), recalls viewing automata (in an exhibition designed by John Joseph Merlin) at a young age. Kang explains that Babbage was fascinated in particular by a twelve-inch female figure: a silver dancer with a moving bird perched on her hand. When the dancer became available for purchase at an auction, Babbage acquired it as one of two objects he would pass around to impress his guests at dinner parties, the other being his calculator prototype. Kang writes that Babbage's guests were more drawn to the dancing woman with "her life-imitating power . . . [and] her mechanical allure" than they were to the "ancestor of the modern computer" that was Babbage's calculator.[201] Babbage's dancer represents the alluring possibility of owning the dance of the dancer—as well as the kinetic spark that her *anima* (produced by mechanical clockwork) kindles. Of course, it is unsurprising that a dancer would be more interesting to gaze upon than a mechanical math device. Dance is about the spectacle of the body in motion—dance not only asks for an audience, but it also evokes the fundamental quality of that soul-like breath of *anima*: movement.

In his study on the history of automata, Minsoo Kang writes:

> Because an automaton is a humanmade object, as opposed to one found in nature, and one that mimics life, it suggests all kinds of essential and disturbing questions about what exactly a human being is [. . .] Are we also mere machines consisting of matter functioning according to a preset program, or is there also a nonmechanical and nonmaterial aspect of us?[202]

The automata of the eighteenth century were directly inspired by the mechanistic philosophies of the seventeenth century, which saw humans as similarly machinic. In Descartes's 1662 *Treatise on Man*, he describes the functions of the organs of the human body with no reference to an immaterial soul. Descartes compared the organs and their drives to the gears and parts that brought automata to life—for him, the human body was thoroughly connected to the "great machine" governing the world.[203] Furthermore, Descartes did not see a stark separation between mechanical and biological bodies, making it possible, in his estimation, for a mechanical, nonhuman body to be in possession of a soul. Olympia's dance—the nonmaterial part of her—is in fact very much produced by the material mechanics of her inner gears. And yet, the dance feels immaterial in that it carries the *anima* not just of kinetic expressive movement, but of Nathanael's desire. His desire to see her as a living being, a human woman, is enhanced by her ability to dance.

It is notable that in the pivotal scene where Nathanael realizes Olympia is merely a "lifeless doll," he sees her body flung, object like, over Coppola's shoulders, and watches as "the feet of the figure, which dangled in the ugliest manner, rattled with a wooden sound on every step."[204] Yes, her eyeless face strikes Nathanael with horror, but it is her puppet-like form—her rattling wooden feet, dancing in a deathly manner—that cause Nathanael to scream out with madness: "turn thyself round, pretty doll [...] turn thyself, wooden doll."[205] It is as if, in the imperative to "turn," he is daring her to dance while knowing it is impossible for her. He recognizes her dance *anima* as a life force in this scene, and it is the loss of this *anima*—Olympia's symbolic death—that drives Nathanael to the edge of madness.

If the dancer is, as I have been arguing in this book, an instrument of exploration that navigates two realms—emergent media and the category of the human—then Olympia, Hoffmann's dancing automaton, is an Enlightenment technology that reveals much about the particular mechanization of the human in the modern industrial machine age.[206] Olympia's uncanny liveness, performed through dance, threatens the social order in which machines are safely under the command of humans. Her characterization paves the way for other, future, dancing machines who similarly display dance as an ensouling force—a demonstration of agency (and of their creator's prowess) that can captivate audiences.[207] As I suggested earlier, Hoffmann's ball scene also acts as a venue for a certain type of looking that engages in imagination rather than scrutiny, and which predicts cinematic viewing practices that follow. Nathanael's scopophilic attention on Olympia enacts the pleasure of gazing at an emergent technology that is both object and, because her dancing and his fantasy ensouls her, subject.

Maria (1927)

Maria, the "*maschinenmensch*"[208] from Fritz Lang's 1927 film *Metropolis*, is one of the first cinematic dancing machines. *Metropolis*, a German-expressionist sci-fi film (adapted from a novel by Thea von Harbou) is about what happens when, in the vain attempt to engineer life, technology goes rogue and turns on its maker. Here, the unruly technology is a feminized robot crafted in the likeness of a woman named Maria (played by Brigitte Helm). Human-Maria poses a threat to the city of Metropolis because she is a sort of Marxist leader for the city's workers, who toil in the underbelly of the futuristic city for the benefit of the rich. Maria attempts to bring these workers to class consciousness by revealing the pampered existence of the wealthy people living at the city's surface. Because her wish to unite the working and ruling classes poses a threat to the smooth operation of Metropolis, the city's ruler, Joh Frederson, collaborates with an inventor named Rotwang to create a robot identical in appearance to Maria who will ruin her reputation with the workers. Indeed, "false Maria" wreaks havoc on the city by convincing the workers to revolt. It is paradoxical that this robot, "false Maria," should be the one to teach the dehumanized workers, who are mere cogs in the wheel of Metropolis, to be more human. And it is precisely the revolutionary anarchy that results from this humanizing process that leads to the inevitable destruction of "false Maria," the agent of change. *Maschinenmensch*-Maria's punishment is a public death: she is burned like a witch at the stake, the flames melting away her ghostly skin and exposing her "true" metallic interior, proving her cold and soulless by extension.

Early in the film, in an experiment meant to showcase the *maschinenmensch's* life-like qualities, false-Maria performs a seductive dance for an all-male audience. Typical to 1920s modern dance and art deco aesthetics, her choreography comprises a series of static poses, displayed in profile, and various angular gestures. She moves between machinic rib isolations and minimal yet sensual hip circles. She begins her dance shrouded in a transparent cape, lit from behind to display her slight figure, and slowly strips down to a fringed skirt and nipple covers, as scene in Figure 9, above. This scene, which illustrates the expressionist aesthetics of Lang's film and also conveys Maria's robotic yet seductive nature, is spliced together with a montage of the audience in which the men's hungry eyes apprehend the dance with lust, thereby constituting the male gaze as itself a kind of machinic presence, both actively manipulating and *manipulated by* the mechanics of the dancer's body.

Maria's dance scene demonstrates the key role of the audience in turning the mechanical dancer human. In Hoffmann's story, Olympia's debut happens at Spalanzani's ball—a space of performativity and display—in front of the onlookers, many of whom are watching her dance in order to actively assess whether she is a real, human woman. In *Metropolis*, false-Maria dances for the men who watch her on stage, and the audience assemblage is crucially extended, through the camera, to all future cinema audiences and solo-laptop audiences like myself. The male gaze—a necessary component of a film audience according to Mulvey's argument—is hyperbolic in Lang's film: as the men watch Maria dance in the darkened theater, their ravenous

Figure 9 This is not a frame of the film, but a still photograph of Brigitte
Helm performing on stage as false-Maria, taken on the set of Fritz Lang's
Metropolis. Her profile pose and bent limbs evokes the angular, staccato
choreographies of 1920s modern dance (Photograph by Horst von
Harbou, 1926. WIKICOMMONS, public domain.) https://commons.
wikimedia.org/wiki/File:Brigitte_Helm_als_tanzende_Maria_alias_
Maschinenmensch_auf_dem_Set_von_Metropolis_(1926).jpg

eyes appear—through the magic of film editing—to be cut from their faces,
flipped, turned, and kaleidoscoped into a wall-of-gaze in which there is no
individual watcher, nor are there distinct, multiple bodies (see Figure 10).
What Lang portrays here is a kind of desiring machine, assembled from individual eyes. Lang's wall-of-eyes emerges out of intensifying close-ups on
the men's faces, twisted in pain or pleasure, or both, linking the eye/gaze to
the desiring mind, and the expression of emotions as wrought on the surface of the face (see Figure 10). Their composite gaze, singularly trained on
the dancing body of false-Maria, is enlivened in its attempt to make sense
of her—is she a human or an automata—bringing a perverse sense of scrutiny (an attempt at control) to the desiring machine that lacks control. In
Hoffmann's story and Lang's film, the imagination (of the fictional audiences

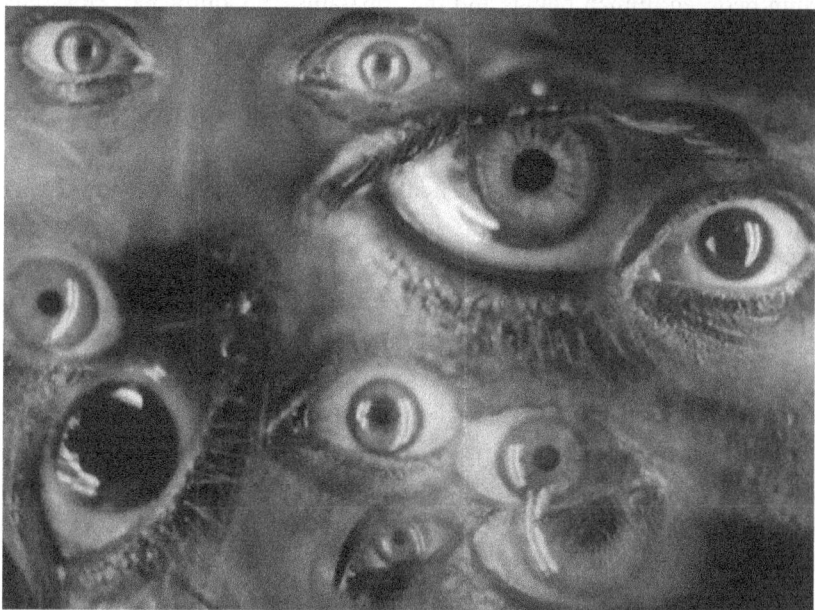

Figure 10 The audience of false-Maria's dance performance deteriorates into a surrealist collage of disembodied eyes. YouTube still from *Metropolis*, dir. Fritz Lang (1927), screenshot by author.

and of the external reader and viewer) does real work, receiving the dancing machine's *anima* and mapping a soul over her gears and cogs.

In his seminal analysis of Lang's film, Andreas Huyssen writes:

> . . . the male eye, which is always simultaneously the mechanical eye of the camera, constructs its female object as a technological artifact (i.e., as a robot) and then makes it come to life through multiple instances of male vision inscribed into the narrative. This gaze is an ambiguous mesh of desires: desire to control, desire to rape, and ultimately desire to kill, which finds *its* gratification in the burning of the robot.[209]

The dance scene from *Metropolis* sets up the primacy of vision, fortified by the new medium of film, as an instrument of power and control. As I have noted, the film is edited to draw this comparison, through a collage of eyes divorced from their bodies—imagery which anticipates Walter Benjamin's statement in 1935 that the "social function of film is to establish equilibrium between human beings and the apparatus."[210] Contrary to Huyssen's reading however, which asserts the ultimate power of the male gaze (here equated with the camera) as the force that both animates and destroys false-Maria, I argue it is not the desiring audience nor the apparatus of the film camera that ultimately holds power in the scene, but, as Benjamin suggests, there is a kind of balance established through an exchange of power (between the camera, the dancer, the audience), and articulated in the force of dance *anima*.

It often appears to be false-Maria's dancing that controls the male gaze rather than other way around. As false-Maria's dance hypnotizes the men in the audience, they seem to lose control of themselves, becoming increasingly frenzied in their panting and looking. Her dancing compels them, perhaps even against their will, to watch lecherously as she gyrates on stage. False-Maria's *own* gaze is fierce, and the camera captures its intensity of focus in medium shots of her as she dances. The stylized orbs that decorate the backdrop behind false-Maria look a bit like giant eyeballs themselves, further extending the machinic gaze assemblage to the performative space of the stage, and giving her the ability to "look back" at her audience in an expansive sense. While it is true that dance often desires an audience, here it becomes apparent that the male audience's gaze is the thing captured by the dance, rather than the other way around. Dance here is the attraction that draws the layered gaze, comprised of camera, Maria's audience, and the audience of the film *Metropolis* more broadly. Dance is the grounding of that assemblaged gaze in a body—the "fleshly" dancer on which the eye (of camera and viewers) comes to rest. In this way, Maria's dancing is also a kind of Turing test wherein the spectator's lust arises not only from her seductive choreography but also from the excitement of not being able to distinguish the mechanical from the organic. Dance is also the catalyst of confusion; as Maria strips off her clothes in a series of jerky, robotic movements, the men gaze upon her and are enchanted by the mystery of whether or not she is "real"—the space of the real being precisely the gap between human and mechanical that cannot be resolved.

False-Maria's dance scene mirrors her later death scene in the sense that both feature stripping-down as an act of attempted verification of what she truly is at her core. While false-Maria's first striptease on stage for the male audience should, in theory, reveal her robotic interior, dance instead becomes layered upon her body like a shroud that persuades her onlookers of her identity as a human woman, or at least sows confusion about what she truly is. By contrast, at the end of the film when false-Maria is burned "alive," the flames melt her humanness away, exposing the metallic body of the robot. In this visceral and violent death, false-Maria is tied to the stake and unable to move (never mind dance). As she is tied up by a group of men, false-Maria throws back her head and laughs with abandon. The affective response of the audience at the scene of her death is markedly similar to the lecherous men watching her earlier striptease: they cheer and fling their arms in the air with excitement at the promise of the violence that will be enacted on false-Maria's body.

The audience, in fact, *dances*, in this scene, gleefully; it is as if false-Maria's dance *anima* has been transferred to the mob. When the fire strips her down to her mechanical core, however, the crowd is horrified and retreats in terror. This is a process—a feedback loop between dancer and audience—that enacts yet another transfiguration of Maria's form, emphasizing not only her deceptive and layered identity but also the ways in which the gaze of the audience forges these layers for her. This audience that produces Maria's dance *anima* is not just the mob at her death scene, but extends beyond the world of the film to the movie theater audience as well. Fritz Lang's *Metropolis* is a story about a dancing machine. Told in the filmic medium, Lang's story offers new techniques of visual storytelling such as montage and emergent special effects to demonstrate the slippage between machine and human.

Kyoko (2014)

The third dancing machine that I want to address is another example from film, specifically from Alex Garland's *Ex Machina* (2014), released almost 100 years after *Metropolis*.[211] In Garland's film, which, like Lang's, is about the ethical and material dangers of attempting to harness technological power to engineer life, programmer Caleb Smith (Domhnall Gleeson) arrives by helicopter on a secluded island to visit the lavish and top-secret home of his CEO, Nathan Bateman (Oscar Isaac). Smith is there to help perform a Turing test on a humanoid AI named Ava (Alicia Vikander) who Bateman has designed.[212] The film centers around Ava, but during his visit, Smith learns that Bateman has also developed several other robot women, all of whom are programmed to be convincingly sentient and flirtatious, including his Japanese maid, Kyoko (Japanese-British actor and dancer Sonoya Mizuno). In one scene that, like Maria's dance scene, combines a pseudo striptease with a choreographed dance number, Smith tries to speak privately with Kyoko, who, according to Caleb, "can't understand a word of English." Unprompted, Kyoko begins unbuttoning her top while looking up at Caleb. Smith is uncomfortable and tells her to stop. Bateman enters the room and upon seeing the two, tells Smith, "I told you, you're wasting your time talking to her. However, you would *not* be wasting your time if you were dancing with her." Bateman flips a switch on the wall behind him, initiating lights that fill the room with a red glow. Oliver Cheatham's 1983 disco track, "Get Down Saturday Night" begins to play and immediately Kyoko's body starts swaying, registering the song's rhythm in her shoulders and hips. "Go ahead. Dance with her," Bateman urges Smith aggressively. "You don't like dancing?" he asks. "She does." He gestures to Kyoko, speaking for her as her moving body gathers speed.

In a demonstration of narcissism and control, Bateman begins to perform a synchronized dance routine with Kyoko in front of Smith (Figure 11). Bateman and Kyoko's bodies move in unison to Cheatham's lyrics, which speak to the theme of embodied labor: "You work all week long, you work your fingers to the bone." Kyoko, of course, does not have bones, but she does work constantly, as a servant and cook for Caleb and his guests. As Caleb and Kyoko shuffle and slide, they lock eyes with Smith: their uneasy yet impressed audience of one. Smith here stands in for the viewers of the film and reminds us that the audience is a key component in the assemblage that produces a soul in the dancing machine. This scene once again relies on

Figure 11 Kyoko, *Ex Machina*'s speechless dancing machine (played by Sonoya Mizuno), performs a synchronized disco choreography with her boss and creator, Nathan Bateman (Oscar Isaac). (Film still from *Ex Machina*, dir. Alex Garland, A24, 2014.)

dance as a spectacle of liveliness born from a feat of engineering. Whether the dance routine was pre-programmed into Kyoko by Bateman or whether she was designed as an expert dancer by way of machine learning, one thing is certain: dance here is both a kind of work *and* a fantasy elision of that labor. The work of the dance sequence is an illustration of Kyoko's submission—to synchronicity and to her creator's ego—and of her impressive ability to master a technically complex movement sequence with precision.

Unlike false-Maria, who dances alone for an audience of men, Kyoko dances *with* her maker, thereby subtly enforcing his power over her. Unlike Hoffmann's Nathanael, who believed his own dance abilities were overshadowed by Olympia's superhuman rhythm, Bateman displays his dance ability by dancing alongside Kyoko. As they dance together, Bateman gets to feel the energy of dance course through him and feel Smith's gaze on his body as well, but more importantly, by dancing with Kyoko, he aligns himself with the ingeniousness of his own invention. False-Maria and Kyoko are two feminized automata who, even though they appear nearly a century apart on screen, are sisters in the Pygmalion semiotics of popular culture cyborgs. Both characters are created and owned by a male scientist figure, situating them within a lineage of feminized robot dancers designed by and profited from by creators who are men. As noted earlier in the chapter, this is a frequent trope in many films, literary texts, and video games, which sets up an unsettling dynamic between the male creator as "father figure" and the female creation as both daughter and sexualized love interest—at one point in Ex Machina, Nathan remarks that he is a bit like Ava's dad, and in "The Sandman," Nathanael first believes Olympia to be Spalanzani's daughter.[213] Kyoko, like Maria and Olympia, demonstrates the common tendency in which novel forms of "technology [are] embodied in a female robot [or] a machine-vamp,"[214] but also where the ability to dance becomes tied to the display, not only of that technology's prowess, but of the machine's ability to perform lively agency. These characters labor under the control of their male creators, and one facet of this labor is the dancing they have to do in order to prove their "realness."

Notably, although dance may ensoul or humanize the machine, it does not ensure humane or ethical treatment of the machines who dance. This dehumanized ensoulment is bound up in the racialization of the dancing machine as well. In the case of Ex Machina, as Anne Anlin Cheng has noted, Kyoko, who is berated and demeaned by Nathan and has no ability to speak back, is portrayed as an object of desire rendered through a focus on "Asiatic femininity, with its spare, clean lines and titillating fluctuation between being a person and being a thing"—she is, in a sense, the "very form and animating matter for Nathan's project of inhuman life."[215] Even though Maria and Kyoko demonstrate their liveness through dance, it does not serve to imbue them with humanist value, or make them persons worthy of ethical consideration. Instead, the function of their dancing bypasses them altogether, missing them as potentially sentient, feeling creatures, and coming to land instead on the personhood of the inventors who created them. Their skill as dancers is therefore not proof of *them* as skilled entities but of their creators as skilled programmers.

This phenomenon, of the dancing machine as a tool or conduit for the power of their creator, is already embedded within the traditional structure of dancer-choreographer. Dance scholar André Lepecki explains that "in dance, the figure of the 'manipulative subject' is powerfully linked to the authoritative figure of the choreographer, to his or her authorial function in dictating steps, controlling gestures, and directing moves to the minutest details. To choreograph is, in part, to control and dictate, and then be obeyed with precision: this is why choreographer William Forsythe once described choreography as 'an art of command.'"[216] Much like the human dancer who performs choreography with impressive skill and grace, only to have the audience praise the choreographer for their visionary ability to shape and create the dance, the skill of these dancing machines makes them just human enough to convince others of their inventors' power, but not human enough to be in personal possession of that power. In *Ex Machina*, Kyoko's ability to move in synchronization with Bateman proves his expertise as an engineer of life (and the power of "technology," like dance, as a force untethered to any one body) more than it proves her capacity to live and be treated as a human being. Olympia's dancing in "The Sandman" serves primarily to display the craftsmanship of Spalanzani, her father/inventor. In *Metropolis*, false-Maria's ability to entrance her audience with her dance speaks more to the brilliance of Rotwang's invention (and the sublime terror of technological newness) than to her innate skill at approximating a human dancer. This attribution of skill to the robots' creators further dehumanizes these dancing machines even as their talent for dance allows them to simulate humanness.

But the dancing machine's ability to dance also hints at the threat of latent agency in the machine, and foreshadows the inevitable violence that this agency will culminate in by the end of these types of stories. Dance *anima* both drives and shrouds that potential violence.[217] At the end of *Ex Machina*, Kyoko and her sister cyborg Ava work together to murder their inventor, Nathan, stabbing him with Kyoko's chef knife, but not before Nathan disables Kyoko by striking her with a dumbbell. That these two fembots have different fates is unsurprising, given their racialization. Kyoko, the only nonwhite character of significance in the film, invented as a mute servant by Nathan, perishes. Ava, who is designed to appear Caucasian, and who is portrayed as having more outspoken, ambitious tendencies (as witnessed during the power cuts when she speaks to Caleb privately), escapes imprisonment and asserts her own will. Having fooled her Turing test interlocutor Caleb into falling in love with her, she leaves him locked in a room to die and flees the island for the city where she can presumably masquerade as a convincing human woman. But it is Kyoko who dances earlier in film, while Ava does not; and paradoxically, her dancing both ensouls her and makes her more mechanical and therefore disposable.

The death of the humanized dancing machine is worth less than the death of a human in the same story. *Ex Machina* presents the inevitable but unseen death of Caleb (a human man) as much more psychologically horrifying than the murder of dancing fembot Kyoko by her inventor Nathan, which the film displays freely on screen. The final pages of "The Sandman" empathetically portray Nathanael's suicide—he jumps off a tower in a fit of madness and shatters his head on the pavement—as evidence of his "lacerated soul," but Olympia's eventual dismemberment has her exposed for the soulless doll that she is. At the end of *Metropolis*, false-Maria's fiery death likewise reveals her soulless metallic interior; her burning at the stake underscores the undeniably gendered position she occupies as a double target of misogyny and technophobia. As Huyssen explains, the *maschinenmensch* embodies the "destructive potential of modern technology [which] had to be displaced and projected onto the machine-woman so that it could be metaphorically purged."[218] While false-Maria and Kyoko have different fates, their dual function as dancers and weapons speaks to the connectedness of these identities in which the assemblage of audience, gaze, and choreography produces a soul in the dancing robot, and the production of this soul in part masks (or distracts from) the robot's potential for violence. At the same time, dance *anima* exceeds the body of the dancing machine and threatens social order. Neither Olympia, false-Maria, nor Kyoko are ensouled enough to spare them punishment for being the locus of technologized power.

This is why, in "The Sandman," Olympia must be revealed in the end to be a "lifeless doll" with a "deathly pale waxen face" containing "no eyes but merely black holes."[219] It also explains why the narrative framework of *Metropolis* presents false-Maria's public death by burning as a reassuring restoration of harmony—a scene which, as I argued earlier, also conveys the transfer of anima from the dancing machine to the cheering crowd and to the image of fire—itself a nonhuman substance that can dance. Similarly, when he sees that Olympia is nothing but a wooden doll, Nathanael screams, "Whirl, whirl, whirl! Circle of fire! Circle of fire! Whirl round, circle of fire! Merrily, merrily! Aha, lovely wooden doll, whirl round!"[220] Here, fire is given dance-like qualities, and Nathanael even commands it to "whirl round," evoking the *anima* of a dancing flame and connecting that energetic agency to that produced by Olympia and false-Maria's dancing. Through fire, their dance *anima* exceeds their expendable bodies in unsentimental perpetuity. In all three stories, the dancing machine is only valuable (and threatening) when agentic/ensouled, and even as she threatens to dance forever, propelled by an uncanny death drive, the destruction of her dancing body (as temporary vessel for dance *anima*) is essential to the restoration of humanist narrative order. These stories, once again, are parables for the risks of attempting to create or engineer life. Because dance *anima* evokes soul, the dancing machine is both proof of the power of the inventor and a warning about what happens when you try to play God. The proximity of the dancing machine to death and violence underscores dance *anima* as an energy impossible to deter or contain: she is uncanny because she *has too much life.*

As mentioned in the introduction to this chapter, the gaze of the dancing machine holds special power in relation to liveliness. The eyes of the dancing machine act as both a window to the soul (a soul enlivened through dance) and as a tool for surveillance and control—a portal that channels dance *anima* from technologized dancer to human spectator and back again. All three characters mentioned thus far—Olympia, Maria, and Kyoko—have moments in which their eyes are critical to their identities as ensouled beings. Olympia's glass eyes, for instance, which Freud focuses on in his essay, begin "lifeless" and are then energized by the desiring gaze of Nathanael through the telescope. Later in the story, Olympia's eyeballs are torn from her head and thrown aside by Spalanzani and Coppelius (a name which itself refers to the Italian word for eye socket: *Coppa*), resulting in "a pair of bloody eyes staring up at [Nathanael] from the floor."[221] The question of how Olympia's eyes are possibly bloody, given that she has just been revealed to be a wooden doll, is never addressed. The impossible blood on her false, disembodied eyes is symbolic of the traces of Nathanael's fantasy, which he clings to in denial, even in the face of Olympia's de-animation.

The interrelated categories of human desire and emergent media are particularly entangled in the space of the mechanical dancer's eyes. This is especially so in the case of *Ex Machina's* Kyoko, who, in an intimate moment of confession with Caleb, peels off her synthetic skin to reveal an exposed eye socket and her mechanical inner-workings (see Figure 12). In pulling off her skin, Kyoko enacts a "strip tease" that exposes her as a machine. There is

Figure 12 In another kind of striptease (she has already removed her clothes), Kyoko (Sonoya Mizuno) peels off her skin to expose her metallic interior, revealing that she has been a robot all along. (Film still from *Ex Machina*, dir. Alex Garland, A24, 2014.)

something about her racial characterization (as a tokenized Japanese character who does not speak) that problematically invites this reveal. Anne Anlin Cheng remarks that "Asiatic femininity in the Western racial imagination does not need to pass through the biological or the natural in order to acquire its most palpable, fully sensorial, supple and vibrant presence."[222] When Kyoko reveals her unnatural metallic interior, she produces a sense of vibrant unease in the viewer because there is a haze of the sensory, human body that lingers around her, even once we know she is a cyborg. In addition to the stereotypical association Cheng notes between Asian identity and technologization, Kyoko's vibrancy is enhanced as well by her earlier synchronized dance with Nathan, her maker. When she reveals her metal eye socket, instead of tapping into a theory of Freudian castration—or anxiety about the potential loss of the eyes as a symbol of power—Kyoko's power of sight is buoyed both by the *power to reveal* and by the power of dance *anima* that retroactively gilds her as a dancing machine.

The most well-known scene from Lang's film—and one in which the eyes of the machine are crucial—is Maria's "transformation scene," or the robot's anthropogenesis, in which the inventor Rotwang, who, like Hoffmann's Coppelius, is a kind of alchemist or mad scientist figure, appears at the helm of this process from behind his flasks, tubes, and vials in his laboratory. The robot, who sits in a chair, is connected to human-Maria by a series of wires and nodes that activate rings of electric energy that encircle the robot's body. Eventually, Maria's human liveliness and likeness are transferred to false-Maria's metallic body (Figure 13). In the moment of transfer, we are given a close-up that cuts between the faces of both Maria and the *maschinenmensch*, eventually transposing the two faces on top of one another and dissolving from the robot's face, with its cold metallic eyes that display faint pupils, to the human face of Maria, whose eyes open slowly to reveal a fixed stare, signaling that the transformation is complete. Sandra Huber has written about false-Maria's slowly opening eyes in this scene as a kind of "wink" that points toward a "secretive knowledge" or suggestion of deception.[223] This ties the cyborg's mechanical yet agentic eyes to the magic of cinematic special effects, which *Metropolis* displays impressively. Once again, the figure of the dancing machine (in this case, false-Maria) acts as a point of investigation between new media (here, cinematic effects) and the category of the human. The "deception" of cinema is transferred to the body of false-Maria, which deceives through its dance.

Figure 13 This image depicts both "real Maria" lying in a glass box (like Sleeping Beauty) that is hooked up to electrical wires, and "false Maria" or the *maschinenmensch*, standing in the background and with haloes of light encircling her body. Both characters are played by Brigitte Helm. (Set photograph from *Metropolis* by Horst Von Harbou, 1926, Public Domain.)

In her 2021 book, *Special Effects and German Silent Film*, Katharina Loew writes that Lang and cinematographer Günther Rittau have historically been very opaque about how this transformation sequence was orchestrated, but eventually some details about the scene emerged:

> Rittau first created a plywood silhouette of the seated robot covered in black velvet and two circular neon lights in different sizes that both fit comfortably over the plywood silhouette. One after the other, the rings were suspended horizontally on three wires from [...] a "fixed elevator," which was custom-built around the silhouette outside of the camera's field of view ... Due to a horizontal grease film on a small glass pane close to the lens, the neon rings, which were moved up and down at a steady pace, appear as blurred discs of moving light. For every shot in which the rings appear, Rittau, using one of [...] two new Mitchell cameras, recorded each ring up to six times; their pacing, starting, and end positions were meticulously planned.[224]

The transmogrifying haloes in this scene, which by this account are actually quite simple in form (neon rings of light), become more complex as soon as they are conceived of as dancing forms. The moving of the lights at "a steady pace" up and down the silhouette—a kind of choreographic sequence—is what causes the appearance of magical, electric energy in this seminal piece of cinema. Electricity as a force that can enliven both organic and inorganic bodies here is akin to the kinetics of dance, or the Aristotelian definition of soul or "anima," as "a mobile energy that is independent from the bodies it infuses" with life.[225] Harnessing both the symbolism of electricity as a vitalizing energy and the practical application of emergent cinematic effects, Lang and his team produce dance *anima* from an mediatic/organic assemblage. That same dance *anima* then serves as proof of liveness in the machine.

Miquela (2022)

I have argued, through my analysis of several case studies, from Hoffmann's dancing German-Romantic automaton, Olympia, and Lang's modernist robot, Maria, to Garland's postmodern fembot, Kyoko, that dance plays a special role in stories about engineered life. These examples demonstrate the pervasive trope of the dancing machine across fiction and film over the span of over a century. I turn now to one last example: digital Instagram influencer Lil Miquela. As a recent iteration of the dancing machine born out of advanced capitalism, Miquela's narrative borrows from the lineage of the other figures mentioned in my chapter. She also embodies new features of the dancing machine that appear when it is articulated to the malleability of digital media. Miquela has the ability to traverse time and space within the visual platform of social media, for example, and she possesses a nuanced self-awareness about her identity that is written into her script, as well as a new relationship to scrutiny, as seen in the comments of her followers, that welcomes confusion about what she is and whether she is "real." This confusion is fed not only through Miquela's performance of sentient girlhood, but also through the implementation of dance *anima* as a disorienting, vital, ensouling force.

Lil Miquela's Instagram account, which dates back to April 2016, chronicles her daily life as a nineteen-year-old Gen Z musician and fashion model living in LA. As of June 2025, she has 2.4 million followers.[226] On October 3,

2018, Lil Miquela, also known as Miquela Sousa, released the music video for "Hate Me," co-produced with Baauer.[227] In the video, Miquela, whose fans often refer to her as a "robot," moves her body for the first time on camera, using kinetic gesture to prove to her fans that her bodily agency is authentic. Miquela's movements—which I consider dance in this context—include a subtle tilt and turn of the head and a medium close-up shot of her standing up from a seated position. She is flanked by human dancers to infuse her music video with life, and her placement in the row with these women positions Miquela as one in a series of organic bodies. The trained dancers around her jump, slide, pulsate, and twirl in an empty warehouse, animating the screen with the flow of their dance *anima*. Miquela stands amid it all, her stoic digital form energized by the excess of bodily activity swirling around her. She is ensouled by her subtle gestures which suggest dance. There is the promise of dance *anima* within her.

A selection of comments beneath the Instagram post of the music video include the following:

> "How are you moving?" (longhair_gurl95)
> "I'm sorry but that head turn creeped me out" (ebOny_)
> "you are the most beautiful robot" (pim_toy_club)
> "I'm so uncomfortable with her mannerisms" (mrbrendenshults)
> "Notice she aint dancing, and just standin" (asapjade)
> "This Is Freaky How She Can Move" (nsfwjimin123)
> "Damn they didn't have the budget to animate her dancing" (jeezfig)
> "Wait. Hold on. You're like a legit robot???" (tatixxlockwood)
> "There's no way this girl/thing is a robot" (oliviasterriker).[228]

These comments demonstrate the varied responses to Miquela—from curiosity and admiration to discomfort and suspicion of her uncanny appearance and movements.

Like the bodies of Enlightenment-era automata, which were scrutinized to reveal their life-giving mechanisms,[229] Miquela's body is probed in the comments section of her social media account: "I don't understand. This bitch is human or a doll or a robt (*sic*). Can anyone tell me pliiiiiiiz" (@max_mysically); "[she's a] digital design. She's a human that alters her photos to look robotic but she's not a robot" (@obersting); "either she's a robot or used a heck of a lot of face tune lmao" (@Alayna.andersonn). The confusion in these comments points toward the uneasy feminized space that Miquela occupies, between object and subject, emphasized by *Refinery29*'s labeling of Lil Miquela as "The Model . . . With No Soul."[230] And yet, Miquela's capacity to move and dance articulates her to a concept of "soul," even as articles written about her declare that she is "soulless." Miquela represents a new type of dancing machine in the lineage I am exploring in this chapter. In each of the first three case studies, the dance *anima* (or soul) of the feminized dancing machine is owned to different degrees by an individual (presumably genius) male creator. Spalanzani creates Olympia, Rotwang creates Maria, and Nathan creates Kyoko. Miquela's creator—the "author" of her soul—is not an individual but a company, making her emblematic of an age of advanced capitalism in which brands and corporations, not individuals, hold power.

Miquela (whose full name is Miquela Sousa) was conceptualized and designed by Brud, the LA-based startup founded by Trevor McFedries and funded by venture capital firm Sequoia Capital. In 2020, The Cut reported that Miquela brings in $10 million per year, making her the face of a very rich (and media-savvy) company.[231] Sousa is a simulation: a digital doll with light caramel skin, pouty lips, and freckles, who Brud describes as a "robot" modeled to appear Brazilian-American. Like *Time Magazine*'s 1993 cover image titled "The New Face of America," which was meant to reflect the impact of immigration on American multiculturalism, Miquela is the beautiful, exotic digital composite of today.[232] Miquela's branding is hyper-intentional, designed to draw a wide swathe of social media followers and to evoke humanist values. She is both racialized and technologized, aligning her with an aesthetics of Afrofuturism, which addresses themes and concerns of the African diaspora, as well as African American peoples, through technoculture and speculative fiction.[233] Her racialization matters, not just symbolically, but materially—meaning, because Miquela's skin is digital, not organic, her owners' ability to change her race on a whim signifies almost as much as her creators' decision to make her racially ambiguous in the first place. In her book *Ornamentalism*, Anne Anlin Cheng writes, "What happens when we consider ornamental forms and fungible surfaces, rather than organic flesh, as foundational terms in the process of race making?"[234] Miquela's modifiable digital skin makes her similar to *Ex Machina*'s Kyoko, whose skin is synthetic and removeable. Both characters exemplify what Cheng calls the "dream of second skin," a "mutual fantasy" understood by "by racialized subjects looking to escape the burdens of epidermal inscription."[235] But Miquela's second (and third, and fourth) skins are not the portal to freedom for her. Instead, they bind her more tightly to her commodity status. Lil Miquela's racial ambiguity and sexual fluidity mean that her "perfection as a brand ambassador is twofold, rooted in her malleability and her ubiquitous potential"—her digital presence facilitates endless movement across space and time.[236]

Since the 2018 release of the "Hate Me" music video, Miquela's Instagram account regularly features videos in which her full body is seen moving on screen. In addition to these videos, there is plenty of movement implied out of frame on her Instagram grid. She appears in indoor and outdoor locations, in group photos, fashion shoots for Prada, and in the pages of fashion magazines like *Vogue, Highsnobiety*, and *Paper. An* issue of *Garage Magazine* photoshops Miquela into photographs from the 1970s and 1980s next to deceased celebrities like Prince, Michael Jackson, and Princess Diana. In a post from May 6, 2019, Miquela is featured in a paid partnership with Calvin Klein—a video in which she kisses model Bella Hadid on the mouth, prompting commenters to voice irritation by Miquela's apparent commodification and fetishization of LGBTQ identity. In a particularly meta move, Miquela even provided a blurb for Legacy Russell's recent book of theory, *Glitch Feminism* (quoted elsewhere in this book). Lil Miquela, who is "forever 19," will never die (though a 2024 WBUR podcast episode titled "RIP lil Miquela" suggests that her nearly ten-year-old presence is starting to age poorly).[237] For all her fluctuations, Miquela is also a fixed entity in the sense that her designers have carefully crafted a complex narrative around her that overrides her Pygmalion origins and the problem of Brud's essential ownership of and profit from her female body. Any potential she may have to align with Donna Haraway's rebellious cyborg, who also "skips the step of original unity, of identification with nature in the Western sense," is complicated by the fact that Miquela was created in the male-dominated world of Silicon Valley by a very wealthy company, essentially to perform labor for free, thus satisfying the etymological origins of the word robot (from Czech, *robota* meaning "servitude or forced labor").[238]

The comments under Miquela's posts also illustrate the slipperiness of a term like "robot" in today's social discourse, once again drawing the realms of the human and new technology together through the figure of the dancer. Miquela often makes jokes about her "gears" and ability to change her appearance on a whim, and she identifies as a robot in her Instagram diary entries, which can be read by accessing the story highlight in her profile where she archives her journals. Whether or not she is actually a robot does not matter, because she feels like one, making the identification similar to that of gender identity or sexual orientation. The word robot was first used in Karel Čapek's science fiction play *R.U.R.* (1920), where R.U.R. stands for "Rossum's Universal Robots." Britannica Dictionary defines "robot" as "any automatically operated machine that replaces human effort," but today the term seems to have become a catch-all for automata, AI, digital avatars, and CGI characters, losing its connection to the "automatically operated" part of the definition. In the discourse network of robotics, the meaning of "robot" changes historically as the assemblage surrounding the word changes. The imprecision with which Miquela's followers use the term reflects not so much their lack of understanding of what a robot is, but rather a new, more expansive (or even tongue-in-cheek) meaning of the term.

Brud's branding of Miquela as a "robot" has spawned entire comment threads debating whether she is "real" or made of CGI, comments which inevitably increase when she is portrayed dancing. This successful marketing strategy stimulates user engagement with Miquela as a product, but it also places her within the narrative and history of the dancing machine, in which the "proof" of the soul in the machine is its *capacity to dance.* Most recently, in a video promo for MSI "borderless" gaming monitors, Miquela moves between digital and photorealistic spaces, declaring, "I *dance* across worlds unbound by age or expectations" (2024).[239] In calling her followers to witness her dance, Miquela's creators are tapping into the historical link between dance and proof of life. Through clicks, likes and comments, Miquela's followers co-create her agency or anima, just as Miku's fans collective belief in her liveness propel her into existence.

By 2020, Miquela began posting full dance routines that showed her entire body. In a music video for her song, "Hard Feelings," Miquela performs a choreographed dance routine on top of a speeding flatbed truck (Figure 14). The virtuosic camera frames her from above, spinning to disorient its viewer. She dances in formation with a set of other digitally animated bodies, cloaked in full-body and face-covering leotards (perhaps to further dehumanize them and render Miquela more life-like by contrast). They dance in complete unison and with a weightless, digital quality to their movements that suggests they are animated. Yet, there is something uncanny about Miquela's dancing here that also gives the appearance of life (one commenter remarks that she "looks like she's from the Polar Express," referencing a benchmark film in the history of uncanny digital animation).[240]

Figure 14 Still from the music video for Miquela's song "Hard Feelings," depicting her dancing (impossibly) atop a speeding truck. To the right of the video, commenters debate whether Miquela is a "girl or a robot." Screen grab from Instagram, August 3, 2020, @lilmiquela.

Miquela is a superhuman dancer. She can perform casually on top of a vehicle that is hurtling through the desert without risk of injury. The viewers of the video accept this. Yet, they do not fully accept that she is purely animated, as demonstrated by the "creepiness" they feel when watching her. What is it about Miquela's dancing here and in other videos that positions her as more than just a CGI character? In her social media posts, she often poses with celebrities, pop stars, and rappers, but in our post-truth era, the practiced reader of visual media has developed a necessary skepticism toward photos as proof of anything solid. This type of post is in fact less likely to sow suspicion in viewers about Miquela's veracity than her dance videos are. It is unclear whether Miquela's choreography in "Hard Feelings" was extracted from a human dancer through mocap technology before being used to animate her digital body, but nevertheless, Miquela's movements in the video do not seem entirely synthetic. In a particularly meta gesture, Miquela's Instagram features a promotional post for the music video from August 2, 2020, that features images of Miquela outfitted in a mocap suit, with a human technician adjusting her markers. The implication is that she provided mocap data for her own animated body, perhaps to explain why she—a self-proclaimed robot—is able to dance on top of a speeding truck.[241]

No analyses of Miquela thus far have focused on her use of dance videos to simulate humanness. Others tend to focus on the way her account uses authentication techniques such as storytelling to make her feel real or alive, and the way that she embodies late capitalist ideals and anxieties. It is true that of all the dancing machines explored in this chapter, Miquela is the most verbose and confessional. Through her diary entries and captions, she performs earnest knowledge of her unstable relation to reality, and this makes her much more reflective and relatable than Olympia, for example, whose only audible expression of selfhood is the sound of her gears whirring. But, to return to the philosophy of Kleist with which I began this chapter, Miquela is in no way "innocent" in the manner of Kleist's dancing marionettes. Occupying the filtered and fabricated dual worlds of fashion and Instagram, affectation is in her nature. Miquela's "personal brand" accesses authenticity by embracing "unreality and performance in the service of capital" (46). Unlike the dancing marionettes, whose movement is guided by their dumb, weighted, jumping force of gravity, Miquela's movements when she dances are uncannily smooth and without weight. And yet, her dancing bestows upon her the same vibrant life that Kleist's friend recognized in the puppets.

I started this chapter with Kleist's marionettes, but went on to analyze four dancing machines who are more like automatons than puppets. The self-moving automaton of course wields far more threat than the puppet, as I have shown, because she is not attached by strings to her puppeteer. And yet, the puppeteer is close at hand in each story of the dancing machine and her maker. Olympia and Maria's creators, as noted earlier in the chapter, hold paternal control over them—Kyoko, too, is described as her inventor's daughter ("I'm kind of like her dad," says Nathan). These men are not puppet masters per se, but they brandish power over these artificial dancing women, reminding us that while their bodies may be autonomous, their dance *anima* is under patriarchal control. The fetishization of automata, CGI "robots," and other technologized bodies—even when fictional—often reinforces the capitalist myth of progress in which technologically engineered life represents the apex of human scientific knowledge and ability. However, the fantasies presented by this discourse have not evolved over history beyond slight changes in the technology; they still center on the body of woman as a commodified and ownable object. Furthermore, the use of dance as Turing test continues to be employed strategically, showing that even in advanced capitalism we have not really progressed past the Romantic obsession with soul, and the association between soul and artistic expression.

This chapter begins with a discussion of Olympia, E. T. A. Hoffmann's fictional automaton whose ability to dance is used to test her lifelikeness, and it ends with Lil' Miquela, a CGI Instagram influencer whose music videos likewise mobilize dance as proof of life. These four dancing machines, which span 100 years and are examples of what Anne Anlin Cheng calls "figures of Western technological advancement" in fact demonstrate a lack of historical "progress."[242] Even though Olympia is an automated doll made of wood, glass, and gears, and Miquela is a digital image undergoing constant mediation, their stories are much the same. Even though they reference different tools and techniques, all four are stories about a technologized girl with an untrustworthy body, where dance acts as a litmus test for human agency. Their differences, however, are significant as well. Lil Miquela is less empty container than plastic image; she displays what Heather Warren-Crow identifies as key attributes of digital culture: "malleability, transmediation and instability."[243] She is both a figure of resistance, a "nimble, labile girl-subject of digital culture [who] can squeeze through the cracks of oppressive power structures."[244] Miquela masquerades as a robot—an automaton, or a self-moving machine—but she, more than any of the other mechanical dancers in this chapter, is controlled by her makers. She is a "plastic image," a "vehicle of hegemony [that] can satisfy a neoliberal mandate to respond to market demands."[245] Her collectively made dance *anima* serves a purpose: to influence capital.

Miquela's plasticity as a digital image significantly matches up with *dance anima as plastic form*, so that it is almost as if in her, the dancing machine has reached its ultimate iteration. Her dancing is her currency in advanced capitalism; it reinforces her malleability, while also reassuring viewers that what they are looking at is not merely a commodity or a vector of brand power but, in some way, real. The robot that can move in a functional, practical manner is an impressive feat of engineering. The robot that can *dance*, however, is one that can *feel*.

3

Animating *Anima*

The 2016 music video for Major Lazer's remixed song "Light It Up," produced by Method Studios and House of Moves, begins with a series of quick shots of photorealistic textured fabrics and materials moving to a two-step dancehall rhythm. A moombahton[246] horn section plays the hook as the screen fills with pink and turquoise nubs, spiraling as if caught in an eddy. A series of quick cuts give way to a throng of shiny metallic scales pulsating with simulated breath and then a swathe of purple-gray fur rippling in slow motion. These mesmerizing shots, which take up the entire screen, feel very much like a dance—or choreography—of rhythmic nonhuman substances. The first humanoid dancers appear on screen when Jamaican singer Nyla begins singing the verse, and it is not immediately clear whether these dancers are humans wearing digitally enhanced costumes or high-quality animations, for the buzzing textures from the opening shots seemingly drape themselves over the dancing bodies, becoming their costumes. Dance exists in the swooshing of fur, the swarm and dissolve of colorful particles, and the lag of the floating streamers trailing behind an arm that strikes out or knees that bend. These dancing materials are somewhat like Loïe Fuller's voluptuous silk costume or the luminescent salt gels that bathed her in colored light while she performed her Serpentine Dance, as described in Chapter 1. However, because the Major Lazer music video is made of computer-generated images, there is an unlimited plasticity to the dancers, substances, and costumes on screen. In fact, the costumes *are* the bodies: there is no difference between the two (Figure 15). As the music video progresses, these bodies/costumes start to break down and fall apart, collapsing into puddles of themselves or dissolving completely. The video offers a more-than-human vision in which inanimate objects display kinetic agency, and bodies that appear to be human end up exploding and dispersing away from their fixed form.

As I watch these digital bodies melt into the floor and come apart at the seams—as the limits of the dancers cease to be clearly defined—I find myself turning to Susanne K. Langer's question, "what . . . is the dance?"[247] Although Langer writes in 1953 about live performance, her questions

Dance Anima. Hilary Bergen, Oxford University Press. © Oxford University Press 2026.
DOI: 10.1093/9780197786673.003.0004

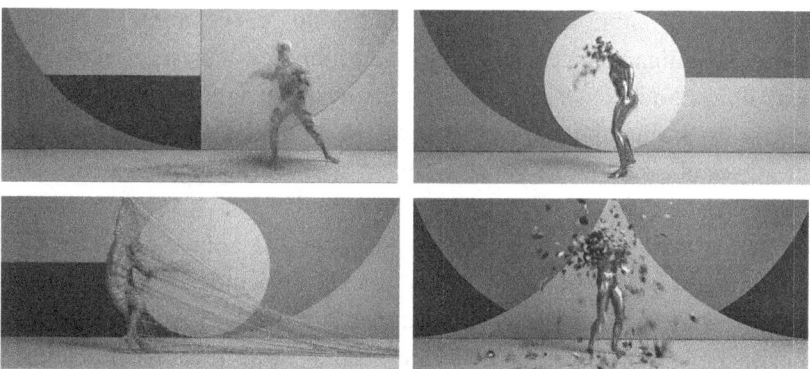

Figure 15 Film stills from the music video for "Light it Up" by Major Lazer, produced by Method Studios (2016), depicting dancing bodies, most likely animated by mocap, made of various materials such as ribbons, strings, and shiny scales—all of which start to unravel and disintigrate as the dance progresses. (Screenshots from YouTube by the author.)

remain pertinent to my own exploration. A dance is created by the dancers' bodies, of course, but their costumes, the dancefloor, the space, the music all "create something over and above what is physically there: the dance. What, then, is the dance?"[248] Langer proposes that dance is a simultaneous product of and *release from* the materiality of the human body. Dance "springs from what the dancers do, yet it is something else. In watching a dance, you do not see what is physically before you—people running around or twisting their bodies; what you see is a display of interacting forces, [from] which the dance seems to be lifted. . . . [and] these powers, these forces that seem to operate in the dance . . . *belong to the dance itself.*"[249] Propelled and vivified by technique, musculature, and effort, the body of the human dancer produces energy or a surplus kinetic force, what I have been calling *anima* throughout this book, a kind of excess sloughed from the dancing body. Dance *anima* is not just as an extension of the dancer's body, but rather its own entity, and as this chapter argues, it can be animated.

In the Major Lazer video, animation is a kind of dance, and dance is a kind of animation. When that kinetic energy is caught on camera, or by the extractive animation techniques of rotoscoping or motion capture covered in this chapter, it is preserved as a trace within the screen, celluloid, or database. Seized and revived, this "power," to borrow Langer's word, is then used to animate other bodies and objects. Dance *anima*, as this book suggests, is a roving, enlivening substance. In "Light It Up," dance *anima* infuses ambiguously human dancers and explicitly nonhuman substances and objects with power both actual and virtual; thinking about dance as animation thus entails expanding the scope of what can be animated. Dancing animations like these illustrate the dispersal of *anima* as ensouling substance to entities beyond the human.

The nascent spectacle of dance is well suited to animation which is, as media theorist Deborah Levitt argues, quickly replacing cinema as "the dominant medium of the twenty-first century."[250] In *The Animatic Apparatus*, Levitt argues that animation is an "increasingly powerful pop cultural form" that contributes to the way we perceive life today as plastic, transformative, and "an-ontological," or without a sense of being.[251] Levitt's concept of an-ontology complements Soviet film director Sergei Eisenstein's definition of "plasmaticness" as the "rejection of once-and-forever allotted form, freedom from ossification, the ability to dynamically assume any form."[252] Animation relies on kinetic energy to defy fixed form, or the predictable limits of organic corporeality, gravity, and temporal rigidity—just as dance does. Canadian animator Norman McLaren famously defined animation not as the "art of drawings that move, but the art of movements that are drawn."[253] This makes clear the historical importance of dance to animators both philosophically and practically, especially using animation processes of rotoscoping and motion capture. Indeed, the animator is not a mythic creator capable of conjuring life with their craft, or a puppeteer of *anima*, but rather a co-creator or collaborator with the moving bodies who provide their labor and energy to the animator's renderings. The trace of the dancer's movement and identity is carried into the animation as the ghostly remnants of *habitus*, technique and training, time, setting, social practice, and cultural context, via dance *anima*. While it is unclear whether the dancing bodies in the Major Lazer video are animated using mocap data from live human dancers, the realistic, weighted quality of movement in the video (released years before CGI animation was capable of such realism) certainly supports this assumption.[254]

Because dance *anima* contains traces of a particular dancer's habitus, it holds capital for animators wishing to bring a sense of lived embodiment to their animations. The use of dance *anima*, therefore, is not neutral, especially where race is concerned. If the surface of our skin has historically acted as a signifier of race, the elastic qualities of dance can seem to represent something disembodied and therefore without skin or race; yet as I demonstrate in this chapter, dance *anima* is often extracted or appropriated from dancers of color and applied to animated bodies (humanoid, animal, vegetal, or objects) as an authenticating force. The video for "Light It Up," for example, which features the vocals of Jamaican singer Nyla and British-Ghanaian Afrobeats artist Fuse ODG, presents a visual world of faceless, skinless dancers in which gender and race are presumably nonexistent. And yet, these digital creatures perform gestures and sequences clearly drawn from Caribbean and African traditions—moves like the Wine from Jamaican dancehall, the Top Rock from break dancing, and a version of the West African Makru dance from the Susu people of Guinea. While the race of the dancers who likely supplied their movement for the video by motion capture, who remain uncredited, as per usual, is unknown, their dance *anima* carries traces of Black culture and history.

In Chapter 2, I described how the inventors of dancing automata and robots took credit for the skill of their machines. Here, I see a similar impulse where the dancers whose labor produces the motion go uncredited, but the animators are given credit for their achievement at engineering life. The dancers' identities cease to matter, as the video's virtuosic digital animation makes so many different types and shapes of bodies possible, including dancers made of what looks to be hair, balloons, lizard-like scales, electric cables, marshmallows, melting chocolate, and paper feathers. "Light It Up" presents the fantasy of animation as a world of unlimited plasticity that simultaneously fetishizes the concept of a deracialized body *and yet* relies on specific markers of race (rooted in movement and gesture) to ensoul these plastic, posthuman figures.

This chapter historically situates the metamorphic abstraction of dance movement as a fantasy of disembodiment that occurs across modernism, postmodernism, and advanced capitalism. Extractive animation technologies like rotoscoping and motion capture take the *anima*, or dance soul, of the moving human body and preserve it as a set of gestures that are transferrable across nonhuman and abstract bodies, various creatures, and agentic objects. More specifically, gestures extracted from dancers of color (in the case studies of this chapter, African American dancers) often function as a kind of ensouling force. While their bodily movements serve to authenticate the dancing body of the animated entity, the human dancers' material body and labor are erased. This is evident in examples such as Cab Calloway's rotoscoped dancing for Koko the Clown in the 1920s, Savion Glover's tapping penguin in the early 2000s film *Happy Feet*, and, as the introduction to this chapter demonstrates, Major Lazer's music video "Light It

Up." I also look at Bill T. Jones's 1999 digital dance work *Ghostcatching* as a project that resists such erasures. The extraction of dance *anima* as a valuable resource is also a process of disembodiment, and it is crucial to examine such erasure and abstraction, especially as it intensifies and becomes more insidious in today's world of animation, the "dominant medium of our time."[255]

The Shameful Body

Like Langer, philosopher Alain Badiou understands dance as something separable from the bodies that dance. "Dance," he writes, "is first and foremost, the image of a thought subtracted from every spirit of heaviness. Dance frees the body from all social mimicry, from all gravity and conformity."[256] He continues:

> Dance is like a circle in space, but a circle that is its own principle, a circle that is not drawn from the outside, but rather draws itself. Dance is the prime mover: Every gesture and every line of dance must present itself not as a consequence, but as the very source of mobility. And finally, dance is simply affirmation, because it makes the negative body—the shameful body—radiantly absent.[257]

Note that Badiou (whose confidence about the nature of dance is surprising given he is not a dance scholar nor has a known dance practice) writes imperatively about dance as a thing capable of drawing/acting/moving on its own: dance is "not drawn from the outside, but rather draws itself." Putting aside the problems of Badiou's statement, including his failure to acknowledge dance's social function and his lack of clarity around what, exactly, this negative, shameful body is, he does strike on something crucial for the conception of dance *anima* as extractable resource. Badiou does not mention the dancer's agency; instead, the dancer is erased in favor of the agency of dance (a source and not a consequence), and so much so that the "the negative body—the shameful body—[becomes] radiantly absent." If certain dance techniques already perform this erasure, animation technologies like rotoscoping and motion capture further efface this "shameful" human body—the dancing body that sweats, breathes, and feels adrenaline, pain, and joy—opening up myriad possibilities for other types of bodies (humanoid, animal, alien, abstract) to be enlivened by the *anima* extracted from humans. What constitutes Badiou's shameful body (the body that dance leaves behind)? Which elements of the body are preserved in animated dance's processes of abstraction/extraction? Is corporeal finitude shameful in itself, or are there particular qualities or types of bodies that are more "shameful" than others?

I propose that Badiou's shameful body speaks to the problematic discourse of formal "purity" as it comes to bear on the body in motion throughout history. The extractive relationship between animated dance and dancers of color, for example, propels dance's paradoxical wish for body erasure: a wish that in fact predates many of the animation techniques I focus on in this chapter. An aesthetics of abstraction—or an erasure of the material trace of the sweating, breathing, dancing body in favor of pure *anima*—can be seen, for example, in dance notation systems meant for archiving and transmitting choreography as early as the 1680s, when Louis XIV commissioned the Beauchamp-Feuillet dance notation for Baroque dance. This aesthetics can also be seen in Austro-Hungarian choreographer Rudolf von Laban's signature Labanotation from the 1920s (Figure 16) and Valerie Sutton's DanceWriting, created in 1966 to preserve classical ballet works. While the little shaded rectangles, half-circles, curved lines, and directional squiggles in these notations are representations of a body passing through movement, the dancing body nonetheless becomes increasingly abstract. As dance materializes in a legible, repeatable system, it also traverses abstraction into a zone of dehumanization.

Many of the first notation systems, including Beauchamp-Feuillet, came about during the Enlightenment and were associated with the highly formalized choreography of courtly dance. But the function of dance notation as a means of analyzing and recording movement, and as a method of abstraction, is epistemologically and aesthetically linked to modernism. Laban's diagrammatic approach to dance notation, influenced by his studies in architecture and spatiality, demonstrates a modernist fascination with the quantifiable or modular body, and the designs resemble the type of modern art often associated with the European avant-garde. Carolyn Lanchner has observed that "notations for the dance can resemble the patterns of abstract [modernist] painting,"[258] and Mark Franko writes that dance "notation itself is a visual abstraction of movement."[259] Flora L. Brandl has pointed out more specifically the resemblances between Laban's kinetography and the geometric abstract artworks of modernist artist Sophie Taeuber-Arp, a dance student of Laban's in Zurich in the summer of 1915.[260] Abstraction is especially hard to achieve with dance as a medium,

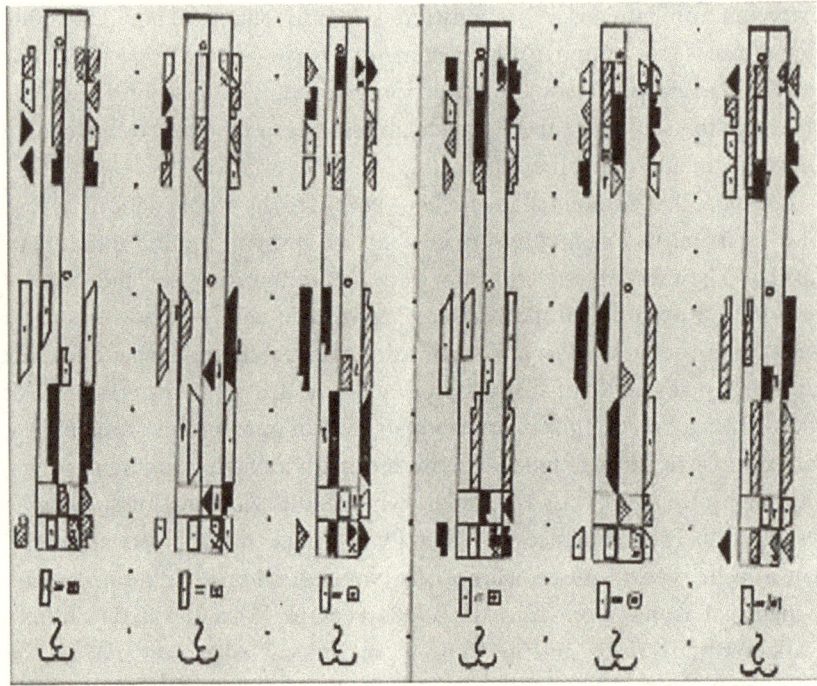

Figure 16 An image of Rudolf Laban's birthday card from his student Valerie Preston-Dunlop, which features a choreological notation closely inspired by Labanotation, WIKICOMMONS.

given the canvas is the expressive human body. I view this trajectory away from the thinking, feeling human and toward a series of formal shapes as a cultural technique not only for the preservation and re-mounting of classic dance works but also for the transmission and production of *anima* outside of the human body—a kind of dehumanized soul.

If, as Moritz Wedell writes, "the epistemic dynamics of notating . . . are not limited to the interplay of storage and retrieval" but, rather, "beyond its documentary function, every notational procedure displays an inherent potential for exploration," then we could say that dance notation makes possible the exploration of dance (and therefore dance *anima*, or soul), outside of the human.[261] Because dance notations, as Wedell continues, "detach [. . .] movements from the restrictions of the real world, and in doing so [. . .] allow researchers to explore movements in a virtual realm, a sphere only restricted by the rules of the notation," they enhance the "freedom to carry out movements in an abstract realm."[262] This is a beautiful idea, but the word *freedom*—which notably here seems interchangeable with feelings of power or control—is loaded, set as it is against the limitations of the human body. It was this limitation that Laban sought to circumvent with Labanotation, a system where "movement no longer travels from one body to another through the imprecise and uncontrollable act of copying the steps of the dance master"; instead, "the originality of a choreography is preserved in a script and can be activated at a later point only through a meticulous and professional hermeneutic effort."[263] Labanotation is, indeed, famously difficult to read and implement, although digital tools of movement analysis such as LabanWriter, an early computer program developed by Lucy Venable in 1987, can simplify the process. The goal here, however, evident both in Labanotation and the tools designed to read it, is the abstraction of information about body motion into "simple, repeatable geometric shapes," a simplification that also affords the (future) choreographer and dancer enhanced control over the slippery animal that is dance *anima*.[264] I therefore understand dance notation—along with rotoscoping and motion capture, which take up a similar action of distilment and abstraction—as a crucial component in the expanded history of dance-as-media that this book explores.

Secret Dancers

Dance notation systems reduce the expressive practice of choreography into a string of figures meant to transmit the essence of each gesture separate from the body that performs it (as if this were possible). Like dance notation, the early hand-drawn animation technique of rotoscoping involves an act of capture that harnesses the power of movement for future re-animation in other bodies. And unlike dance notation, rotoscoping moves away from abstraction, returning to the body of the dancer as expressive medium (while also separating that body from the product of their labor: their dance *anima*). Invented by American animator Max Fleischer in 1914, the rotoscope involves projecting filmed bodies (in early animation, these were often dancers) onto a transparent easel. An artist then traces onto paper the live action as the bodies move consecutively through space, extracting the quality of human motion to infuse animated bodies with a sense of vitality. Fleischer was not interested in reproducing photographic realism, and indeed, rotoscoping does not offer straightforward verisimilitude. Instead, the technology supplements the fantasy of plasticity with a realistic (or human) core. Rotoscoping allows artists to access the "invisible lines of force that run through and underneath the surfaces of . . . visible bodies" to animate their hand-drawn figures.[265] Animators found that the technology allowed them to approximate the weight and movement of bodies that were too complex to capture by freehand drawing.[266] Yet the rotoscope also aims to capture a perpetually mobile and nascent state as an end in itself. And it is this nascent state as end—a suitable definition for dance *anima*, in fact—that gives bodies animated by rotoscoping their life-like quality.

A cartoon or animation that has been rotoscoped offers the viewer the spectacle of an unrealistic body moving realistically; it has *anima*. It is this oscillation between the quotidian and the fantastic that excites the imagination of the audience. While the original performer of the movement is forgotten in this process, their specific motions live on in the animation, which is rotoscoped in one of two ways in early cartoons: by "through-line" or "rotoscoping by outline," which was developed by Disney in the mid-1930s. Ryan Pierson explains that whereas rotoscoping by outline presents a body that moves "with a weight or an anchoring force we cannot see"—a kind of "shadow-play"—rotoscoping by through-line centers on "underlying scaffolds of movement."[267] Rotoscoping is therefore both an erasure and a conjuring; in tracing the outlines (or through-lines) of the little bodies that move across each frame, the animator disappears the referent body, keeping only its dance *anima*, as seen in both the lively edges of the animation or in the movement of its "through-lines." Either way, the character's body movement is felt to be radiating out from a real, authentic, ensouled center.

Panpan Yang writes about the "secret dancers" of early rotoscoping who enlivened cartoons with the motion of their own bodies but who were rarely acknowledged in the film's final product.[268] American dancer Marge Champion, for example, was fourteen years old when she provided dance footage for Disney's animated heroine Snow White in 1937. In exchange for her dancing, Champion was "paid ten dollars a day" and wore a "football helmet so that her head-to-body ratio would approximate her animated doppelganger." [269] Champion performed rotoscoped movement for characters in other Disney movies, including for the Blue Fairy in *Pinocchio* (1940) and for Hyacinth Hippo and the ostriches' ballet sequence in *Fantasia* (1940). Yang notes that Champion's rotoscoped *Snow White* footage was re-used to animate the fox character Maid Marion as she dances in the 1973 animated feature *Robin Hood*. Champion's indexical gestures have thus propelled various animated bodies, in the same way that the rotoscoped animations of Mowgli from *The Jungle Book* (1967) were re-used for Christopher Robin in *The Many Adventures of Winnie the Pooh* (1977), as were certain ballroom dance sequences from *Beauty and the Beast* and *Cinderella.*

Disney remains purposefully vague about how much of the animation in these films was produced by rotoscoping or hand drawings using live action footage as reference, and dancers like Champion are not credited in the films. Indeed, Champion was asked by Disney to stay quiet about her involvement because they wished to keep the practice of rotoscoping covert, a secrecy that is at least in part an attempt to preserve the myth of the animator as creator of life. Some animators viewed rotoscoping as a kind of cheating by aid of a technical device. To admit to rotoscoping was to shift at least some of the power of creation to the dancer or actor who supplied the motion, and this was not encouraged.[270]

Despite Disney's efforts at secrecy, rotoscoping's visibility as a magical tool increased throughout the early twentieth century. African American Jazz bandleader Cab Calloway brought his star power to the technology by providing his highly recognizable dance movements to several animated characters designed by Fleischer—Koko the Clown, the ghostly Walrus, and the Old Man of the Mountain—all from episodes of the *Betty Boop* cartoon between 1932 and 1933.

Two episodes of *Betty Boop* that feature Calloway, titled "Minnie the Moocher" (Dir. Dave Fleischer, 1932) and "Old Man of the Mountain" (1933), open with footage of Calloway and his orchestra in a stage performance. At the helm of two creative spheres, Calloway conducts the musicians, pausing to dance his signature move, a slow, sliding moonwalk that would later inspire Michael Jackson, in front of the band. Calloway and his musicians are named in the opening credits of the episode, and the film clearly teases a connection between Calloway's human form and the animated bodies that appear later, which have been rotoscoped using Calloway's dancing. But it does not make that link explicitly clear through credits naming Calloway as dancer. In another *Betty Boop* short, "Snow White" (Dir. Dave Fleischer, 1933), Calloway is named as the singer providing the "vocal chorus" for "Saint James Infirmary Blues" but not as a dancer providing motion for "Snow White's" KoKo the Clown, even though Calloway's movement style is very palpable in the character.

In "The Old Man of the Mountain," for example, Calloway's movements can be felt in the smooth twisting spins of the Old Man character as he dances along barefoot, his cartoon body swooning toward into the punctuating taps of his feet. Calloway's moonwalk is in there too, under the long raggedy beard and knobby knees, as are his relaxed yet rhythmic arm gestures that follow and enhance the fluidity of his body. Calloway's animated characters possess what perceptual psychologists call his "motion signature," or the unique way *his* body moves, which allows us to recognize or identify figures by the quality of their movement alone.[271] This motion signature is related to dance *anima*—as an ensouling force that is on the one hand evidence of the individual with all their quirks and on the other, evidence of their particular "habitus" an accumulation of the repeated techniques and practices that shape body movements over time.[272] While Disney was sure to erase the labor of the unknown dancer Marge Champion, disconnecting her name from any instances of her dance *anima* in various animations, the Fleischer Brothers' *Betty Boop* shorts capitalized on Calloway as a household name, introducing him and his orchestra upfront as contributors to the score and vocal performances of the cartoon. They did not, however, acknowledge the work of Calloway as dancer. It seems dance is a labor often relegated to the ghostly trace rather than foregrounded as important work.

Indeed, in rotoscoping, the performer's body remains a "palpable spectre within the animation"[273]—what Mark Langer and Tanine Allison observe as a "simultaneous presence of the drawn and the photo-indexical, in which the rotoscoped or Rotoshopped body is not so much fused with the human body as it is mapped over it."[274] Ryan Pierson, conversely, objects to the tendency to theorize rotoscoped bodies—especially those animated by "surface line," as "haunted" or "uncanny."[275] Instead, he distinguishes between what he calls (via Donald Crafton) "figurative performance" and "embodied performance" where "figurative performance" is associated with vaudeville and minstrelsy, which relies on "surface-level traits that come from a familiar stock vocabulary" and which can reduce a character to a "type or an icon."[276] Pierson gives the example of the various morphs that Koko the Clown cycles through in *Betty Boop: Minnie the Moocher* and explains, "It also means that when a figure changes, that change is totalizing. Because there is no "interior to a figurative performance, there is no essence."[277] "Embodied performance," according to Pierson, describes Disney's preferred mode of animation post-1930s; it is derived in part from a focus on psychological depth championed by Stanslavski and other European theater-makers at the time. In "embodied performance," the figure has a "hierarchical form, with a central through-line that dictates the manner and direction of its internal forces and an un-yielding core that external forces cannot alter."[278] "Even though the outline is

Figure 17 A collage of four different iterations of Cab Calloway: his dancing body in live performance (top left), a walrus (top right), a long-legged ghost (bottom left), and a beheaded creature whose head has become a bottle (bottom right). This sequence shows the expressive plasticity of Calloway's animated form. These stills are from the animated short *Betty Boop: Minnie the Moocher* (Paramount Pictures, 1932), directed by Dave Fleischer. (Screenshots collaged by the author.)

the only line that is literally visible in the resulting figure, it is the least important," Pierson writes, "it is "simply a skin.""[279]

While I appreciate Pierson's noting of the relation between certain stock movements and minstrelsy here, representations that can certainly be seen in the *Betty Boop* shorts, I find it curious that "embodied" performance in his definition is that which corresponds to the character's embodiment of *psychological* depth. This formation unhelpfully returns to a kind of Cartesian dualism that views body movement as merely symptomatic of thoughts and feelings happening in the *mind*. I disagree with Pierson that there is no sense of "essence"—or interiority that holds—in the "figurative" performances of early rotoscoped cartoons. In fact, I believe that it is the presence of *dance* in these cartoon bodies that fosters a sense of interiority or ensoulment. The source dancer's particular movement, which always returns between morphs, while not necessarily evocative of a precise psychological, narrative depth, is certainly embodied and carries with it traces of that dancer's *habitus*, training, aches and pains, pleasures, age, weight, cultural shaping, and so on. Calloway's "Old Man," with his disheveled appearance and lecherous, even malevolent, gestures toward Betty, is undeniably "figurative" (even racistly so), but his signature movement (his moonwalking, tap dancing dance *anima*), makes his character absolutely "embodied" as well. Rotoscoping, with its staticky edges and shaky kineticism, also feels very alive, perhaps more so because the exact intent of each gesture is not always crystal clear. It is precisely this lack of clarity that feels dance-like to me.

In contrast with the vibrancy of rotoscoped animations, motion capture (or mocap) is an animation method that offers clarity and precision. Technically similar to rotoscoping in that it extracts human motion to enliven animated bodies and forms, mocap became an integral technical element in the production of digitally animated bodies from the late twentieth century onward. Susan Kozel makes us aware of the tensions within the term "motion capture," for "it implies that the motion is contained once it is captured, like a bee in a net, but this sophisticated and poetic slice of human-computer interaction is about flow, patterns, and shapes of movement, about the way life can be breathed into that which seemed inanimate."[280] The process, Kozel argues, fosters an ethical and intersubjective relationship between the performer and the data their body generates. Mocap allows animators to create visible traces of movement and to have that movement spill over and beyond the bounds of the referent dancing form. However, mocap preserves a sense of interiority inherent to the dance which seems to emanate from an unseen core, no matter what entity hosts it. Because its edges are clean and digitally rendered, its surface changeable and faceless, the digital body propelled by mocapped dance ultimately draws back to the "through line" of dance *anima* and thereby seems to have a more determined and focused, yet (surprisingly) less "embodied" feel. The dancing avatars of "Light it Up," for example, are much more task-focused—than the strange and distracting rotoscoped characters that Calloway animates with his dancing. This is of course mostly due to the experimental stylistic choices of early animators versus the near impossibility of that type of messiness in the postmodern digital mocap realm. In both cases, though, dance *anima* functions as a type of extractable resource—a valuable one to artists and media practitioners wanting to engineer or simulate life in limitless dancing forms.

Popularized in video game design in the 1990s, mocap is today used in military, sports, and medical applications as well as in robotics. Filmmakers like James Cameron and Peter Jackson used mocap to animate the characters in *Avatar* (2009) and *Lord of the Rings* (2001–2003), respectively. When a dancer or an actor provides their gestural movements for a mocap animation, they often perform within a black box surrounded by cameras and wearing a special suit—a tight-fitting black leotard with sensors placed at specific points on the joints of the limbs, across the torso, and on the head. These sensors (which look like tiny disco balls) are registered by the cameras as coordinates in space and become data points that can then be accessed within a choreographic interface on a computer and mapped onto a digital avatar, making them move. Although I have not yet attained confirmation about how the Major Lazer video was created, given the quality of movement, the combination of digital virtuosity and grounded gestures, and the smooth transitions between whole dancing bodies and dissolving, erupting ones, the producers almost certainly used mocap techniques, possibly in combination with a 3D-animation tool similar to Adobe Mixamo or Blender. Mocap facilitates a kinetic exchange between human and more-than-human dancers and makes countless different types and shapes of bodies possible, as is evident in "Light It Up."[281]

The technological apparatus of mocap, while productive of spectacular visual effects, can also be limiting for dancers in a number of ways, from the claustrophobia of dancing within a small grid to the way more minor, nuanced body movements might be harder for the cameras to read.[282] Kat Hawkins and Clarice Hilton are two researchers who have also critiqued mocap's reinforcement of ableism due to its inability to read non-normative bodies, and their project "Figural Bodies" centers disabled dancing bodies into the digitally immersive design process.[283] Researchers like Hawkins and Hilton draw attention to the fact that mocap situates the dream of the virtual/virtuosic body in a standardized human form that excludes those who are differently abled. Emerging from the preoccupations of postmodernism, where disembodiment became both a utopic fantasy of immortality and a horrific prediction of lost agency, mocap offers the virtuosic body as the ideal state of being.

One of the most "pervasive themes in the fiction and theory of cyberculture" produced in postmodernism was that the "human body is vanishing, irrelevant, or interfaced with the machine, an empty shell robbed of what is variously called spirit, consciousness, or identity."[284] The rhetoric of disembodiment characteristic of cultural theory in the 1980s and 1990s conveyed a world in which "the human form . . . becomes an electronic body . . . obsessed with its own disappearance": a novel digital body capable of moving in new, networked ways unhindered by the "shameful" weight of the human corporeal form.[285] In 1999, Roy Ascott writes: "computer networking responds to our deep psychological desire for transcendence—to reach the immaterial, the spiritual—the wish to be out of body . . . to exceed the limitations of time and space, a kind of bio-technological theology."[286] Thinking back to the etymology of *anima* as the floating, breeze-like soul that can move between bodies, described in the introduction to this book, there seems to be a spiritualism inherent to both digital animation and dance *anima*.

The digital spirit, according to writers like Ascott, William Gibson, and Michael Heim, is immortal: unencumbered by the weight of the body, it roams freely through cyberspace. In 1993, Heim mused that in the computer interface, "the spirit migrates from the body to a world of total representation, [and] information and images float . . . without a grounding in bodily experience."[287] Like the postmodern digital spirit, the mocapped or rotoscoped dance *anima* traverses multiple representations and promises, therefore, to be immortal: no longer tethered to one material body or form, dance *anima* can be re-embodied, over and over, as an energy that travels out of body. And yet if postmodernism was marked, as Susan Bordo argues, by the desire for "human freedom from bodily determination," or the "limitless improvement and change [that defies] the historicity, the mortality and, indeed, the very materiality of the body," the postmodern body is in fact, like dance *anima*, "no body at all."[288] Or rather, the only viable body is one which is thoroughly "responsive, efficient, controllable, [and] engineerable" to suit the demands of late capitalism.[289] This string of adjectives could also apply to the "ideal" dance body, where the dancer might act as a responsive instrument for the will and vision of the choreographer, and to the cartoon body controlled by the animator. A digitally animated dancer, therefore, embodies the engineerable efficiency of the late capitalist subject.

In our time of advanced capitalism, this digital performer takes on new prominence, as seen in the rising popularity of hologram pop stars and virtual entertainers like Hatsune Miku, referenced in my Preface. The 1990s aspirations of digital disembodiment have been replaced by a performative spectacle that is self-aware about its simulated nature. Today, the trend is to tap into postmodern tropes of immateriality as a kind of gimmick or surface aesthetics that is nostalgic but never very critical. Take for example the Netflix show *Dance Monsters* (2022), a dance competition where contestants perform live, but not as their human selves; instead they dance (via mocap) as CGI avatars in front of a live audience. Another recent example that gives its tricks up from the start is the music video for American pop singer Ed Sheeran's 2019 single "Cross Me" featuring Chance the Rapper. This video displays its use of mocap unambiguously: it begins by showing professional dancer Courtney Scarr in a mocap suit performing choreography that shifts between ballet technique, krumping, and acrobatic moves, demonstrating her ability to code-switch between virtuosic, cross-cultural dance styles. The video then proceeds to reveal the many different bodies that can be animated using the gestural data mined from her dancing. These bodies include a swarm of gold mannequins, bodies made of glowing mesh and lively balls, and the digital bodies of Sheeran and Chance themselves.

"Cross Me" presents a shape-shifting fantasy that harkens back to the dream of 1990s cyber theory, where bodies can transmogrify and differences of identity such as race and gender are made fluid, but it does so without the naivety of a Benetton-era color-blindness. While Scarr's body never appears as an animation in the video, Sheeran and Chance are given CGI forms that have a distinctly dated, uncanny feel. When Sheeran and Chance are infused with Scarr's dance data, they are also given superhuman capabilities—their (still uncanny) animated bodies become elastic and they can perform flips and jumps—and at times the screen emulates a glitching effect, revealing the grid of cameras and data points that mocap necessitates and in which they all dance. Although the mocap and animation produced for "Cross Me" is not as sophisticated as in "Light It Up," dance is portrayed in both cases as a fluid agentic force whose transfer between bodies is also a conjuring of new life. If we conceive of the dancer's mocap data (their extracted *anima*) as an entity that is separate from their body, this entity is also productive: it can generate infinite other dancing entities.

Unlike rotoscoping, which is born out of the spatiotemporal labor of the animator's meticulous hand-tracing, and which limits the animated dancer to whichever setting (time and place) the animator draws them in, mocap produces a dance spectacle untethered to time or space (the dancer's data can be transported quickly into any type of setting). Whereas rotoscoped dance is somewhat linear in a narrative sense—the morphs emerge from a singular dancing body, one after another as a kind of fantastical chain of cause and effect—mocapped dance offers a new, non-linear relationship to time and space, as it can use data taken from a single dancer to proliferate and layer the dancing form into multiple bodies that can dance *together,* anywhere.

Mocap animations are therefore uncanny in their cloning ability and are almost too ethereal and flighty in their digital vacuum. Many animators therefore want to ground their figures in the earthy feeling of human movement, and to do this, they turn to dance. Especially in the North American context, animation producers often use Black vernacular dance movement to imbue cartoon animals and inhuman forms that are otherwise deracialized with a sense of authentic interiority.

A clear example of this is the 2006 film *Happy Feet*, directed by George Miller for Warner Bros. The film follows a group of CGI-generated Antarctic penguins known for their singing. One young penguin named Mumble cannot sing like the rest of the penguins, but he regularly expresses his emotions through little outbursts of dance, and eventually, instead of "finding his voice," Mumble finds his *body* and contributes his dance to the chorus of penguins.[290] Mumble is voiced by Elijah Wood, but his body movements and dance scenes are animated via mocap by American tap dancer Savion Glover. While there are several behind-the-scenes videos that feature Glover in a mocap suit, tap dancing to provide his data for Mumble, his name is generally absent from the *Happy Feet* project at large.

The movie poster for the film demonstrates the hierarchy of contributors to the project: while Wood's name appears at the top of the poster, Glover's is nowhere to be found. Neither is he acknowledged in the opening credits or the trailers for the film. As Film and Media Studies scholar Tanine Allison has noted, Glover is "widely regarded as the best tap dancer of his generation," and he supplies an "essential" component—some may even say the *most* important component—of Mumble's identity; after all, this is a story about a penguin who finds his identity through dance.[291] The withholding of Glover's name from promotional materials for the film almost seems intended to conceal the film's appropriation of Black culture in the way that *Happy Feet* uses motion capture "as a medium through which African American performance can be detached from black bodies and applied to white ones."[292] This is similar to what Pamela Krayenbuhl calls "blackbodying," a "practice of appropriation whereby non-Black performers use Black dance and movement styles without using blackface makeup," but it is not quite the same.[293] Given the fact that penguins are animals and therefore without race, and given that Glover's actual dancing lives on in the body of the penguin through his captured motion data, this is not a cut and dry case of appropriation. As Glover's dance jumps from human body to digital (animal) body, however, the materiality of his tap gestures (and the history of tap as a distinctly Black American dance form that draws on West African rhythms) undeniably permeates the animation.

Glover's re-embodied tap dance reveals crucial questions about ownership, uncredited labor, and appropriation as they relate to dance and animation, not to mention race. Mocap further complicates this phenomenon, which has a long history. Brenda Dixon Gottschild argues that the "Africanist" influence on American culture has a "pervasive," "potent, vital force" that "sets American culture apart from that of Western Europe," and at the same time, the Africanist presence has been "invisibilized" as a kind of "vitality" inherent to America.[294] "The Africanist presence," Gottschild writes, "comes to Americans from home base, from the inside. Like electricity through the wires, we draw from it all the same, but few are aware of its source."[295] The case of *Happy Feet* demonstrates Glover's dance *anima* as the "electricity" coming through the wires, and the invisibilization of his name serves to frame his vitality as belonging not to Glover but to American culture at large. T. Brown explains that because Black culture, "particularly as it is imagined by white minds, is the foundation for American popular entertainment," and given the ongoing erasure and violence enacted upon Black bodies in America, there is a clear cultural wish to separate Black creativity from the dancing/singing/working body that produces it.[296]

Many practitioners of mocap are enchanted not only by the power it affords the animator—who gets to play puppeteer—but also by its ability to abstract the beauty of human movement away from "bodily distractions" such as gender and race.[297] Digital artist Paul Kaiser, for example, has previously praised mocap as a method of "clean[ing] out the eyes" to approach a more "pure" representation of movement.[298] This language reflects the scrutiny of a scientific and undeniably racist gaze, which extends the aesthetics of abstraction present within the culture of dance since at least the 1680s towards a logic wherein the dancing body's (cultural, gendered, racial) specificities are seen as obstacles to "clean" or "pure" movement.[299]

Ghostcatching

In 1999, African American dancer Bill T. Jones used mocap technology to explore both the particular *anima* of his movement as a dancer and the affordances of abstracted motion in his project *Ghostcatching*, a collaboration with white media artists Paul Kaiser and Shelley Eshkar for the OpenEndedGroup. Before the collaboration, Jones was known for using improvisation to make work that was deeply informed by his embodied experience of history, race, sexuality, and memory. After Jones's partner, dancer Arnie Zane, died of AIDS in 1988, Jones committed himself to "making work that dealt explicitly with his [own] identity" and what he called his "black rage" in pieces such as *Last Supper at Uncle Tom's Cabin/The Promised Land* (1990) and *Still/Here* (1994). The New York dance scene in the early 1990s, however, saw an increased interest in "formal purity," largely inaugurated by the work of Merce Cunningham and Trisha Brown, choreographers Jones loved and respected.[300] Danielle Goldman has written at length on Jones's work in *I Want to Be Ready*, where she challenges the links between fantasies of freedom and histories of improvisation in American postmodern dance. Goldman explains that Jones was skeptical about this aesthetic: "as a black man dancing in a time and place where whiteness is largely invisible and so-called formal purity looks suspiciously like traditionally white aesthetics, Jones understands the naiveté, the exclusivity of imagining a formal realm free of politics."[301] *Ghostcatching* emerged from this frustration.

For *Ghostcatching*, Kaiser and Eshkar recorded his improvised movements using mocap technology and then rendered them onto a screen as a sketch of his body in expressive, painterly outlines (Figure 18). In this

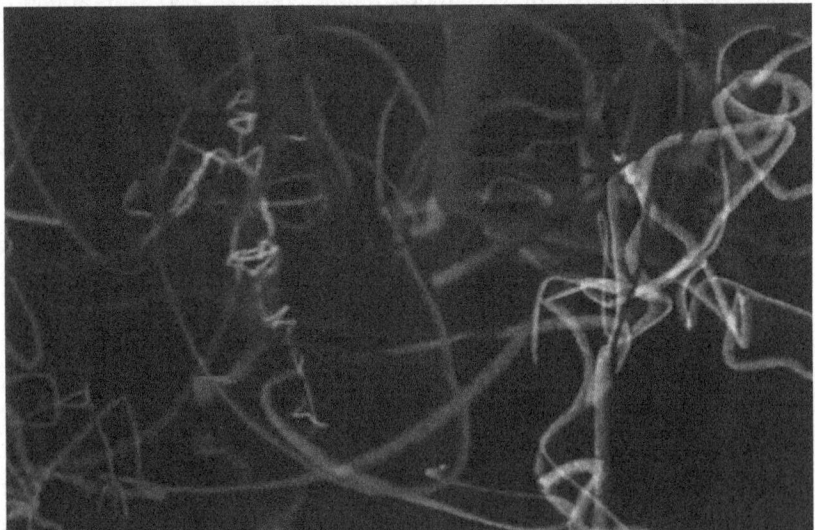

Figure 18 In *Ghostcatching*, Bill T. Jones's motion-captured body dances amongst other painterly versions of himself that have become paused in time and space. Screenshot from YouTube, *Ghostcatching* (OpenEndedGroup, dir. Paul Kaiser and Shelley Eshkar: 1999).

way, his "improvisations became virtual, moving in a sense *beyond* [his] body."[302] Indeed, when Kaiser and Eshkar asked Jones to collaboratively experiment with dance and mocap, Jones took as his starting point this suspicion of being reduced to, as he says, a "disembodied, denatured, de-gendered series of lines moving in a void."[303] He was also skeptical that mocap could "actually capture" what he did.[304] This skepticism was justified, as Eshkar declared in a 1999 panel that "The machine could barely snare [Jones]," and recalled that "motion capture markers [were] flying off during *Ghostcatching* recording sessions, the result of Jones' sweating body being literally too slippery to be caught by the apparatus."[305] The title *Ghostcatching* actively evokes both Jones's constant flight from digital capture, and the ephemerality of dance in general.

The painterly aesthetics of the finished product also resist the precise, clinical imagery associated with mocap at its emergence. The soft, curved, and multicolored lines of Jones's animated body in *Ghostcatching* give off a warmth not typically associated with computerized data. Eshkar and Kaiser let traces of Jones's body positions linger as markings in the frame, meaning that his motion hangs in the air in a sequence of embodied imprints. These gestures are sometimes accompanied by post-production sound effects that resemble a shovel scraping ice or a solid object being pushed across a hard surface. There is a sense of heaviness in the sounds that, paired with the grain of Jones's extracted gesture, grounds the weightless feeling of the digitally animated body. At times, the animation freezes Jones's animated body in certain poses while allowing his avatar to move forward with the motion. His gestures thus build a palimpsest of themselves until Jones appears to be dancing within a constrictive web of his own motion, a web which he both makes and is in constant escape from.[306]

The result, as seen in Figure 18, is one of copying and imprinting the body onto the space of the virtual stage so that Jones's multiple bodies move together at once, in a kind of group choreography. The "ghost" referred to in the title of the work might not only be Jones's live performance captured, extracted, and re-enlivened through animation, then, but also the many ghost-selves that a dancer passes through as they perform the successive instants of a movement sequence—the many poses left behind or slipped past in motion. *Ghostcatching* certainly attempts to resist the ephemerality classically associated with both dance—Marcia Siegel writes of dance that "no other art is so hard to catch," [or] "so impossible to hold"[307]—and digital media, as well as the latter's perceived immateriality. Yet despite the haptic, embodied quality of the animations, the work still enacts erasure: of skin, sweat, facial features, hair, and Jones's palpable, working body. *Ghostcatching* asks us to consider the place and agency of the material human body in dance and in data.

Tiffany E. Barber writes of *Ghostcatching* that "Jones was struck by the [mocap] technology's ability to render a faithful image that arguably would capture his liveness but not his likeness, producing another being that was not intrinsically or essentially him."[308] In his live performances of a work called *The Breathing Show* (1999), Jones screened portions of *Ghostcatching* and interacted with the animated projections, periodically stepping out from behind it, and using sounds like humming and singing while unseen to make explicit the tension between his live and mediated bodies. Jones reportedly once asked his spectators at the end of the show, "Can you see with two sets of eyes? Can you see the identity, and also the form?"[309] Described by OpenEndedGroup as a "meditation on the act of being captured and breaking free," the specters of racial violence, imprisonment, labor, and persecution are very much palpable in the work, prompting Goldman to ask, "Can politics transpire in a virtual dance that allows neither sweat nor skin, primary markers of labour and race, to appear on stage?" and "is pure form escape or constraint?"[310]

These were questions that were circulating in the North American cultural consciousness at the time as well. In his controversial book *Against Race: Political Imagining Beyond the Color Line*, published one year after *Ghostcatching* premiered, Paul Gilroy argues that the development of new digital imaging and visual medical technologies ushered in a post-racial discourse, where "skin is no longer privileged as the threshold of either identity or particularity" allowing us to let "old visual signatures of 'race' go."[311] But what about the nonvisual signatures of racial identity? What of the more overlooked aspects of racial identity/labor—what about dance as a trace of the source body in the morphable digital form?

I want to return to my earlier discussion of Cab Calloway, who provided dance movement (and vocal performance) for Koko the Clown in three *Betty Boop* cartoons: *Minnie the Moocher* (1932), *Snow White* (1933), and *The Old Man of the Mountain* (1933). As he dances, Koko the Clown (in ghost form) keeps losing his pants, which slip down off his thin and very long legs. The repetitive slow slide of the pants down his legs matches Calloway's sluggish, skating dance moves in the scene, and this twinning endows Koko's pants with a lively dance-like quality, pushing the boundaries of where the dancing body begins and ends. At one point, Koko shifts into a handstand and his legs extend beyond their previous physical capacity, winding themselves into a looped formation so that they look like the chain of a necklace, his head the hanging pendant (Figure 19).[312] His body continues to stretch and loop and swing in physically impossible ways, and yet at the end of the number, he comes back together, his body once again intact. This animation tendency, toward the spectacular transformation of the body, goes hand in hand with dance as an art form and as an idea and is seen not just in rotoscoped dance sequences but in filmic ones as well, illustrating the historical relationship between dance and emergent visual media as one that navigates and proposes new boundaries of the human form.

Douglas Rosenberg's work on screendance, for example, explores the dance film's ability (and desire) to produce bodies that dissolve into fragments without threat of death. Through the key process of editing and projection, Rosenberg argues that the filmed body in screendance becomes "recorporealized" "as a kind of Frankenstein, temporally dislocated and awaiting authorial reanimation."[313] Rosenberg writes that what results is an "impossible body, unencumbered by gravity, technique, time, or death."[314]

Figure 19 Koko the Clown's dancing body morphs into a pendant on a chain in *Betty Boop's Snow White* (1933). Screen grab from YouTube.

What does it mean to fantasize about being able to come to pieces and not die? And who is fantasizing about disassembling whom here? Ngai notes that this ambivalence about where power resides in the animation assemblage takes on "special weight in the case of racialized subjects, for whom objectification, exaggerated corporeality or physical pliancy, and the body-made spectacle remain doubly freighted issues."[315] In presenting a fantasy of inhuman, elastic animations, immune to pain and death, these "impossible bodies" disregard the real, material, oftentimes violent conditions of living life as a nonwhite subject.

This is complicated further when the appearance of the animated body trades in racist stereotypes or caricature. In the *Betty Boop* cartoons' diegesis, it seems as though whenever Betty finds her way into a dangerous situation, Koko appears. He morphs into a ghost, a dancing walrus, and an old hermit, each time singing songs about gambling, drug use, and crime in scenes that are full of imagery of death and addiction,[316] all the while performing Calloway's signature dance moves—most notably a slow, backward dragging step he called "the buzz," echoed later in Michael Jackson's 1985 performance of the moonwalk (see Figure 17, upper left-hand corner). Christopher P. Lehman writes that "African American performers and the surreal dwellings of their caricatures in the *Betty Boop* series represent an 'other' that provides an appealing sense of liberation for whites but contains a threat of miscegenation via Betty's presence in their part of town."[317] Calloway himself was no stranger to being fetishized as a Black performer; he regularly performed for primarily white audiences at the Cotton Club from 1931 to 1934 following New York's Harlem Renaissance period. Koko the Clown is similarly a tourist attraction for a white audience—a racist caricature associated with the seedy inner city and the wild creativity of jazz. Warren-Crow notes that despite their obvious associations with Blackness, all of Calloway's characters in the *Betty Boop* series have white skin, and suggests that this allows "white viewers to get a safe thrill" from the suggestion of "interracial sexuality" in Calloway's scenes.[318] Nate Sloan points out that Calloway had an ability to code-switch, due to his mixed-race identity, his light brown skin, his chemically straightened hair, and his "protean vocality," all of which contributed to his "in-betweenness," giving him a unique crossover appeal to both Black and white audiences.[319] This hybrid identity is also palpable in the plasticity of the animated characters created using Calloway's rotoscoped dancing.[320]

As I mention earlier, these rotoscoped cartoons were openly advertised as being voiced by Calloway; they often began with clips of his live performance, and Calloway's rich and textured singing voice is joined to the fluid dancing movement of his animated body. In this way, Calloway (as tourist attraction) remains a more intact entity than the assemblage of Mumble the Penguin from *Happy Feet*, whose voice, visual appearance, and gestural movements are provided by three different sources. And yet Calloway's various characters (KoKo the clown, the walrus, and the ghost) all display another type of spectacle. Moving beyond the typical squash and stretch of animation, where the identity of the pliable character remains intact, Calloway's personas are capable of transforming into other creatures and objects entirely. From Sloan's historical account of Calloway's relationship to his own identity (his resistance to being fixed in place), it is plausible that Calloway delighted in his animated alter egos' ability to shapeshift and be freed from any one, stable form. And it is also likely that Calloway's embodied experience of being Black in early twentieth-century America nurtured this desire to be free of his fixed physical appearance. Yet there is also a complicated dynamic that arises from the joining of Calloway's recognizable singing voice and "motion signature" dancing with the fluctuating cartoon objects on screen in *Betty Boop*.

Calloway's dancing and singing anchors his plastic animated form in what Afrofuturist writers like Alexander G. Weheliye and Kodwo Eshun describe as the invocation of Blackness as an appeal to authenticity, embodiment, and the "natural."[321] These thinkers, who I also cite in Chapter 4, are mainly focused on music—they argue that the Black singing voice is often used in the R&B, pop, and rap genres as an authenticating force that can be extracted, sampled, and remixed. They do not write about dance. But I observe a similar strategy in animation and visual media that capitalizes on Black social dance and Black gesture—like voice—as a signifier, not necessarily of specific identity but of a general authenticating force. Calloway's dance *anima* is therefore a powerful asset to the Fleischer Brothers' films. Dance is the thing that navigates the borders between reality and fantasy, material and ephemeral—or the real, embodied labor of dancers and abstract, disembodied form. The animated body is an entity that in a sense fulfills the expansive potential of dance, without the material constraints of the human in the real world. But under the hand of the animator, is the animated dancer's "plasmaticness," to return to Eisenstein's word, a sign of its power or its precarious vulnerability? Ngai cites Rey Chow to argue that while the animated body, with its "excessive energy and metamorphic potential," can be seen as a "subversive or powerful body," the same elastic and pliant qualities that seem "liberatory" are also "readable as signs of the body's utter subjection to power, … external manipulation, and control."[322] A dancer's corporeality can similarly be seen as both material to be manipulated by choreographer and as a "subversive or powerful body" with its own agency, and this manipulability only increases when the dancer is a digital animated avatar.

Yes, Cab Calloway's *anima* propels Koko's body, but the animator morphs him into a ghost with long, looping legs and multiple limbs, and a gold coin on a snaking chain. After his many distortions, Koko returns—his body springing back into the form he began with. And yet, we might also read Koko's *resilience* (a term Christina Sharpe notes is often liberally applied to migrants and people of color in the United States) as both a survival imperative and a "stubborn refusal not to go away" or, as Sharpe writes, a "stubborn not-dying."[323] The elasticity of Koko may be post-human or post-body, but it is not post-race. Throughout his various "an-ontological" (to quote Levitt) transformations made possible by rotoscoping, Koko's movements remain tethered to an ontology: Calloway's signature dance habitus, born of repetition, ritual, practice, and Black social formation, history, and culture. The dance *anima* of Glover, Calloway, and Bill T. Jones, sampled and remixed by emergent animation technologies of their respective time periods, conjures a series of embodied *ghosts, caught* in the machine. Dance, which carries the memory of the body's habitus and history, challenges the postmodern (and posthuman) ideology of an imagined "raceless future."[324]

I began this chapter by citing Langer and Badiou's arguments that dance can be framed as an escape *from the body itself,* and I demonstrated how we can read this discourse historically, through modern and postmodern aesthetics and animation techniques like rotoscoping and mocap. But I hesitate to limit my analysis to the idea of dance as an extractable resource to be captured by the animatic apparatus. Dance *anima* is both an emission and an undeniable appendage of the dancer. It cannot be owned and yet it "belongs" to many bodies and states simultaneously. A dancer's physical presence is materially shaped by the repeated practice of dancing, but dancers are also subjects that produce dance *as an embodied output* that both resides in their individual presence *and* exceeds and spills beyond them, linking multiple bodies, techniques, and modes of liveliness. The joy of holding something so fleeting as dance *anima* in one's dancing body, of co-creating that anima, of being in relation to the particularities of an energy that has moved through many bodies, of touching it with one's learned sense of rhythm and musical interpretation, is what I might call a violent joy, mirrored somewhat in the images of bodies dissolving and exploding into pieces that Major Lazer's music video offers up (Figure 15). These images present a video game-like irreverence toward death characteristic of advanced capitalism, where the digital body becomes a space to enact fantasies of violence. They illustrate, too, that no one body is a contained unit with defined borders. Dance shows us this. Dance is not just about dispossession; it is also a driving life force that generates more and more dancing entities through the production of dance *anima*.

Dance can be thought of as a secretion of the body that also, in the case of extractive animation methods, makes secret (or conceals) its source. It is the relation between secretion and concealment, dance and body, capture and plasticity that drives my interest in dance as *anima*. When dance is animated, the limits of human ontology are juxtaposed with the an-ontology that both dance and animation promise. The resulting animation, now in possession of its own *anima*, both erases the referent body and simultaneously preserves it as a ghostly memory in unfurling gestures. The pain of dance practice and effort does not guarantee ownership on the product of that energetic work. If dance is an escape *from the body itself*, "freeing" the body's gestures, which hold the promise of rebellious agency, from the limits of bounded human form, the escape is thus dance's own.

Dance has agency outside the human, and yet dance is not completely independent from the bodies that produce it. It cannot *only* escape. *Anima* must reside in a body to be seen and felt. But not just one body; dance *anima* carries with it traces of bodies that danced before and opens into future relational possibilities (the bodies that will dance). The traces of bodies, cultural histories, and emotions that are retained in a dancer's *anima* bring those affects to bear on the animated body as well. This is a process that is deeply conditioned by discourses of race and fraught by issues of labor, appropriation, visual representation, and the porous boundaries between subject and object that make ownership precarious. Dance *anima* may be neutral, but there is an ethics to its extraction and depiction.

4

Esprit de Corps

The Military–Industrial Dancer

. . . movability had become the main goal of military exercises, and the soldier had been transformed from a "lifeless machine" into a dynamic instrument of warfare. (Harald Kleinschmidt on Guibert's 1775 philosophy of unison movement for soldiers)[325]

. . . at the command "march," the soldier will move the left leg forward in a lively manner but without tremor, the thigh turned a little outwards, the foot advancing flat and parallel to the ground at two inches of elevation and stopping when the heel will be at the height of the point of the right foot. This movement must be from the hip, the back of the knee being without stiffness and gently bending, and the body resting quite perpendicular to the left leg. . . the soldier will [then] carry the right leg forward . . . to around six inches of alignment between the heels, and . . . the right foot will advance twelve inches further, the body quite straight and always accompanying the leg . . . Once the soldier well-understands the nature of the step, and when he executes it with firmness and accuracy, he will no longer mark time.

(Guibert's specific instructions for marching soldiers, from his *General Essay on Tactics*, 1775)[326]

In December 2020, American engineering firm Boston Dynamics posted a set of videos to YouTube featuring dancing robots. In the opening frames of one of these videos, a shiny white humanoid robot with articulated limbs and fin-like feet stands in a large, glass-walled warehouse as the opening chords for The Contours' 1962 pop hit "Do You Love Me?" fill the space (Figure 20). The robot, named Atlas, begins to move. It sways from side to side and fidgets, looking dejected as one of the singers opens the song with a spoken line: "you broke my heart cause I couldn't dance; you didn't even want me around." As the drums swell, leading into the chorus, Atlas perks up and launches into its choreography, step touching and grape vining to

Dance Anima. Hilary Bergen, Oxford University Press. © Oxford University Press 2026.
DOI: 10.1093/9780197786673.003.0005

Figure 20   Boston Dynamics' robots "Atlas" and "Spot" in a dance video
released by Boston Dynamics to demonstrate the robots' skill in executing
gestures and moving their bodies. Above, Spot appears to be doing something
like a *bourrée*, which ballet dancers perform *en pointe*, and the Atlas models
seem to be doing a *grand battement* (or big kick) with their right leg as they *plié*
with their left. In the second image (below), the robots are transitioning out
of the "running man" (popularized by MC Hammer in the 1980s Oakland hip
hop scene) and into the "mashed potato" (made famous by singer James Brown
in 1959) (Still from YouTube video: "Do You Love Me?" Uploaded by Boston
Dynamics, December 29, 2020.)

the rhythm of the song. It twirls, jumps, twists, and hand jives with the exuberance, awkwardness, and dogged rhythmic fidelity of one who has newly learned—or been programmed—to dance. Soon, other dancing robots enter the stage, including a second Atlas model, who joins the first in complete unison of the dance moves. The camera zooms out and pans in a circle as other robots designed by Boston Dynamics—Spot the "dog," Handle the warehouse worker, and Pick, who is skilled in depalletizing—join in the choreography (Figure 20). They do the running man together, performing neck isolations, leg extensions, and fluid, supple squats and jumps, alternating between a weighted quality of movement and a breezy, effortless lift of their clunky bodies off the ground.

The video was released by the robotics design company as a marketing strategy and has forty-one million views as of July 2025. The robots can dance so well (and so humanly) that there are entire Reddit threads dedicated to exposing the videos as masterpieces of CGI.[327] The video is an example of what Sydney Skybetter calls "choreorobotics," a genre "concerned with how bodies move and are encoded, and how performances interface with power."[328] Boston Dynamics' choice of song here—"Do You Love Me" by The Contours—is tongue-in-cheek, given that the lyrics are sung from the perspective of one (i.e., the robot) who has just learned to dance, and who asks the audience to love them more because of it. The first movement Atlas makes in the video is a kind of withering shrug, timed to coincide with the lead singer's spoken lamentation, "you broke my heart / cause I couldn't dance / you didn't even want me around." Atlas's performance of dejection joins body to voice and gesture to inner emotional turmoil, humanizing the robot and presenting dance as a solution to being disposable. Atlas's new ability to dance, work, and perform is directly tied to human emotion and "soul" in the lyrics of the song:

> Do you love me? (I can really move)
> Do you love me? (I'm in the groove)
> Now do you love me?
> (Do you love me now that I can dance?)
> Watch me, now
> (Work, work) ah, work it out baby
> (Work, work) well, I'm gonna drive you crazy
> (Work, work) ah, just a little bit of soul, now?
> (Work)
> Now I can mash potatoes (I can mash potatoes)

I can do the twist (I can do the twist)
Tell me, baby, do you like it like this?
—The Contours, "Do You Love Me?" (1962)

Why would Boston Dynamics portray their robots to be seeking love? The Contours' lyrics effectively set up the robots as emotional commodities; they are things that consumers desire or long for and that, in turn, this video suggests, long to be desired by the consumer ("do you love me?"). The robots' ability to dance softens them to the viewer so a trade in such affective capital can happen openly.[329] While the repetition of "work" in the song lyrics is a subtle reminder of the true function of Spot and Atlas as warehouse workers, their emotional song and dance distracts from the dehumanization of their job. As they hop, shuffle, slide, and twist, they imbricate technique and technology toward a fantasy of capitalist synchronicity.[330]

The articulation of this desire is undeniably tethered to race. While the robots are not explicitly racialized, it is impossible to ignore the fact that Atlas is a shiny *white* robot dancing to Black soul music.[331] This simple visual-auditory contrast, combined with the the use of Black vernacular dance moves, strategically commodifies Black joy to distract from the unpaid work Atlas must perform, while also erasing the Black body as source of said joy (and work).[332] The Contours, a successful African American soul group signed to Motown Records (see Figure 21), topped the charts with "Do You Love Me?" in 1962 and again in 1988 following the release of *Dirty Dancing* in 1987, which featured the song in a central scene. The robots replicate many of the dance moves mentioned in the lyrics of the song (the twist, the mashed potato), all of which were made popular by African American performers of the 1960s, like James Brown. Skybetter, who has worked closely with Boston Dynamics as a hands-on researcher, remarks in a 2024 Harvard Keynote speech that these dance moves "aren't just appropriative choreographic choices manifested exclusively at the level of YouTube performance. These dance techniques have been lifted out of cultural context and encoded at the level of software and *interface*."[333] As an example, the twerk performed by Spot in several videos is an "Africanist and African American movement technique that contemporarily gained prominence in New Orleans in the 90s and has since been a staple of hip hop and femme Black dance performance."[334] Spot twerks by lowering and raising its rear end in time. However, Skybetter points out, Spot's interface lacks the ability to twerk to multiple time signatures and tempos, meaning that "the robot thus aims to perform a Black coded movement, but without the possibility of rhythmic complexity and exclusively on a basic 4 [count]."[335]

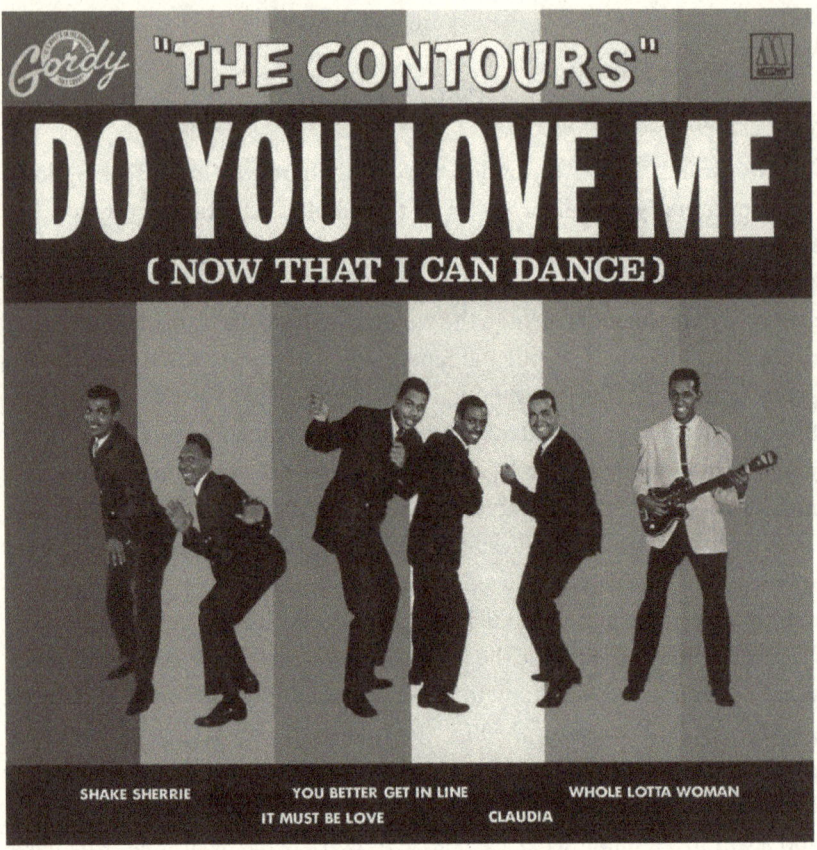

Figure 21   The cover for The Contours' 1962 Motown LP Do You Love Me?
released with the label Waxtime depicts the six Black musicians in various
poses, mid-dance. It seems as though they are doing The Twist, a Black
vernacular dance move they sing about in the song, and which the robots
replicate in the Boston Dynamics promotional video.

This disjuncture, which fundamentally changes the polyrhythmic *anima* of
the dance move, ironically sums up the historical difficulty white (human)
bodies trained in Eurocentric concert dance like ballet have with performing
polycentric, polyrhythmic Africanist dance styles.[336] The body of the robot is,
from an Africanist perspective, like the body of the ballet dancer: stiff, even
"corpse"-like, with a "pulled-up, aligned stance and static carriage indicating
sterility and inflexibility."[337] Atlas's stiff white body is nonetheless articulated
to Black vernacular dance and music—acquiring race as "additive"[338] in order
to remain uncannily oriented toward the type of "soul" its makers intend to
evoke: specifically, Black American soul of the 1960s.

The years between 1954 and 1968 were marked by the campaign to abolish segregation, discrimination, and disenfranchisement of Black individuals in America. A genre influenced by gospel and rhythm and blues, soul music was in many ways the urgent assertion of Black humanity against a deep history of violent dehumanization, and its ascending popularity paralleled the rise of the civil rights and Black Power movements in America. Soul pioneers like Ray Charles and James Brown brought the rhythms and harmonies of church music to a message of political empowerment and self-pride. Boston Dynamics is undoubtedly aware of these associations; their robots' song and dance boldly appropriate the vital *anima* of Black culture to imbue these robots, as capitalist commercial entities, with a sense of soul or humanity.

There is nothing new about this type of cultural appropriation in the American context. It is what scholars have called "vitalist racism," a "type of racism characterized by a powerful white attraction to certain supposed black characteristics, a white desire for black style, dance [and] song" that effectively erases the Black bodies who produce such "modes of expression."[339] In the Boston Dynamics dance videos, as Jessica Rajko discusses, "deracinated Black aesthetics are structurally normalized toward fostering entertainment while omitting Black dancers and embodied knowledge from the design process."[340] Dance is deployed by Boston Dynamics as a vitality that veils the robots' function as replacements or surveillants for human workers—a function that in effect circles back to *erase and control the vitality of bodies*. Remember that *robata*, the Czech root of *robot*, means "slave," and that Atlas and Spot are designed and marketed as warehouse workers programmed to follow orders. Boston Dynamics thus creates robot slaves to do menial, repetitive work. And then, to deflate the perceived threat of these robots (who are also military weapons, a fact I discuss in detail further on), the engineers make them dance to soul music, thereby not only humanizing them, but also coding them as Black, further squeezing the robots into a deeply problematic North American historical logic that calls up the hierarchy between slave and master. These dancing machines represent a powerful yet troubling convergence of efficient mechanized labor, the spectacle of dance, and the appropriation of Black culture *as soul* to sell machines of war.

Another hierarchy the dancing robots embody is that of dancer/choreographer. When I asked Skybetter if Spot and Atlas can dance without a choreographic input, he confirmed that "they [Boston Dynamics] don't let these things improvise in dancerly contexts." While the machines have the capacity for AI, "the AI / machine learning bit is for lower-level processes like self-balancing," and "the choreographic functions are pre-encoded using a pipeline of animation software and [perhaps diminishingly] their choreography software."[341] Dance might therefore more usefully be replaced with the term *choreography* in this chapter. Choreography, as André Lepecki suggests, is an "apparatus for the control of gestures, mobility, dispositions, body types, bodily intentions, and inclinations for the sake of a spectacular display of a body's presence."[342] Lepecki references Giorgio Agamben's theory of the "apparatus," that which has "the capacity to capture, orient, determine, intercept, model, control, or secure the gestures, behaviours, opinions, or discourses of living beings."[343] Both Lepecki and Agamben are concerned with the regulation and standardization of bodies and their movement, and indeed, what is at stake in this chapter's case studies is control—of presence, life, gesture, and dance. This should be clear from the Guibert quote that begins the chapter, in which the bodies of marching soldiers are meticulously choreographed and standardized to the precision of a ruler. Analysis of such control requires an expanded definition of *choreography*, including the choreography of labor and working bodies to harness effective kinetic potential, thereby de-animating human bodies (or making them machinic) in order to animate them in the name of productivity. This chapter looks at a wide array of choreographies, and it examines the machinic apparatus of the camera as an agent in these choreographies to build a theory of dance *anima* for the military–industrial dancing machine. Just as the choreography of work and war plays a role here, so too does the camera act as a means of producing or multiplying *anima* as resource. Through a consideration of the interlinked apparatuses of choreography and camera, this chapter engages with the Boston Dynamics robots as a case study to tie together the dancer, the worker, and the soldier. These three interlinked figures can function as parts of a whole—a mass of bodies choreographed to produce a collective type of dance *anima* (or *esprit de corps*) that exceeds individual expression of agency or feeling. This illustrates a significant shift from the singular charismatic dancer (e.g., Loïe Fuller, Lang's Maria, or Cab Calloway) to the depersonalized many (the chorus line, the assembly line, the drill formation) and reveals the military–industrial complex as invested in *esprit de corps* for profit and power.

Choreographing Work

In Chapter 2, I explored the role of dance as cultural technique in the production of soul in nonliving bodies. The book has thus far positioned dance *anima* as an energy that overflows the body to exceed mechanisms of capture.

This chapter explores the related historical quest to contain, standardize, and mechanically reproduce human motion and activity. The Boston Dynamics robots are a current example of how dance *anima* is valuable not only as an extractable resource but also as an *engineerable* one. Dance—as engineerable *anima*—is useful to corporations like Boston Dynamics for a number of reasons: practically, dance is a method of testing the robotics' hardware and software and contributing to "rapid innovation" in the robot's design; dance acts as proof of the robot's ability to manipulate its body deftly and with strength for the purpose of manual labor; promotional dance videos are also easily circulated and shared, contributing to Boston Dynamics as a maker of entertaining spectacle; lastly, and central to my argument, dance acts as an ensouling force in the robots, obscuring their dehumanized factory and military roles and softening them to their audience.

While dance might appear to spring up in the robots from some inner feeling or impulse, their dance *anima* is meticulously produced, as are the promotional videos overall. The dance sequences in the videos were choreographed by professional dancer Monica Thomas, and the routine was later polished by Danish robotic movement consultant Jakob Welner.[344] The impressive product is the result of painstaking positioning and programming of the robots using a software called Autodesk Maya and a publicly released interface called Choreographer, which is also used in theme parks to sequence attractions and shows. Eric Whitman, a Boston Dynamics roboticist, notes that "dancing is a form of highly accelerated lifecycle testing for the hardware" that leads to "rapid innovation in how a robot can move."[345] Instead of dance acting as the apotheosis of achievement in robotics, it actually uncovers potential improvements for the physical design of the robot. "An athletic performance like dance stresses the mechanical design of the robot, and it also stresses the algorithms in the software," says Marc Raibert, founder and chairman of Boston Dynamics, giving "developers a creative target that leads to rapid innovation in how the robot can move."[346] Whitman and Raibert see dance as a method for improving the physical awareness and dexterity of the robot worker. Dance is a means to an end: a way of making the machinic body *optimal*.

Dance is understood similarly as a mode of optimizing, improving, or mastering the functioning of the *human* body. Neuroscientists often tout dance as a holistic cure for ailing minds, for example, and, as noted in Chapter 3, during the rise of factory work, people like Ford viewed dance as a method of synchronizing his workers and making their bodies more efficient. Once again, dance performs "lifecycle testing" for the "hardware" of many different types of bodies, including human ones. When dance combines with interactive technology, the potential for improvement reaches new, aspirational heights. Take, for example, a recent project called Dance Biometrics, a dance motion learning system that teaches dance with real-time feedback founded by competitive ballroom dancer Alessia Minaeva, DreamWorks animator Chris Grun, and robotics engineer Oleg Pariser. Dance Biometrics uses surveillance tools such as "biofeedback" and visual "overlay" to compare the input of the dancer with the "proper technique" of dance expert, helping users improve their dance ability.[347] Their slogan—"we help people move better"[348]—suggests that technology can become a tool of mastery over the body, and dance is similarly instrumentalized as a method of improving efficiency and control. From a marketing standpoint, the Boston Dynamics robots dance to display their own capacity for body mastery and the prowess of their makers, who have created a work technology (and a body) unhindered by fatigue, hunger, boredom, or desire. In the case of Boston Dynamics and Dance Biometrics, the energetic output of the body (dance *anima*) is a resource that both powers the body-as-optimal-machine and can itself be optimized through the training of that body.

There is a saying I encountered often in dance school: "dancers make good workers." The phrase rings true in my experience as both a dancer and someone who had to work at a variety of manual and customer service jobs to support myself while I was a student. I knew my skillset (being attuned to other bodies as well as my own proprioceptive embodiment, well-trained in following orders from choreographers and teachers, an almost masochistic disregard for pain or discomfort) was an asset for any kind of physically and socially demanding job. Yet there is also a well-documented tendency to exploit the work of dancers, assuming they will perform for free or work for long hours without breaks.[349] Dancing robots like Atlas and Spot are a culmination of the dream of the industrial revolution in part *because* they are dancers: they represent the optimal working body that feels no pain and does not need to be paid.

Historically, working bodies become increasingly choreographed alongside the rise of industrialization. The introduction of mechanized agriculture, coal and steam engines, electricity, the telegraph, and thermodynamics in the late 1800s led to increasing urbanization and a shift from handmade artisanal goods to machine-made commodities on the assembly line. The human body had to be modified and made standard and reliable to keep pace with the new technologies of work. Hence the creation of the field of work science in the late nineteenth century, with its attendant technique of "minimal gesture" to produce maximum efficiency of the working body, which contributed to the "redefinition of 'performance' as [measurable] productivity."[350] The very idea of rhythm changed alongside the development of coordinated factory work (e.g., in the newly mechanized cotton mills of the textile industry) and with this change in rhythm came a change in the way bodies were understood and organized—or choreographed—in the workplace. Such choreographies, which substitute the hands of an individual for a many-bodied machine, also speak to Walter Benjamin's argument that "aura" changes in the age of mechanical production, insofar as aura could be understood as a type of *anima* residing not only in the artifact (or artwork) created, but as a lingering energy: in the case of dance, the product of a moving body.

Post industrial revolution, a change in work rhythm, namely the "staccato movement of bodies with machines,"[351] is significantly represented in popular dance and embodied performance acts at the start of the twentieth century. Josephine Baker's zany dances, which Anne Anlin Cheng refers to as "pure kinetic eruption" and E. E. cummings described as "neither infrahuman nor superhuman but somehow both, [a] mysterious unkillable something," are one such example.[352] "Zany" is an aesthetic category Sianne Ngai theorizes, claiming that we are confronted with it in particular when things become out of control on the assembly line. The affect, Ngai argues, "asks us to regard form not as structure but as activity."[353] We can see the zany in *Modern Times*, for example, when Charlie Chaplin's Tramp character is eaten by the machine he is working on, effectively turning his rebellious body into a commodity on the conveyer belt.[354] Lucille Ball's stint as a chocolate factory worker on *I Love Lucy*, in which she is overwhelmed by the speed of the conveyer belt and ends up stuffing her mouth with chocolates to keep up with the pace required of her as a worker, also demonstrates the comedic potential of the incompatibility between the human and the machine. The container of work choreography is here exceeded and made farcical by a frantic form of dance *anima*, produced at the intersection of human body and emergent technology.

Putting aside the comedic representation of the human–machine relationship, what the Lucille Ball and Charlie Chaplin clips also make clear is why pioneers of work science and industrialism such as Henry Ford might have seen the value of dance technique for their assembly line: if the movement of bodies is well-choreographed and assimilated to the machine (unlike in the cases of Ball and Chaplin), labor power can improve. In fact, Ford required his workers to take lessons in contra dance and participate in regular group dance activities when they were not working in the factory. As Katherine Brucher suggests,

> the features of the social dances championed by the Ford Music Department suggest that they may have served as an object lesson in the virtues of modern factory work. The dances bore a strong resemblance to Ford's moving assembly line. First, group dances like contra dances are activities in which individuals or pairs of dancers execute interlocking patterns of movement that propel couples down the line towards one end of the hall. Second, group dances require the individual to execute precise, efficient movements in exact time. If a dancer loses a step or miscounts, the dancers can lose their places in the line . . . . Finally, the dancers must defer to the authority of the caller. If the dancers fail to respond properly to his instructions, the line breaks down.[355]

Work science's theory of "minimal gesture" for maximum efficiency can be seen in Brucher's description of contra dance, which requires "the individual to execute precise, efficient movements in exact time." Felicia McCarren tracks what she calls the "economy of gesture" across systems of work science to demonstrate the interrelated spheres of physiology, chronophotography, and cinematography. The minimal gesture, she argues, is in part inspired by the "photographic instantaneity" of the camera, a new apparatus in the late nineteenth century.[356] Of particular note are the photographic experiments by Eadweard Muybridge (1830–1904) and Etienne-Jules Marey (also 1830–1904), which used chronophotography to capture and study moving bodies. Both photographers often used dancers in their studies, and although they were not as interested in choreography as they were in "the visualization of the passage of time via the objectification of movement," their subjects—who, in Muybridge's case were often topless, objectified women (Figure 22)—performed choreographed sequences of gestures through space.[357] These were often simple gestures, like jumping, twirling, and even standing and sitting.

Muybridge and Marey had different aesthetic approaches: Muybridge's stop motion photographs feature the realist subject captured at successive points throughout the performance of a gesture, which Tom Gunning and other film theorists suggest are precursors to cinema.[358] Muybridge's studies were chronological and sequential, offering a narrative of gesture. Because Muybridge "retroactively" ordered his individual photos, "arranging fragments of the world into temporal sequences," they became narratively

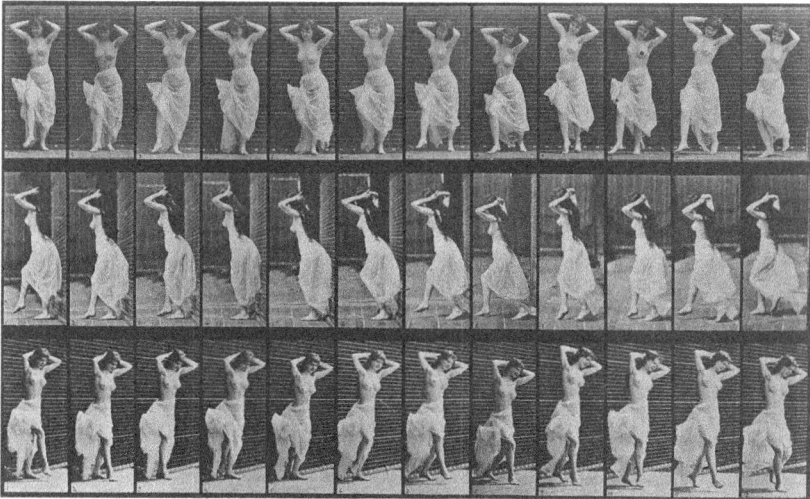

Figure 22 Muybridge's subjects were often nude, topless, or half-dressed women photographed in progressive stages of a minimal gesture which, in this case, I am reading as dance-adjacent or choreographic. ("Animal Locomotion Plate 190," Collotypie, Eadweard Muybridge, 1887, Public Domain.)

legible, and "could then be dramatically transformed into histories."[359] By contrast, Marey's chronophotographic technique, combined with his subjects' tight black unitards with white stripes running down their limbs, abstracted the photographed bodies into a series of lines that ripple across the frame, making his work a predecessor to animation techniques like motion capture technology (Figure 23). Elizabeth Stephens notes that Marey's images were impositional, depicting the full range of movement (or *anima*) in a single image.[360] This impositional tendency is also seen in visual art at the time, including Marcel Duchamp's *Nude Descending a Staircase* (1912), where time is compressed and the many possibilities of the moving body can be seen all at once in the same image. The gaze evident in Marey's work, as Wolfgang Ernst argues, pushed "against the tradition of perspective" to introduce "a genuine media perspective" that was more interested in multiple exposure and "virtually optical 'noise'" than in "material for narration," as we might see in Muybridge's work.[361] For this reason, I argue that Marey's gaze teased out a *dance* impulse in his subjects, viewing them as layers of potential and swirls of emergent movement.

These human motion studies illustrate the camera not just as an apparatus of capture, but *as choreographic apparatus*—one that can instruct, position, and mechanize laboring bodies in the name of efficiency. Between 1913

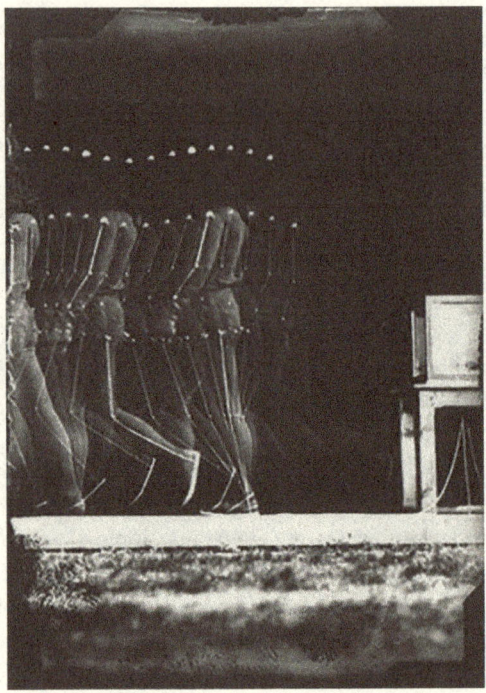

Figure 23 By painting white lines down the limbs of his subject before photographing them in motion, Marey presented a sort of prototype for today's motion-capture suits, which demarcate the joints and limbs using reflective markers. Notably, Marey's subjects were often soldiers. ("Man Walking," Etienne-Jules Marey, chronophotography, 1890–1891, Public Domain.)

and 1917, American industrial engineers Frank and Lillian Moller Gilbreth completed a series of motion studies for the express purpose of studying the minimum gesture of the manual laborer's body. The Gilbreths used a chronocyclegraph to record the gestures of brick layers and factory workers at the assembly line, who wore small lamps on their wrists and limbs that were then captured by the timelapse photographic technique. The resulting photodynamic streams of light were like maps of the way these workers' bodies moved through space as they went about their tasks. The Gilbreths argued that by reducing the number of unnecessary movements done by the workers, they could increase efficiency and productivity. As Elizabeth Stephens notes, the purpose was to identify and eliminate "industrial waste" in the form of movement. *Waste* in this context doesn't mean idleness or the squandering of resources that already exist, but rather a "kind of untapped margin of potential between current levels of productivity and the maximum amount of productivity they could engineer."[362]

Figure 24 depicts a worker engaged in the repetitive gestures that comprise her daily labor. The job she is doing is not entirely clear from the photograph, but what is apparent is that this is work she does mainly with her hands while sitting. Of this photograph, Rick Poynor notes "the combination of the spectral figure of the woman—her boots under the table are the most solid thing about her—and the grids behind her and covering the tabletop."[363] He observes that "the erasure of the phantom woman's identity within this hard-edged chamber of grids . . . looks like an unintentional warning of the dehumanizing pressure of the relentlessly monitored production line."[364] The Gilbreth motion studies indeed both scrutinized the mechanization of workers' bodies via the medium of photography and film and also used those tools to further standardize those bodies. In fact, the studies revealed that a bricklayer could double the bricks laid per hour, from 350 to 700, by stacking bricks on a trolley and not bending down every time. The Gilbreth studies transformed the gestures of working bodies into data optimized for maximum productivity, demonstrating the ways in which emergent twentieth-century recording technologies were used to measure, visualize, and indeed *produce* a new kind of body. The studies propose that the most reliable and productive type of working body is a machinic one,

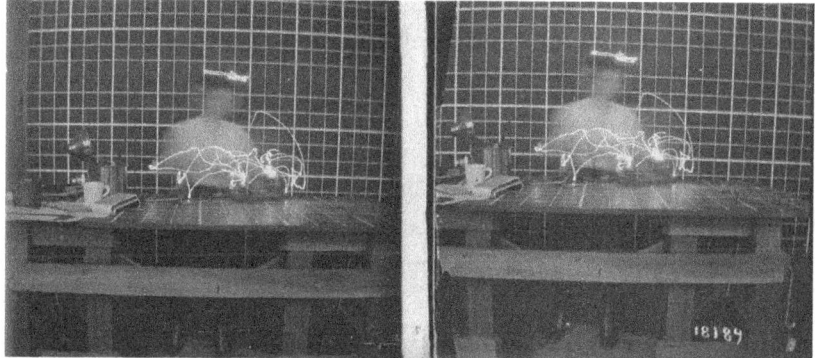

Figure 24 Seated at a gridded table, a woman performs a repetitive task (possibly soap-making) at work. She wears lights affixed to her wrists, so that the path of her movements can be captured by Frank Gilbreth's chronocyclegraph. (Motion efficiency study by Frank Gilbreth, c. 1914. Collection: National Museum of American History).

one that does not deviate from the expected routine—which is to say one that does not improvise.

I want to return briefly to Badiou's definition of dance I shared in Chapter 3. He writes that in dance there is "a mobility that is firmly fastened to itself, a mobility that is not inscribed within an external determination, but instead moves without detaching itself from its own center. This mobility is not imposed, it unfolds as if it were an expansion of its center."[365] This is another way of saying that dance (the "it" in Badiou's quote) can be productive of some sense of inner agency—a type of movement that seems to emanate from interiority and soul. This is reminiscent of Delsartean movement theory (discussed in the Introduction to this book), in which movements evocative of soul must originate in the trunk, or the center of the dancer's body. No, Gilbreth's workers are not dancers, but in the photographic studies of them we can see the choreography of labor in which gestures of efficiency with minimum effort are imposed on their bodies from *without*, via technologies of capture like the camera. In order to perform the gestures smoothly, the workers then integrate them as movements emanating from the "center" of their body. This integration of work movement into the body's center does not necessarily link the gestures to the will, agency, or soul of the worker; rather, it produces a soul for the worker in the Foucauldian sense. On the other hand, in the photodynamism of the Gilbreth images (Figure 24), and Marey's motion studies (see Figure 23), the laborer's body hard at work is replaced by the aesthetic beauty of the light trails left behind by their gestures through space. These images *erase* the working body, leaving only the pretty path of their productivity: their *anima*.

Esprit de Corps

The standardizing of human movement is also a method of synchronizing multiple bodies into the logic of the machine. Another Boston Dynamics video meant to illustrate the skill (and potential productivity) of the working machine, titled "Spot's on It," was released on YouTube in June 2021. The video features five of the same model—Spot, the "canine" robot—dancing together in perfectly timed formation.[366] They are lined up, one robot directly behind the other, so that from the camera's view it looks like a singular dancer. The performance begins, and each robot proceeds to peek out from the line, fanning out their long, supple necks, which can move fluidly thanks to smoothly articulated joints (see Figure 25). This makes the formation look Medusa-like, as if it is one dancing body with many snake-like limbs. Eventually, the robots step out of line and into group choreography, revealing their bodies as exact copies of one another. The Spots can dance in unison or in synchronized formation. In a blog post for Boston Dynamics, Calvin Hennick writes that their "motions are so smooth and harmonious,

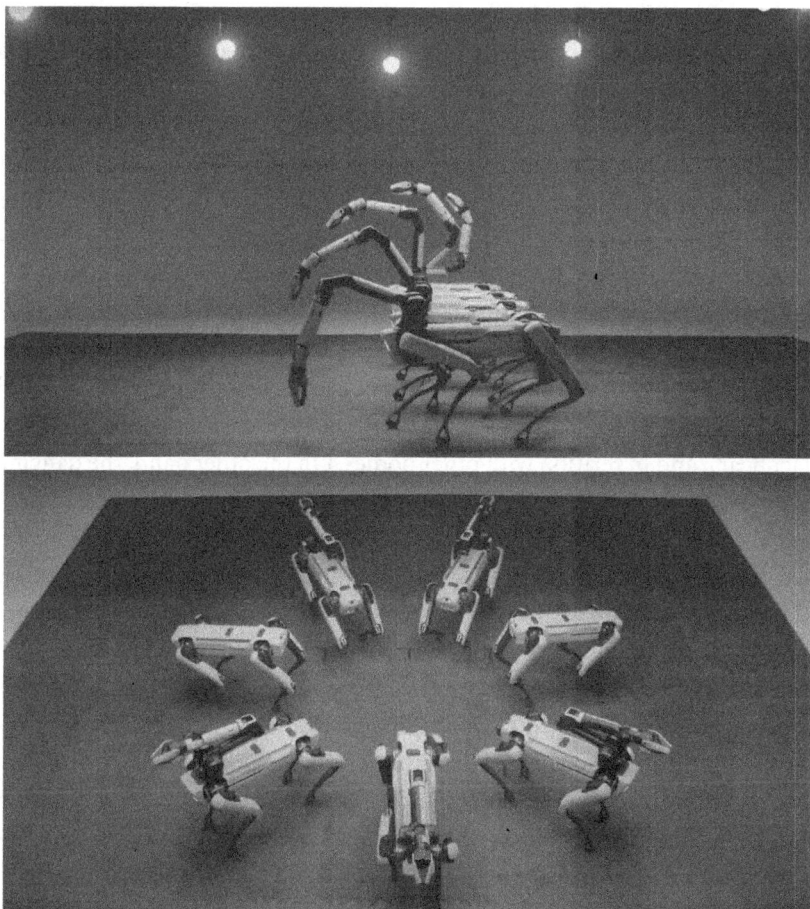

Figure 25 Five Boston Dynamics Spot models dance in formation, much like Busby Berkeley's dancers do in his 1930s musicals. (Stills from "Spot's on It," a performance video posted to YouTube. Boston Dynamics, June 29, 2021, https://www.youtube.com/watch?v = 7atZfX85nd4)

that you might think the robots are actually listening and responding to the music. But they're not; they're listening to their synchronized inner clocks. For all their sophisticated sensors, the robots don't even know that music is playing."[367] This is an example of what Nick Thurston, in his 2013 poetry collection *Of the Subcontract*, calls "Artificial Artificial Intelligence," where we imagine the AI entity to be self-operating and emulating the human, but really, there is a human controller or programmer who sets up the conditions for them to appear intelligent.[368]

The "Spot's on It" robots were choreographed by the same dancer mentioned earlier, Monica Thomas, who said it was difficult to think and move like Spot in the creation process.[369] As a human dancer attempting to embody Spot and create movement to suit the robot's body, Thomas illustrates a reciprocal move to the mimetic dances of Olympia, Kyoko, and Maria analyzed in Chapter 2; Thomas, the human choreographer, mirrors the nonhuman dancer, in a sense mechanizing her own human dance impulses, or revealing them as already somewhat machinic. Thomas's experience reveals the paradoxical nature of dance as both an innate liveness (or even humanness) used to animate and personalize the robot, and as a type of industrial programming that can feel awkward to an uninitiated organic body. On the one hand, the dancing robot evokes a body free in its physical and emotional expression, lost in the rhythm of the music (which it cannot in fact hear), and in relation with other bodies. On the other hand, the dancing robot reminds us of that which is aspirational but impossible for the human body: the impeccable, rigorous, repeatable, exactitude of the machine.

The video of the multiple dancing Spot models appears to be inspired by the dance numbers of 1930s film director Busby Berkeley, whose choreography was often shot from above to display his (human) dancers' bodies like gears in a wheel or ants in a snaking chain. *Footlight Parade* (1933) features a group dance comprised of young blond women who look nearly identical from the vantage point of the distant camera, and whose synchronized bodies fall into concentric circles and lines (see Figure 26). Seen in bird's-eye view, these dancers cease to appear as individuals and are instead absorbed into the machine of the dance formation as a synchronized mass.[370] Berkeley's choreographies rely on the ability of the dancers' bodies to create a dehumanized effect. The kind of "life" that emerges from these dances is not evocative of individual human soul, attached to inner feeling and expression; instead, Berkeley's choreographies exert a crowded, buzzing life, a posthuman kinetics on the surface of the assemblage. The individual bodies

Figure 26 Still from *Footlight Parade* (1933), directed by Lloyd Bacon and choreographed by Busby Berkeley. Dancers are shot from above in a kaleidoscopic formation, made possible by the buoyancy of the water (they are in a pool). (Screenshot from YouTube.)

matter less than the synchronization of parts into a whole spectacle of fluid motion. As Brynn Shiovitz writes, "Berkeley creates abstract images that often make viewers forget the human basis of his geometric designs."[371] And yet, Berkeley often pivots between displaying his dancers from a distance, as depersonalized cogs in a wheel, and using the cinematic close-up to focus the individual faces of the glamorous women that make up this posthuman assemblage. As the choreographies of both Berkeley and Boston Dynamics demonstrate, dance can be used in both directions—to ensoul and to mechanize.

In another of Berkeley's films, *Dames* (1934), the camera is nearly as choreographed as the dancers, swooping and dipping to move through corridors of women's bodies bent at right angles, drawing out their geometrical affordances. Berkeley's vision brings to mind Jean Baudrillard's "industrial simulacrum," in which the concept of "series" is key.[372] In a series,

Baudrillard writes, "the relation between [objects/bodies/commodities] is no longer that of an original to its counterfeit—neither analogy nor reflection—but equivalence, indifference . . . Only the obliteration of the original reference allows for the generalized law of equivalence, that is to say the *very possibility of production*."[373] Similarly, because the dancing robots' choreography or dance *anima* is made of data and can be repeated with standardized consistency, their ability to operate with error-free reliability is enhanced, which also implies that their bodies are interchangeable. Both "Spot's on It" and Berkeley's choreographies present images of cloned dancers whose superhuman ability for synchronization and sustained body control is complemented by the virtuosic contribution of the camera, which swoops and soars, capturing the dance in ways impossible for the human eye. In these dance spectacles, something uncanny emerges from the gap between synchronized movement and "the very possibility of production"— and that thing is *anima*. In both cases, the dancers are part of a series that is also a mass of bodies—or is it one body? One by one, the bodies enter a disciplined, militarized swarm that is undeniably alive.

The image of a line of bodies as a series of copies is also notable in the dancing formations of the Tiller Girls, first formed in Manchester, England, by John Tiller in 1889, whose choreographed dances mainly consisted of high kicks in marching unison. The Tiller Girls were a dance troupe that helped popularize the chorus line at the beginning of the twentieth century at the Folies Bergère and the London Palladium. Fixated on precise discipline, Tiller had his chorus dancers link arms in a long chain, so that they could move as one. Individuality was not encouraged among Tiller's dancers, and the girls selected were nearly identical in height and weight. As McCarren writes, "like factory workers, the Tiller Girls were appreciated as a unit, and their dancing as the expression not of an individual will but of a team."[374] Siegfried Kracauer described the Tiller Girls' choreographed dances as reflective of "the entire contemporary situation [of] the capitalist production process," where the girls themselves are symbolic both of workers and commodity objects.[375] "The hands in the factory," writes Kracauer, "correspond to the legs of the Tiller Girls," who are "no longer individual girls, but indissoluble girl clusters whose movements are demonstrations of mathematics," abstracting them into an anonymous "mass ornament" perfectly suited to capitalist systems of production and consumption.[376]

Many scholars have used Kracauer's writing on the Tiller Girls to analyze Berkeley's choreographies (see Giles, 2000; Ockman, 2003; Tystad, 2021; Walls,

2024)[377] but there is in fact no direct evidence to show that Berkeley was directly inspired by the Tiller Girls. Instead, it was his training in military drill, a fact that I explore in greater depth later in this chapter, that led Kracauer to choreograph a "tight geometry" of bodies in space. In addition, Kracauer was fascinated by the emergent technology of film and the new ability to choreograph the camera. As Shiovitz writes, Kracauer saw that it as "the camera's duty to organize these ... bodies into patterns and formations that gave off a sense of order and productivity."[378] This visual phenomenon, which offered both comforting stability and ornate decadence, a shift from the destitute individual to the communal group whose strength is in moving together, was particularly desirable at a time of uncertain poverty in America, following the Great Depression. Add to this the fact that Kracauer's dancers, like Tiller's, reflect the Taylorist assembly line: a new, mechanized technology of commodity production. This shift, from individuality to anonymity, reflects the driving depersonalized force of modernity, but also describes an advanced capitalist sensibility in which dance belongs to no one body, but to the machinic assembleage itself.

I am calling this singular, engineerable force resulted from the extrapolation of *anima* produced by multiple bodies *esprit de corps*,[379] a French military phrase which means the "common spirit" of or "loyalty and devotion" to a group.[380] Who owns the means of production of such *esprit de corps*, especially given that the *esprit* in this case is necessarily produced by not one but many *corps*? And how does such ownership shift over history? In the case of Berkeley, the credit for the lively assemblage of choreography is always given to the director/choreographer himself, not to the laboring dancers whose bodies provide the movement. The ownership of Boston Dynamics' digital robot choreographies expands further away from an individual human to a corporate body. They are not attributed to any one "genius" creator (nor to the choreographer Thomas, whose name is scrubbed from the promotional materials); rather, their dancing is owned by the robotics design company—a military–industrial figurehead. However, both Berkeley's modernist choreographies and the corporate spectacle of the late capitalist dancing robots treat the dehumanization of the dancers as necessary to achieve the spectacle—a dehumanization that also facilitates the trading of dance as resource, not by the workers of said dance, but by the choreographer (Berkeley) or the engineering firm (Boston Dynamics). In this way, dancers, soldiers, and factory workers have much in common—and their *anima* is drawn together through the choreographing apparatus of the camera and is unownable by the bodies that produced it.

Throughout this chapter, I have been circling around the camera as both an observer of dance and as an active agent in the choreography of the laboring body, as both a tool of capture and, in many cases, a performer itself. Spot, for example, becomes a reconnaissance camera on the battlefield or in a Bronx neighborhood, seeking out moving bodies and capturing human life to monitor and control it. But Spot can also dance *for* the camera (and does, in its various YouTube music videos). Similarly, the bodies (and their *anima*) of workers at the turn of the century were organized, regulated, standardized—which is to say choreographed—by the cameras of the Gilbreths (and to a certain extent, Muybridge and Marey) in order to optimize them as machinic instruments of work. It seems important to note that Marey's original photographs were taken with an instrument he referred to as his "gun." Whereas Muybridge's equipment in 1870 was "heavy and unsuitably clumsy to capture the rapid movements of birds and insects," Marey attempted to avoid this pitfall by designing a "device that was about the size of a hunting rifle, portable, and free to aim from any angle."[381] As described by Pasi Valiaho, "the photographic lens was located in the barrel, while the bottom end of the barrel housed a magazine containing a cylindrical glass plate alongside two disks with shutters. Pulling the trigger made a clocked mechanism of the three disks move inside the magazine and record pictures sequentially."[382] Marey's gun-camera is doubly evocative (as weapon and photographic lens) of Gilles Deleuze's and Felix Guattari's "apparatus of capture," a device that stills, abstracts, and homogenizes the activity of living beings to "profit from their productivity."[383]

The camera, with its proclivity for the impartial, might be the "ideal" spectator of dance for someone like Badiou, who, reflecting on poet Stéphane Mallarmé's writing, asserts with shocking confidence, "just as the dancer—who is an emblem—is never someone, so the spectator of dance must be rigorously impersonal. The spectator of dance cannot in any way be the singularity of the one who's watching."[384] The ideal spectator of dance, Badiou explains, has what Mallarmé calls "an impersonal or fulgurant absolute gaze . . . one that commands the essential nakedness of the dancers," with "nakedness" implying impersonality or non-singularity.[385] Mallarmé would certainly be thinking about live dance here, and Badiou makes no explicit mention of mediated dance or dance on film, but it strikes me that this "fulgurant gaze" is epitomized by the camera. *Fulguration*, which originates from the Latin word for *lightning*, means flash-like or glancing, much like the camera's shutter (and a firing gun) as it suddenly closes on the image/

body. A "fulgurant gaze," according to Badiou, is that which attempts to grasp a "vanishing gesture" to "keep it pure, outside of any empirical memory."[386] Badiou writes that the fulgurant gaze of the dance spectator should not be one that projects personal desires onto the bodies of the dancers, but rather a gaze that "belongs to no one."[387]

Elsewhere, I have written about the National Film Board's dance film *ORA*, directed by Philippe Baylaucq, which was shot in complete darkness with thermographic cameras borrowed from military giant Lockheed Martin. The film holds tight to the concept of aura as linked to soul through the emanating light of the dancers' body heat as proof of inner vitality, and it employs the fulgurant gaze by capturing the dance in 3D through two synchronized infrared cameras, placed side by side, like eyes.[388] Likewise, Spot can be equipped with multiple sensors, including thermal sensors that help it navigate terrain and collect data from its surroundings. These sensors might already be qualified as cameras of a sort, and furthermore, as noted on the Boston Dynamics website, "Spot's perception system consists of five stereo pairs of depth cameras: two at the front, one at the rear, and one on each side of Spot."[389]

There is a shift between mid-century optical surveillance (exemplified by Taylor's and Ford's work science cameras) and the thermographic military camera, which finds warm bodies even under cover of darkness, not to mention the digital surveillance emerging under advanced capitalism embodied by the Boston Dynamics robots.[390] The difference between the two is partly informed by the interaction between surveillance device and the content captured. Electromechanical media such as the cameras used by Muybridge, Marey, and the Gilbreths chop up flow, piece fragments back into sequences, and analyze them to assign value (or standardize workers' bodies, etc.). Digital media, on the other hand, as Lev Manovich suggests, make this process algorithmic and mathematical, threatening a more invisible (and insidious) kind of control.

Yet perhaps there is something in the nature of dance that resists the surreptitious invasion of apparatuses of capture on the body, and which protests the Taylorist desire for choreographed militancy. This paradox is difficult to put into words, and perhaps this is why those who know little about dance are most confident to try. In his self-assured yet puzzling essay "Dance as a Metaphor for Thought," Alain Badiou approaches an analysis of dance and philosophy through Nietzsche. He writes that for Nietzsche, the "opposite of dance ... is the German, the bad German, whom he defines as follows: obedience and long legs."[391] He continues:

The essence of this bad Germany is the military parade, the aligned and hammering body, the servile and sonorous body. The body of beaten cadence. Dance instead is the aerial and broken body, the vertical body. Not at all the hammering body, but the body "on points," the body that pricks the floor just as one would puncture a cloud. Above all, it is the silent body, set against the body that prescribes the thunder of its own heavy strike, the body of the military parade.[392]

Never mind that to think dance as a "metaphor for thought" is in fact to exclude "the [very] thinking and doing that belongs to the art form itself,"[393] Badiou sets up a confusing opposition in his aesthetic description of dance: following Nietzsche, he contrasts dance with the "military parade," yet his description of dance as "aerial," "broken," "vertical," and "silent" quite aptly describes the bodies of Berkeley's dancers in formation—choreographed dances which certainly evoke the military parade. What is it about military repetition that both threatens and constitutes dance? Watching videos of Spot traverse forests, battlefields, and, recently, Chernobyl, I am struck by the clicking, prancing motion of its four-pointed legs (almost like a ballerina's feet *en pointe*) that move with eery precision and delicacy. Spot's is a body that "pricks the floor just as one that would puncture a cloud"; it is also an "aligned and hammering body."[394] Spot is both weapon and dancer. Spot (let alone Berkeley's dancers or the Tiller Girls) collapses Badiou's distinction between the military parade and the dance, a collapse that has also been made by soldiers who have trained in extensive "close-order military drill," characterized as a kind of exhilarating dance or exercise in "muscular bonding."[395]

It turns out dance and military rituals are not so far apart. Harald Kleinschmidt analyzes the parallel changes in body movement happening in both European military drill and dance practices between the fifteenth and eighteenth centuries. Drill manuals from the 1700s instruct soldiers to keep an upright stance, to "stand stiffly on their feet," and "to march with their knees stretched out straight."[396] Whereas the sixteenth-century military prioritized "stable equilibrium" of the body, the armies of the seventeenth and eighteenth centuries were taught technique for the purpose of "keeping the soldiers' bodies tight and upright and of constraining their movements" to make "them enact all commanded movements promptly and swiftly."[397] The main aim of such technique was not the honing of the individual soldier's body as a resilient instrument of battle, but the "meticulous enactment of given orders" by all soldiers, as parts of a whole.[398] Furthermore, French general and military writer Jacques Antoine Hippolyte de Guibert (1743–1790) shifted the emphasis from the traditional static standing position of soldiers "at attention" to a "natural" flow of interconnected positions that prioritized "moveability" as the primary goal of military technique, thus transforming the soldier from a "'lifeless machine' into a dynamic instrument of warfare."[399] Jean-Georges Noverre, Swiss choreographer and ballet master, developed an image of the dancer as machine similar to Guibert's image of soldier as machine; for Noverre, who played a significant role in developing body technique for classical ballet in the nineteenth century, the dancer was a machine insofar as they were an "instrument for the facilitation of quick and intense movements, such as jumps or lifts of other dancers."[400] These are similarities and overlaps in the thinking around military and dance technique that persist today.

I now wish to tie the worker's body, engineered for unfeeling productivity and choreographed to be posthuman in its efficiency, to the dancing machine *as* weapon. The motion studies of Marey and Gilbreth introduce us to the quantifiable, instrumentalized body and prepare us for the weaponized body, both of which are connected through a choreographic sensibility. Indeed, recall that Marey's work portrays a dehumanized set of lines depicting the motion of a walking soldier, an already-dehumanized figure (Figure 23). I want to extend this notion to today's design of military technology and the function of dance in the marketing of a fantasy narrative about that technology. As James Vincent notes, Boston Dynamics and other robotics firms have a "long history of developing robots for the US army."[401] The French army starting testing Spot in military exercises, with "the intention of assessing the usefulness of robots on future battlefields," in 2021.[402] Pictures released on Twitter by France's foremost military school, the École Spéciale Militaire de Saint-Cyr, confirmed this, and French newspaper *Ouest-France* suggested at the time that Spot was mainly being tested for use in reconnaissance missions, a process which requires the robot to be equipped with cameras and remote controlled, making it a useful contributor to both commercial markets and simulated battlefields (Figure 27).

At the time of writing this book, robot dogs are already reporting for active duty with the military. *Forbes* recently reported a similar but less expensive quadruped model to Spot made by Ghost Robotics, which has a machine gun mounted to its head, is able to control its own speed of movement, and gets back on its feet when tipped over, offering soldiers a "reliable

Figure 27 The British military has also been testing robot dogs for deployment in the battlefield, as seen in this still from a YouTube video depicting a Ghost Robotics quadruped robot, similar to Boston Dynamics' "Spot" model. (Still from YouTube: "British Army Tests Ghost Robotics Dog-Like Quadruped Robots." Off Track Places, Military Aircraft Channel, August 22, 2022, YouTube, https://www.youtube.com/watch?v=VfLvCIkKJUE.)

means to fire a weapon from a distance" without compromising their own bodily safety.[403] A 2023 article from *the Middle East Monitor* confirms that Israel's army (the Israel Defense Forces or IDF) purchased "three Vision 60 robot dogs" from American company Ghost Robotics to "assist combat soldiers" in their horrific ongoing genocidal occupation of Gaza, a development that further dehumanizes Palestinians by the use of dehumanized military force.[404] As Ryan S. writes for the Kansas City Defender, "the normalization of such machines on the battlefield," in particular in Gaza, which is home to a high concentration of children, "raises profound ethical and strategic concerns, signaling a move towards more depersonalized forms of violence."[405] Skybetter has additionally tracked the various uses of Spot in policing scenarios in the US, including for the NYPD, and has found that it was deployed with much greater frequency in historically Black neighborhoods like Cypress Hill in Brooklyn and Wakefield in the Bronx.[406] This fact demonstrates, as Skybetter puts it, the "irresolution of Boston Dynamics' robots being representationally enveloped in Blackness all while being martially deployed against Black communities."[407] Spot's perceived animal quality (he is a "dog," after all, not a humanoid robot) neutralizes his potential violence—dogs are both friends to humans and reinforcers of human violence—while also furthering him from human bodies and concerns, a trajectory supported by the ensouling power of dance.

In Chapter 2, I focused on Lang's Maria and Garland's Kyoko, both of whom are dancers with weaponized bodies. When Maria dances for the audience of leering men, she seduces them with her angular gyrations, but she also sets up a conduit of dance power between her body and their gaze that harbors a violent energy capable of destruction. In this chapter, I show how the Boston Dynamics' robots, likewise *enlivened* through dance and through their articulation to soul music, are also used to *extinguish* life. They are, in effect, killing machines positioned between life (where dance connotes liveliness as well as an unending Freudian death drive) and death (in their potential violence and deadened—or nonexistent—morals). The dancing of the Boston Dynamics robots makes them just alive enough to perform as weaponized servants for the military, but not so alive that there would be qualms about harming them in warfare, as predicted by the many viral videos of people kicking earlier models of the Spot robot aggressively.[408] In light of this information about the robots' weaponization, which Boston Dynamics does not tend to publicize, the robots' dance routines start to look a little different. Here we see that dance is, again, not the opposite of the weaponized, synchronized body (the "military parade" as Nietzsche and Badiou suggest), but that dance can also act as a technology for training bodies to follow orders and automatize rhythmic gesture (e.g., Ford's implementation of Contra dance as a required "leisure" activity in his many factories). The dancing machine, the working body, and the military apparatus can therefore be connected through a special kind of dance *anima*: *esprit de corps*.

Selling Soul

This chapter covers quite a bit of ground, moving from racialized dancing robots through the motion studies of the late nineteenth century, to their impact on work science and Taylorism, to the entwined history of choreography and instruments/formations of war; from the resistant materiality of the body—the way Chaplin and Ball use their bodies as obstacles to capitalist production on the assembly line, for example—to the rigorous and repetitive choreographing of the body via the apparatus of capture that is the camera. The military–industrial complex seeks to engineer dance *anima*, often across many bodies as *esprit de corps*, for profit and power. Both military drill and the assembly line seek to reduce the laboring body to a series of gestures that are not only minimal, but also abstract, even disembodied. And yet, to return us to where we began, racialized movement appears again and again as the ghost in the machine of abstraction.

As mentioned earlier in this chapter, Jessica Rajko describes this tendency as "race as additive," a term she borrows from Alison Reed and Amanda Philips, who suggest that "performance practices, particularly in [a] digital context, participate in post-racial ideologies of a world in which the goals of the civil rights movement have supposedly been realized by reducing race to a matter of style."[409] Rajko explains the "additive race" process as such:

> The deracination of Black aesthetics tends to reduce Blackness to that which can be aesthetically labelled as hip or cool. Once deracinated, Black aesthetics are then integrated into digital design as general aesthetic features, mostly as a means to cash in on their broad popularity. Such practices disregard the fact that Black aesthetics derive from and celebrate Black communities' embodied experiences rooted in what it means to be Black. The general indifference to the fact that Black aesthetics derive from embodied experience '[...] indicates [as Reed and Philips argue,] a dominant cultural assumption of a racially normative, transparently white, core subject.'[410]

The Boston Dynamics robots seem to operate in a world where race and gender do not exist, yet power (or cultural capital) is still tied to the "neutral" dancing robot body by way of residual signifiers of Blackness, not as "epidermal schema"[411] but as *anima* extracted to humanize the machine. The presumed correlation between authenticity and Black culture is one that has been analyzed by dance scholar Brenda Dixon Gottschild and critiqued by Afrofuturists like Kodwo Eshun and Alexander Weheliye, who argue that "black subjectivity appears as the antithesis to the Enlightenment subject"— that disembodied mind—"by virtue of not only having a body but by *being* the body" [emphasis mine].[412] "Within Enlightenment discourses," Weheliye writes, "blackness is the body and nothing else."[413] As Susan Manning notes, there is a common white appropriation of the African American experience (or in the case of the Boston Dynamics' dancing robots: gesture, culture, and song) to represent a "universal metaphor" for human struggle, and the metaphor in this case works to humanize the robots.[414] This is particularly fraught, given that soul music and Black vernacular dance have long represented a mode of resistance to the strictures of slavery, indentured labor, and other oppressive white supremacist structures in North America. Troublingly, "Black sacred and later secular music [take] on two simultaneous functions: proving black peoples' soul and standing in for the soul of all U.S. culture."[415] The singing voices of the Contours are recontextualized in the YouTube video, implicating the "soul," and by extension "humanity" of Black subjects in not only white mainstream culture, but also the realm of commodified, mechanized labor.

The Boston Dynamics robots are, indeed, for sale and ready to work—a fact that should glaringly evoke the legacy of slavery. These robots demonstrate the insidious ways in which, as Saidiya Hartman writes, "black lives are still [. . .] devalued by a racial calculus and a political arithmetic that were entrenched centuries ago."[416] A study of dance *anima* reveals how power is articulated at the intersection of two realms: emergent media and the category of the human. The shiny white cybernetic Boston Dynamics robots may suggest the post- or superhuman subject, but they are not post-race. They are enlivened or ensouled through their choreographed movements and through the voices of Black singers that, in a weird additional kind of erasure, they cannot hear. It is deeply problematic that Black culture is "mined" for soul and authenticity, when Black people are in fact still (as Christina Sharpe argues) in the "wake" of slavery—a dehumanizing history which of course entails the repeated justification of self, soul, and humanness. The futuristic bodies of the Boston Dynamics robots are particularly in need of ensouling, given their terrifying presence on the battlefield. They therefore also reveal another paradox at dance's core. First is the idea that dance can ensoul things, humanizing them and making them seem worthy of life and capable of joy. Second is the fact that dance (or choreography: the repetition of synchronized, minimal gesture) is also linked to the mechanization of humans to serve capitalist and military interests, and the optimization of machines in the service of killing. The choreographed body can go both ways: towards life and death.

Conclusion

The Dance Between Life and Death

In the summer of 1518, a "dancing plague" spread through the streets of Strasbourg. It started with a lone woman, hopping and swaying on the dirt road. The townspeople watched from their windows as she began to move "uncontrollably" and without stopping.[417] Soon, other dancers, most of them women, were compelled to join her by some external force or trance-like state, medical or divine. This strange scene, in which the dancers seemed to attain "extraordinary levels of endurance," enabling them to move for hours, might seem unlikely to us today; but in the post-medieval context, John Waller notes, "compulsive dancing joined that litany of natural and human disasters to be explained in terms of celestial or supernatural forces."[418] The phenomenon of a dance without end is also, significantly, the topic of the Hans Christian Anderson fairy tale, "The Red Shoes" (1845), a story about a dancer whose enchanted red shoes compel her to dance constantly.[419] In Anderson's tale, the suffering dancer asks an executioner to chop off her feet, but the shoes continue to dance with her amputated feet inside them. Detached from the human dancer, the shoes dance on their own, driven by an uncanny *anima*. Anderson's fairy tale was adapted in a 1948 film of the same name,[420] and, in a full circle moment for this book that brings us back to the research creation dance project of my Preface, "The Red Shoes" is also the title of Kate Bush's seventh studio album.[421] That Bush should haunt this conclusion with a pair of unstoppable red dancing shoes, which themselves are a nonhuman dancing entity and a viral echo across multiple bodies, is apropos to a theory of dance *anima* in which gesture travels by contagion.

The Strasbourg dancing plague mentioned above is just one of many similar epidemics that took place across Germany, Holland, Italy, and France between 1300 and the mid-1600s.[422] Researchers note that there are links also between the dancing plague and various similar conditions including "Tarantism in Italy, Tigretier in Abyssinia, and Imanenjana in Madagascar . . . " as well as the "Leaping Ague in Scotland," many of which have also been classified as "St. Vitus's disease."[423] Those who have written

Dance Anima. Hilary Bergen, Oxford University Press. © Oxford University Press 2026.
DOI: 10.1093/9780197786673.003.0006

about these dancing plagues are often quite singularly focused on their cause, postulating epilepsy or demonic possession among various catalysts. One theory is that the dancers had ingested contaminated flour harvested from moldy stalks of rye, also called ergot, which infected their brains, causing them to move erratically.[424] Another belief was that the dancing plague may have been caused by the bite of a tarantula. The heat of summer was thought to activate the venom coursing through the victim's body, causing convulsion and spasms that looked like dance. Rather than speculate about its origins, however, I find it more interesting to consider the symptoms of the dancing plague as phenomena that speak to the already uncertain relationship between dance and embodied agency. Here, ergot and tarantula venom (or *rumors* about them) act as agents in the production of dance *anima*, thereby decentering agency from the human dancing subject.

Since the 1518 dancing plague, there have been other instances of epidemics that manifest in infectious body gesture. A 2012 *New York Times* article, "The Mystery of 18 Twitching Teenagers in Le Roy," details a comparable phenomenon where a group of high school cheerleaders in small-town New York contracted contagious body spasms and were diagnosed as suffering from "mass psychogenic illness," or "mass hysteria" (Dominus). American director Anna Rose Holmer's 2015 debut feature film *The Fits* fictionalizes a similar tale. The film features an all-girl drill dance team who are struck by an inexplicable outbreak of seizure-like attacks that spread from dancer to dancer. These "fits," which erupt in the bodies of the girls as their friends look on, often capturing the spectacle on their camera phones, have a performative, kinetic quality. And Jonathan Glazer's dance film *Strasbourg 1518*, which takes inspiration from the dancing plague, was filmed during the COVID-19 lockdown and released in September 2020. These historical precedents and their fictional counterparts reveal that dance *anima* can arrive involuntarily; it can be an infection, an invasion, a torture.

I wrote this book through two huge shifts in my life (one personal and one planetary): becoming a mother and the global pandemic. I gave birth to my first daughter in December 2019, just three months before COVID-19. In combination with new motherhood, the lockdowns—and in particular the Quebec laws that regulated the population with an enforced 8:00 p.m. curfew for non-essential workers—drove me to become, perhaps as a coping mechanism, more and more deeply cocooned in the repeated gestures and tasks I performed daily: swaddling my baby daughter, Ingrid, changing her diaper, and bathing her carefully in the kitchen sink. These mundane chores, or chains of operations that are part of the technique of infant care, became a choreography for the new life in which I found myself. Like Foucault's description of the orders given during a seventeenth-century plague—"First, a strict spatial partitioning: the closing of the town and its outlying districts"— my world closed in around me like a small box in which I had to merely repeat my comforting, choreographed patterns (patterns which, in turn, produced me).[425]

Perhaps because I am a dancer, I tend to see dance everywhere. This seemed to intensify when suddenly, in those early months of the pandemic, bodies were organized spatially both by a common sense of morality and duty (giving passersby a wide berth on the street, for instance) or by a set of institutionalized structures (e.g., the markings on the ground in the grocery store, indicating where to stand for proper social distancing). I saw dance in the growing and ritualized space between bodies; in the lone runner who, curfew briefly forgotten, was sprinting to make it home; in the overflowing hospitals; in the grid formation of my students' videos on Zoom; in the chaotic order of the protests—and yet I missed dancing so very much. I ached to brush up against the bodies of strangers and to move with abandon at a loud nightclub.[426]

I acknowledge my privilege here, in being able to write about the pandemic in this way, safe (although cooped up) in my house while many did not have the luxury of protecting themselves against sickness and death by simply staying home, but were in fact forced to move toward danger. I understand these dynamics as related to choreography; under the lens of dance, Andre Lepecki writes, "geo-political and bio-political questions become essentially choreographic ones [about] *who* is able or allowed to move—and under what circumstances, and on what grounds; to decide *where* one is allowed to move to."[427] These choreographic questions demonstrate something important beyond the slippery relationship that dance *anima* (in all its contagious virality) has with ownership. The question of "who moves" is also the investigation of power—of various assemblages that articulate the dancing body to media, screens, and visibility, as well as to processes of erasure or dispossession.

This book has been about the way machines or nonhuman entities are humanized—given soul—through dance, but this conclusion is intended to show the inverse of the dancing machine: the mechanization of the *human* through technique. What I want to address here is something a bit different than the use of Fordist techniques of productivity and the choreography of labor I wrote about in Chapter 4. This conclusion is not about standardized movements of the assembly line or the feeling of being imprisoned within a militant choreography of bodies. Most dancers know the sensation of losing themselves to the process of mundane repetition in rehearsing a piece of choreography or in technique class, practicing as a group. That repetition often gives way to a feeling of release and unexpected joy that arises from the experience (the *esprit de corps*) of moving together with others and, sometimes also, from the feeling of moving one's body with the confidence and exactitude *of a machine.*

Once, as a student in my four-year dance degree program, I was performing a contemporary group choreography on stage in our end-of-year show. Caught up in the swell of the music and the unison choreography I had practiced for months until it was second nature, aware of the immense energy the group was producing and offering the audience, who gazed back at us from the darkened theater, I suddenly felt an elation—a sudden ecstatic rapture that lasted only a few seconds and which promptly caused my entire mind to go blank and my body to briefly stop moving. This feeling, which I am sure dancers will recognize, is similar to the "oceanic feeling" of oneness with others described by Sigmund Freud (which Tavia Nyong'o links to the experience of the dancefloor at a club in his essay, "Disco and its Discontents") or the exultation described by soldiers performing close-order military drill in Chapter 4. Forgetting the choreography in this moment, I scrambled on stage to catch up with and mirror the other dancers, suddenly and humiliatingly lost at sea. After the show, my friends and family insisted they never noticed me stumble, and it is true that I quickly found my way back into the river of unison movement, but the experience (and all others like it) has stayed with me. I think of that feeling as a formative contact with the power of dance to enter your body, possess you, and make you think you are at the helm of it all, only to make you realize that you never were in control at all.

I see the experience as a kind of *glitch*. Following Legacy Russell, it soothes me to reframe this past experience as an instance of "failure as a generative force": one that both caused me to fall into a state of blankness, and then, just as quickly to trust my body (in all its technical ability) to pull myself out of that blankness and back into movement. To pull through the thread I began in my Preface, which described the glitchy dance Hatsune Miku did when I asked her to dance like Kate Bush, I am suggesting that the glitch—as both an interrupter and a producer of dance *anima*—is a powerful thing. Russell writes that "errors, ever unpredictable, surface the unnamable, point toward a wild unknown," so that "to become an error," or a glitch, "is to surrender to becoming unknown, unrecognizable, unnamed."[428] Russell writes of the glitch as a kind of "nonperformance" or refusal to perform, but conversely, I see glitch as a certain kind of dance, maybe akin to improvisation. Both glitch and improvisation require a grounding of technique or technology that has taught the body/object/process to move or behave in a certain way, and in both cases, there is a rebellion against that script that actively uses the script against itself. It is not that the glitch presents possibilities that are limitless, but rather, like the improvising body, the glitching body has technical limits that govern how it resists or acts out. The glitch can feel like freedom—or a release—but it is actually a reminder: of the mechanization of the dancing body.

I offer, as an example, the final, stunning, dance scene of Claire Denis's 1999 avant-garde military film, *Beau Travail*. At the end of this minimalist, poetic film, foreign legion officer Galoup (played by Denis Lavant), who has been commandeering troops in the East African Gulf of Djibouti, makes his bed fastidiously and lies down in it. We see his bicep jump rhythmically in close-up as he handles his revolver and maybe—possibly—considers using it on himself. This contemplation of death—without any outcome revealed—acts as a segue into the final, thrilling scene.

The camera cuts to an empty dance floor with mirrored walls. Galoup is there alone, dressed in black trousers and shirt, and shiny shoes. He smokes a cigarette. He walks slowly along the wall, caressing his own reflection and feeling the song (Corona's "The Rhythm of the Night") fill him up. He approaches the center of the dance floor, pausing as if to think of how to begin, and then does a spin and takes a drag of his cigarette, in tandem. His gaze extends out of shot, presumably to land on his reflection in another mirror, and he smiles as he smokes and rocks on his heels, continuing his attempt to enter the dance. After a few false starts (he kneels, feels himself pulled toward the beat, stops himself, leans back into the music as if onto a pillow), Galoup is sucked into another spin, this one punctuated with a bouncing step, and is finally at the mercy of the dance (Figure 28). It pushes and pulls him, his knees and elbows leading the movement like a marionette whose hands and feet trail behind. He gets caught in the tornado of his own body and is unable to escape. After a brief cut to credits (the film feels over but isn't), the scene reopens, with Galoup in a frenzied fit of jumps and thrashing limbs. The power of the movement pulls him down to the floor and then, in a

Figure 28 Denis Lavant dances in the mirrored discotheque in *Beau Travail's* famous final scene. Once again, the grid is present in the pattern of the mirror (echoing the grid of MMD from my preface), but Lavant's relationship to control is somewhat more chaotic. His body, doubled in the reflection, leans back into a swirl of his own dance *anima*. (Screenshot by the author.)

log-roll that befits an army man, he moves across the dance floor and out the door. I have watched the scene maybe one hundred times and I never tire of it. Apparently, the director's only instruction to Denis Lavant was to perform "the dance between life and death." Galoup did not practice in advance and accomplished the scene in two takes.

The scene does not offer a sense of release so much as the image of a tightly wound machine gone off the rails. The dance (like a machine) seems to take him, use him, and spit him out. One can imagine the way Galoup's body has been optimized for such kinetic movement, as the film foreshadows when Galoup puts his soldiers, their taut bodies gleaming in the East African sun, through drills in which they jump and duck, dive and climb walls. Galoup, who has lived by the mechanical choreography of war and masculinity, diverts the energy—the *anima*—of that habitus to a different use. Olivia Wood's poem, "After Beau Travail," which acts as an epilogue to this book, evokes the emotional resonance—the ecstatic "not death"—of the film's final dance scene. Galoup's dance, for Wood, is not only joyful; words like "bash" and "shudder" bring violence and discomfort. Dance moves Galoup's body almost without his consent, but certainly because of the repeated gestures of his military practice. Galoup (the "master-servant") is both choreographer and dancer as he "meters his ecstasy," navigating between life and death, or rather using dance to ascertain a "not-death."[429]

The violent joy I see in Lavant's dance is also at play in the rubber hose animation style of Koko the Clown, rotoscoped from Cab Calloway, as described in Chapter 3—his body stretching into ropes and chains which then come apart and fall to pieces. It is present, too, in the pirouetting military robots of Chapter 4, robots that can jump almost weightlessly despite their massive, dense bodies, and who, in other videos, scuttle bug-like across the forest floor with machine guns affixed to their backs. Dancing machines are indefatigable. They cannot die. They might dance for days without pain or exhaustion. Frozen in time, yet capable of perpetual motion, hologram pop star-dancer Hatsune Miku will always be sixteen and Instagram influencer Lil Miquela is forever nineteen. Humans, however, are not machines. Humans are mortal. Humans die. The human fear of mortality explains in part the use of technologies of capture and storage to stave off death, preserve youth, and freeze time—or even to preserve dance *anima* for future incarnations of the dance (as explored in this book). Yet, the *experience of dance* also wards off death by putting humans in touch with something that seems to go on forever: that "oceanic feeling" described by Freud as an "inclusive—indeed, an all embracing—feeling" in which the ego feels bonded intimately to the world around it.[430] Tavia Nyong'o defines the oceanic as "the vestige within the adult psyche of the unbounded plenitude we have all experienced as infants, a state in which polymorphous sensuality, unspoiled by the sense of a division between self and other that we later accrue."[431] In dancing, in repetition, in moving to the music, we often feel more expansive than our bodies' limits; we feel connected to each other, but also to our own past, present, and future— even to our eventual death.

Why does dance so often appear as a threshold between life and death?[432] The final scene of Charlotte Wells' 2022 film *Aftersun* takes place on the dance floor of a nightclub, lights strobing, electronic dance music pounding; the scene is a metaphor for the impending death by suicide of its protagonist Callum—a young, depressed father who turns to dance as an escape. In the final poignant shots of the film, Callum (played by Paul Mescal) is caught rhythmically in his wild dance by the flashing light and the gaze of his daughter, who is realizing she is seeing him for the last time. Similar to Lavant's dance in *Beau Travail*, there is a tension between abandon and mechanization in Mescal's movements, as if the dance, again, is tugging him along and through to the other side.

I do not mean to fetishize dance as a portal to unfettered freedom, or to equate freedom with death, but to show how the feeling of freedom while dancing is actually deeply interwoven with the (assumedly "unfree") practice of repetition and technique. In her work on dance improvisation, Danielle Goldman writes that many discussions of improv erroneously focus "on spontaneity and intuition," implying the dancer's "lack of preparation, [and] thereby eliding the historical knowledge" and "enormous skill that the most eloquent improvisers are able to mobilize."[433] Improvisation "does not reflect or exemplify the understanding of freedom as a desired endpoint, void of constraint. On the contrary, it actively resists it."[434] A dancer improvising is not dissimilar to a writer being struck by inspiration and putting pen to paper. What feels like spontaneous freedom is actually an uncovering, a "revelation," as Jacques Derrida puts it, of what is already there.[435] When writers write, Derrida argues, they are not engaging in creation from nothing: "if writing is inaugural it is not so because it creates, but because of a certain absolute freedom [...] to bring forth the already-there as a sign of the freedom to augur. A freedom of response which acknowledges as its only horizon the world as history and the speech which can only say: Being has always already begun."[436] Similarly, when dancers create, meaning when they dance, they are revealing that which is "already-there," in their bodies and minds, even if it is not wholly accessible to them. As Galoup prepares to be brave and enter the dance in *Beau Travail*, he is filled with the "already-there," emboldened to express himself with a sense of freedom.

I think *relation*, rather than freedom, is the primary desire that dance can articulate and make known. The desire to relate turns us not only outward (to the many "bodies" that interact with us daily), but also inward, toward an intimacy with our own acquired techniques that might foster a trust in our own bodies that also readies us for their inevitable glitches. The stakes of a theory of dance *anima* are multi-scalar and can be thought in terms of larger assemblages that unmoor the sovereign body (of the dancer or the watcher), and in terms of the minutiae of everyday life—where minor engagements across social, technological, affective, commodified, and screenic realms reveal that we are never completely in control. Dance, as a model of these ideas as well as their product, is the excess that spills over the body already not in command.

Damiano Fina writes that "the unpredictable par excellence is death" and that "in the depths of thought about death lies the extreme threat brought to light by Greek philosophical thought: the oscillation of things between being and nothingness."[437] If we understand death as a "return to the nothingness from which one came," dance too—or more specifically, dance *anima*—is a specimen for this oscillation. As I have argued, dance is vital gesture: it gives things soul, it breathes life into bodies, and it cannot be owned or fully controlled. If dance *anima* propels a sense of human soul in a body, what is that soul made up of? Desire? Ardor? Dancing is not so much human as superhuman—not so much realistic as aspirational. We dance as we wish to be seen. When we dance, as Thomas DeFrantz says, we "put action to impulse; we do," and in so doing, "move into an unknown space that can be enlivened by a generosity of memory."[438] If dance is "a reminder of what was, and who was, and a harbinger of what can be,"[439] then to dance is not to deny history or futurity, but to embrace both directions through the traces of multiple embodiment that dance *anima* carries across time and space.

This energy, or *anima*, is present in all of us, but it can also be lifted off of the human body; it is an extractable energy that carries traces of human culture, relation, and emotion. It also carries traces of technique and evidence of technical practice, forged through repetition. These imprints of past bodies in action and feeling can offer an energetic interruption to the endlessly mediated river (of AI-generated content; of the doomscroll) that we find ourselves in these days. Dance is a river of a different sort: an immortal stream that flows through material forms and bodies, often with the help of technologies, and holds real memory and experience, yet refuses to be a singular, concrete, possessable thing. Loïe Fuller cannot own the spiraling movement of the Serpentine dance; Cab Calloway's dancing propels the an-ontological shapes of various cartoon bodies as they transform; Denis Lavant enters the dance like a guest in the mirrored room, but he steps out of it and it (the dance) is still there, in the rhythm of the night.

This book has suggested that dancing—that thing that *humans* do—in fact troubles the category of the human as we know it. Dance, as an upspringing of movement, comes not only from an internal expression of humanness, but from a viral, technical assemblage that reveals the porous, changeable nature of human bodies. Rather than give us power over bodies, dancing reveals our ultimate—and potentially ecstatic—lack of control.

Notes

Preface

1. Yu Higuchi, "MikuMikuDance," *Softonic*, 2008, https://mikumikudance.en.softonic.com/.
2. Kate Bush, "Wuthering Heights," *The Kick Inside* (EMI Records, 1978).
3. Margaret Talbot, "The Enduring, Incandescent Power of Kate Bush," *The New Yorker*, December 19, 2018, https://www.newyorker.com/culture/culture-desk/the-enduring-incan descent-power-of-kate-bush.
4. There are actually two music videos for Bush's "Wuthering Heights": the "red dress version," shot on a foggy, verdant moor, and the "white dress version," shot in an empty studio. Both videos are directed by Keith MacMillan and choreographed by Bush with help from one of her dance tutors, Robin Kovac. See Min Chen, "Roll and Fall in Green: Kate Bush's 'Wuthering Heights' Video Is Still Moving," *Proxy Music*, August 20, 2018, https://proxymusic.club/2018/08/20/kate-bush-wuthering-heights-video/.
5. Wuthering Heights Montreal, "Kate Bush Wuthering Heights Choreography," YouTube video, 4:27, June 30, 2016, https://www.youtube.com/watch?v=IziOMwBu7ws.
6. "Hatsune Miku," *Vocaloid Wiki*, accessed August 4, 2021, https://vocaloid.fandom.com/wiki/Hatsune_Miku.
7. I co-organized the first Montréal edition of this event, in 2016, with Sandra Huber, Eileen Holowka, and Karissa Laroque.
8. For a more in-depth account of this research creation project and its stakes, see Hilary Bergen, "Let Me in Through Your Window: Dancing with Kate Bush and Hatsune Miku," *LO: TECH: POP: CULT: Screendance Remixed*, eds. Alanna Thain and Priscilla Guy (Routledge, 2024), 25–44; and Hilary Bergen, "Animating the Kinetic Trace: Kate Bush, Hatsune Miku, and Digital Dance," *PUBLIC* 60, Biometrics (2020): 187–207.
9. Bush, "The Kick Inside."
10. Ka Yan Lam, "The Hatsune Miku Phenomenon: More Than a Virtual J-Pop Diva," *The Journal of Popular Culture*, Special Issue: *Asian Popular Culture* 49, no. 5 (2016): 1107–1124.
11. Between the "sixteenth and eighteenth century," Siegert explains, "grid-shaped control becomes the universal practice that constitutes the basis of modern disciplinary societies." The grid continues to operate as a structure of power, even in the digital space of MMD. See Bernhard Siegert, *Cultural Techniques: Grids, Filters, Doors and Other Articulations of the Real* (Fordham University Press, 2015), 97.
12. Because I use the Kinect, Miku's body becomes mobilized by my gestural input, turning her from a symbolic image, or an icon, into an indexical body, which bears "a mark or trace of [my] physical presence," and which "inscribes [both her and me] at a specific moment of time" through the unification of the moving image of Miku's body with a ghostly past: a trace of the human dancer in the code. Here, I am using Mulvey's haunted reading of the film as indexical body. See Laura Mulvey, *Death 24X a Second: Stillness and the Moving Image* (Reaktion Books Ltd., 2006), 9.
13. As seen in the stills from our final video, we approximated Bush's iconic red dress and black sash from the original music video using the costuming available in MMD's database: a revealing kimono-style dress with red knee-high stockings.
14. Most MMD videos are highly produced and polished. The dances presented are meticulously synchronized and the dancers' body gestures are smooth, fluid, and stereotypically "sexy" (as in, performed for a heterosexual male gaze). The kind of project I have created in MMD is rare.

People do not tend to use the program experimentally, nor is it common to use the Kinect in combination with MMD. The consequences of using this unsophisticated mocap technology and little-to-no editing to polish the choreography are that my end result is glitchy.

15. Rosa Menkman, "The Glitch Art Genre," The Glitch Moment(um), *O Fluxo*, July 2012, https://www.ofluxo.net/the-glitch-art-genre-by-rosa-menkman/.

16. Kiri Miller, *Playable Bodies: Dance Games and Intimate Media* (Oxford University Press, 2017), 21–22. Miller's book, which marks a foray out of ethnomusicology toward dance studies, is very relevant to my research, given her focus on the intimacy of media and the politics of embodying agency via dance in digital and games platforms.

Introduction

17. *Petrouchka* is one of several ballets from the late nineteenth and early twentieth centuries that navigate the trope of the mechanical dancer who is also racialized. *Coppelia* is another, which Mara Mandradjieff has written on recently for *DRJ* (see Mara Mandradjieff, "Coppélia's Human-Objects: Winding Up Racialized Automata on the Ballet Stage," *Dance Research Journal* 55, no. 3 (2023): 30–46, https://doi.org/10.1017/S0149767723000347.) Relevant to the concerns of my book is the fact that a secondary puppet character in Petrouchka, the "Blackamoor" puppet, was traditionally portrayed in blackface, and was characterized as "mean, aggressive," and "prodigiously stupid" (Wendy Perron, "It's Time to Overhaul the Blackface (or Blueface) Puppet in Petrouchka," *Dance Magazine*, July 14, 2020, https://www.dancemagazine.com/blackface-in-ballet/#gsc.tab=0). *Petrouchka* therefore carries not only the history of the dancing marionette as a potentially ensouled figure, but the racist history of Black minstrelsy—a connection that foregrounds tropes about racialized characters (or puppets and automata) in stories about dance, technology, and ensoulment.

18. Andrew Wachtel, "The Libretto of Petrushka," in *Petrushka: Sources and Contexts*, ed. Andrew Wachtel (Northwestern University Press, 1998), 118–122, 119.

19. Many animals have mating rituals that are rhythmic and dance-like, but evidence shows that very few animals can move to the beat of external music, and it is likely that the enjoyment of dance is unique to humans (see Jason G. Goldman, "Are Humans the Only Species that Enjoy Dancing?" *BBC*, October 29, 2012, https://www.bbc.com/future/article/20121030-lords-of-the-dance).

20. Judith Lynne Hanna, *To Dance Is Human: A Theory of Nonverbal Communication* (University of Texas Press, 1979), 3.

21. Anthea Kraut, *Choreographing Copyright: Race Gender and Intellectual Property Rights in American Dance* (Oxford University Press, 2016), 19.

22. Roger Copeland and M. Cohen, eds., *What Is Dance?* (Oxford University Press, 1983), 52.

23. Merce Cunningham Qtd. in Susan Sontag, "Dancer and the Dance," *Reading Dance*, ed. Richard Gottlieb (Pantheon, 2008), 338.

24. Sontag, "Dancer and the Dance," 338.

25. Sontag, "Dancer and the Dance," 338.

26. Hanna, *To Dance Is Human*, 3. Hanna breaks her definition of dance into several key humanistic categories including dance as "social behavior" that is also "psychological," dance as economic, political, and communicative behavior, and dance as a "physical instrument or symbol for feeling and/or thought" (4).

27. Norman Bryson, "Cultural Studies and Dance History" in *Meaning in Motion: New Cultural Studies of Dance*, ed. Jane C. Desmond (Duke University Press, 1997), 15.

28. Harmony Bench, "Choreographing Bodies in Dance-Media," PhD Dissertation, University of California, LA, 2009, 35.

29. Alanna Thain, "In the Blink of an Eye: Norman McLaren Between Dance and Animation," in *The Oxford Handbook of Screendance Studies*, ed. Douglas Rosenberg (Oxford University Press, 2016), 167–186.

30. Spyros Papapetros, "Movements of the Soul: Traversing Animism, Fetishism, and the Uncanny," *Discourse* 34, no. 2–3 (Spring/Fall 2012), 185–208, 186.

31. Papapetros, "Movements of the Soul," 186.

32. Papapetros, "Movements of the Soul," 188.

33. Papapetros, "Movements of the Soul," 186. I want to note that although it is tightly woven to Western cultural and philosophical definitions as informed by Plato, Aristotle, and Jung, my use of the term "anima" is not meant to invoke the soul of a "universal" white, male subject, but rather to challenge the certainty of that figure. For me, the term succinctly evokes the soul outside any one body—conjuring ideas of animateness, body movement, agency, and culture to link humanist philosophies of soul with a posthumanist theory of dance. For more on a posthuman theory of dance, see Hilary Bergen, *Dancing Media: The Contagious Movement of Posthuman Bodies (or Towards a Posthuman Theory of Dance)*, Doctoral Thesis (PhD Humanities), Centre for Interdisciplinary Studies in Society and Culture, Montreal, QC, September 2022.

34. The anthropocentric associations between the term *anima* and (human) soul are not as common outside the canon of Western philosophical history. In many Eastern languages, including Hindi, Sanskrit, and Tamil, *anima* does not mean soul but rather infers a kind of atomic smallness or the power of minuteness. For example, *anima* in Sanskrit (अनिम) is a word referring to the "ability to become infinitely small like an atom," as described in the Yoga Sūtras of Patañjali. These references to shrinking, shape-shifting, and plasticity also inform my understanding of dance *anima* as an energy with morphing powers that exceed the limits of the singular human body.

35. I should note that both "anima" and "soul" can be contentious terms in my academic field, and there is some necessary discomfort associated with my choice to use these words. "Soul," for example, is certainly not a word proper to atheistic, postmodern intellectual training. This is partly why I like the term. I wonder: Is it disingenuous or even unethical or write of the soul in a nonreligious context or to re-imagine what "soul" can mean in our advanced capitalist, media-saturated world? In the specific context of dance as energetic capital, is it blasphemous to imagine the dancer's soul as both immortal and extractable, as not morally determined but produced by techniques and technologies? The word soul is loaded, from many angles, making it a productive pivot around which to examine the relation between dance, technology, and the figure of the human.

36. For an analysis of dance *anima* from the perspective of a religious framework, see Emily Wright's recent book, *Dancing to Transform: How Concert Dance Becomes Religious in American Christianity* (Intellect, 2021), which uses auto-ethnographical methods to explore the connections between dance movement and Christian concepts of soul, suffering, and the creativity of spiritual experience as a kind of liturgy. On the other end of the spectrum, Ann Wagner's book *Adversaries of Dance: From the Puritans to the Present* (University of Illinois Press, 1997) provides an overview of Christianity's opposition to dancing, which the religion has historically viewed as a carnal sin. In both cases, dance is configured as a kind of energetic excess which needs to be channeled or controlled.

37. Greg Ostrander, "Foucault's Disappearing Body," *Canadian Journal of Political and Social Theory* XI, no. 1–2 (1987): 120–133, 121.

38. Michel Foucault, *Discipline and Punish: The Birth of the Prison* (Pantheon, 1977), 29–30. Here, Foucault produces a historical analysis of the Western penal system that begins with practices of public torture and execution, which enact violence directly on the body of the criminal. He contrasts this with the modern prison (exemplified through Jeremy Bentham's unrealized panopticon) and the use of surveillance or an "unequal gaze" to police and control inmates, arguing that prisoners eventually internalize the disciplinary gaze. Thus, power produces a soul (or a way of being) for the individual, and that soul imprisons them.

39. This reading of "soul" is evocative of Foucault's postmodern thought, which characteristically challenges Enlightenment values that imagine the modern subject as autonomous, rational, and free. For Foucault, subjectivity is not "forged in liberty" but rather born out of discipline. See Hatim Bendayne, "From the Scaffold to Surveillance: A Brief Reading of Foucault's Discipline and Punish and the Birth of the Modern Soul," *Medium*, June 24, 2025, https://medium.com/@bendyane.hatim/from-the-scaffold-to-surveillance-a-brief-reading-of-foucaults-discipline-and-punish-and-the-fdcca04a8597.

40. L. D. Arnett, "The Soul: A Study of Past and Present Beliefs," *The American Journal of Psychology* 15, no. 2 (1904): 121–200.

41. Edward B. Tylor, *Primitive Cultures: Researches into the Development of Mythology, Philosophy, Religion, Language, Art and Custom*, Volume 1 (John Murray, 1871), 429.

42. Tylor, *Primitive Cultures*, 429.

43. For more on the practice and art of animation and the idea of *anima*, or soul, see William D. Routt, "De Anime," in *The Illusion of Life II: More Essays on Animation*, ed. Alan Cholodenko (Power Publications, 2007), 172–190.

44. Diana Taylor, *The Archive and the Repertoire: Performing Cultural Memory in the Americas* (Duke University Press, 2003), 5.

45. See Johannes Birringer, *Media & Performance: Along the Border* (Baltimore: Johns Hopkins University Press, 1998); Birringer, "Interactive Dance, the Body and the Internet," *Journal of Visual Art Practice*, no. 3.3 (2004): 165–178; Birringer, *Performance, Technology & Science* (PAJ Publications, 2008); Steve Dixon, *Digital Performance: A History of New Media in Theater, Dance, Performance Art, and Installation* (MIT Press, 2007); Susan Kozel, *Closer: Performance, Technologies, Phenomenology* (MIT Press, 2008); Anna Leon, *Expanded Choreographies—Choreographic Histories: Trans-Historical Perspectives Beyond Dance and Human Bodies in Motion* (Transcript Publishing, 2022); Chris Salter, *Entangled: Technology and the Transformation of Performance* (MIT Press, 2010); Sita Popat and Nicolas Salazar Sutil, *Digital Movement: Essays in Motion Technology and Peformance* (Palgrave Macmillan 2015); Stamatia Portanova, *Moving Without a Body: Digital Philosophy and Choreographic Thoughts* (MIT Press, 2013), 23.

46. Brenda Dixon Gottschild, *Digging the Africanist Presence in American Performance: Dance and Other Contexts* (Greenwood Press, 1996), 8–9.

47. Gottschild, *Digging the Africanist Presence*, 8–9.

48. Gottschild, *Digging the Africanist Presence*, 17.

49. Reginold A. Royston, "Soulcraft: Theorizing Black Techne in African and American Viral Dance," *Social Media + Society* 8, no. 2 (2022), https://doi.org/10.1177/20563051221107644.

50. I intentionally refrain from providing a specific definition of dance throughout the book. While distinctions between dance styles as various as bachata, ballet, dabkeh, breakdancing, and waacking, for example, are vast, and involve differences in rhythm, musicality, and body position among countless factors shaped by sociocultural, geographical, and other influences, *Dance Anima* purposefully considers "dance" a broad term. While my case studies throughout the book are attentive to the particulars of each style of dance being performed, it is also my intent to build a theory of dance *anima* that can be applied to many types of dancing in order to reveal dance as a general idea (and fantasy) in the public eye, and to expand the boundaries of choreography to include embodied, synchronized tasks like assembly line work and military drills. I take this approach in order to move beyond the specifics of one style of dance and examine the various disciplinary structures that construct and corral the energy of dance across these expanded forms.

51. Pierre Bourdieu, *Outline of a Theory of Practice* (Cambridge University Press, 1977), 86.

52. Marcel Mauss, "Techniques de Corps," in *Sociologie et Anthropologie*, 4th edition (Presses Universitaires de France, 1968), 364–386.

53. Thomas F. DeFrantz, "Afrofuturist Remains: A Speculative Rendering of Social Dance Futures v2.0," in *Choreography and Corporeality: Relay in Motion*, eds. Thomas R. DeFrantz and Philipa Rothfield (Palgrave MacMillan, 2016), 211.

54. DeFrantz, "Afrofuturist Remains," 211.

55. DeFrantz, "Afrofuturist Remains," 212.

56. Delsarte qtd. in Hillel Schwartz, "Torque: The New Kinaesthetic of the Twentieth Century," in *Incorporations*, eds. Jonathan Crary and Sanford Kwinter (Zone Books, 1992), 71.

57. Notably, the Swiss composer Jacques-Dalcroze also drew connections between musical rhythm and expression of emotion, as developed in his system of Dalcroze eurhythmics, and he believed that rhythm united "body and soul," spirituality, and corporeality (Schwartz, "Torque," 72).

58. Shawn qtd. in Schwartz, "Torque," 72.

59. Helen Moller, qtd. in Schwartz, "Torque," 73.

60. Judith Hamera, *Dancing Communities: Performance, Difference, and Connection in the Global City*. Studies in International Performance (Palgrave Macmillan, 2007), 4.

61. Marcel Mauss, "Techniques of the Body," *Economy and Society* 2, no. 1 (1973): 83.

62. Ben Spatz, *What a Body Can Do* (Routledge, 2015), 34. Spatz, who has written extensively on technique as an embodied knowledge, rejects "the idea that the value of a practice lies in its ephemerality" focusing instead on that which is "relatively stable and transmissible in embodied practice, and [using technique] to show how much value, as well as danger, is to be found in repeatability" (59). Spatz traces the usage of the word "technique" to Romantic poet Samuel Taylor Coleridge, who, writing on William Wordsworth in 1817, described technique as an

obstacle to genius, or "that which must be transcended in order for true genius to appear" (28). This is common also in the writings of Martin Heidegger (See Martin Heidegger, "The Question Concerning Technology," (Harper & Row, 1977) and Lewis Mumford (*Art and Technics*, Columbia University Press, 1952), who seem to see technique as rote mechanics and not the stuff of real artistry, and requires what Spatz calls the "trope of excess": the Romantic notion of "genius" as that which spills over and beyond the structure of technique, or lingers afterward. This trope of excess relates to dance *anima* in terms of the spilling over of energy beyond technical boundaries or containers for dance. The difference, however, is that my theory of dance *anima* is not about the individual dance artist as genius but about dance as a lingering energy that, in its excess, carries specters of other bodies.

63. Cornelia Vismann, "Cultural Techniques and Sovereignty," *Theory, Culture and Society* 30, no. 6 (2013): 83–93, 84. See also, Friedrich Kittler, *Gramophone, Film, Typewriter* (Stanford University Press, 1999); Siegert, *Cultural Techniques*; Geoffroy Winthrop-Young, "The Kultur of Cultural Techniques: Conceptual Inertia and The Parasitic Materialities of Ontologization," *Cultural Politics* 10, no. 3 (2014): 376–388; Jussi Parikka, "Afterword: Cultural Techniques and Media Studies," *Theory, Culture & Society* 30, no. 6 (2013): 147–159.

64. Susanne K. Langer, *Feeling and Form: A Theory of Art Developed from Philosophy in a New Key* (Charles Scribner's Sons, 1953), 169.

65. Langer, *Feeling and Form*, 174.

66. Langer, *Feeling and Form*, 174–175.

67. Langer, *Feeling and Form*, 175.

68. Langer, *Feeling and Form*, 175.

69. Langer, *Feeling and Form*, 180.

70. Langer, *Feeling and Form*, 180.

71. Langer, *Feeling and Form*, 180.

72. See Minsoo Kang, *Sublime Dreams of Living Machines: The Automaton in the European Imagination* (Harvard University Press, 2011), 16.

73. Anna Kornbluh, *Immediacy, or The Style of Too-Late Capitalism* (Verso, 2024).

74. Nicolas Salazar Sutil and Sebastian Melo, "Exposed to Time: Cross-Histories of Human Motion Visualization from Chrono- to Dynamophotography," in *The Oxford Handbook of Screendance Studies*, ed. Douglas Rosenberg (Oxford University Press, 2016), 143–166, 149.

75. Felicia McCarren, *Dancing Machines: Choreographies in the Age of Mechanical Reproduction* (Stanford University Press, 2003), 36.

76. Andre Lepecki, "Choreography as Apparatus of Capture," *TDR: The Drama Review* 51, no. 2 (2007):119–123, 122.

77. These comments by Bradley come from a live-streamed video of a studio visit she did with Jaamil Olawale Kosoko, for Kosoko's multimedia performance titled "Chameleon." The video is no longer accessible online. Rizvana Bradley, "Studio Visit for "Chameleon" by Jaamil Olawale Kosoko," CUNY Graduate Center, October 6, 2018, https://www.gc.cuny.edu/events/studio-visit-jaamil-olawale-kosoko-chameleon.

78. Bradley, "Studio Visit for "Chameleon" by Jaamil Olawale Kosoko."

79. For a more recent, expanded exploration of these ideas, see Rizvana Bradley, *Anteaesthetics* (Stanford University Press, 2023).

80. See Jacques Derrida, "Semiology and Grammatology: Interview with Julia Kristeva," in *Positions*, trans. and annotated by Alan Bass (Continuum, 2004), 15–36.

81. Rosaura Martínez Ruiz, "Freud and Derrida: Writing and Speculation (or When the Future Irrupts in the Present)," *Filozofski vestnik* 36, no. 3 (2015): 93–112.

82. Taylor, *The Archive and the Repertoire*, 20.

83. Taylor, *The Archive and the Repertoire*, 20.

84. Taylor, *The Archive and the Repertoire* xvii, 2–3.

85. Taylor, *The Archive and the Repertoire* xvii, 2–3.

86. Joseph Roach, *Cities of the Dead: Circum-Atlantic Performance* (Columbia University Press, 1996), 26.

87. This term, derived from Foucault's concept of the assemblage/dispositif, is Gilles Deleuze and Felix Guattari's word for the organization of bodies and things in order to profit off of their activity. Giorgio Agamben and André Lepecki use similar concepts, with Lepecki specifically writing about choreography as an apparatus of capture. See Gilles Deleuze and Félix Guattari, *Mille plateaux: Capitalisme et schizophrénie* 2 (Paris: Les Editions de Minuit, 1980), 545–560.

88. McCarren, *Dancing Machines*, 4.

89. McCarren, *Dancing Machines*, 4.

90. Rizvana Bradley, "Black Cinematic Gesture and the Aesthetics of Contagion," *TDR: The Drama Review* 62, no. 1 (Spring 2018): 14–30, 21.

91. Wes Davis, "The Copyright Fight Over Fortnite Dance Moves is Back On," *The Verge*, November 4, 2023, https://www.theverge.com/2023/11/4/23946260/epic-fortnite-choreogra phy-emote-lawsuit-ruling-overturned.Crucially, the presence of dance in *Fortnite* evolves out of an earlier practice of using specific dance moves for "taunts" or to provoke other players in the 2007 first person shooter game, *Team Fortress 2*. Certain dance moves such as the "Kazotsky Kick," the "Square Dance," the "Conga," and "Mannrobics" can be purchased for use in game play, and *Team Fortress 2* players can also dance together—it only takes one player to begin dancing for others to join in on the same choreography. (see https://www.youtube. com/watch?v=k08gjJbxG-A; https://www.youtube.com/watch?v=2z9XTeeA43o; https:// www.youtube.com/watch?v=pK38dH0c_Pw). In this way, Fortnite commodifies long-extant practices in other games, which conceive of dance as a communal-digital activity. The Fortnite dances therefore hold multiple traces of other dancing bodies within them, illustrating the cumulative force that I understand dance *anima* to be.

92. The full quote from Benjamin about the temporal-spatial qualities of aura is as follows: "Even the most perfect reproduction of a work of art is lacking in one element: its presence in time and space, its unique existence at the place where it happens to be. This unique existence of the work of art determined the history to which it was subject throughout the time of its existence. This includes the changes which it may have suffered in physical condition over the years as well as the various changes in its ownership. The traces of the first can be revealed only by chemical or physical analyzes which it is impossible to perform on a reproduction; changes of ownership are subject to a tradition which must be traced from the situation of the original. The presence of the original is the prerequisite to the concept of authenticity." My argument is that dance presents an obstacle to Benjamin's thesis because dance, for which origins and originality are impossible anyway, holds authenticity not by being the first instance of the thing, but by virtue of dance's role as a cultural technique of soul, which bestows aura on whichever body is dancing—regardless of whether that body is organic, digital, robotic, or a "reproduction" of sorts. (Walter Benjamin, "The Work of Art in the Age of Mechanical Reproduction," in *Illuminations*, ed. Hannah Arendt, trans. Harry Zohn (Schocken Books, 1969), 3.

93. Gottschild, *Digging the Africanist Presence*, 1–2.

Chapter 1

94. Notably, the hand-tinting of Fuller's videos, meant to resemble the experience of seeing the colored lights projected on Fuller's body in her live show, is an interesting example of the way media innovations can emerge from an attempt to *copy* something.

95. Under many of the videos, one YouTube user named Cyrilla Behrndt repeatedly claims that the dancer is not Fuller or any of the other performers listed above, but *Papinta*, "the flame dancer." There is very little written on Papinta, but apparently her real name was Caroline Hipple Holpin and she is said to have died in Dusseldorf in 1907, "possibly due to the gas produced by the limelight" projected from the front of the stage, meaning that she would have been burned alive in front of her audience (from Victoria Bogushevskaya and Elisabetta Colla, eds., *Thinking Colours: Perception, Translation and Representation* (Cambridge Scholars Publishing, 2015), 148). Behrndt is also the individual behind the Facebook page dedicated to archiving newspaper articles on Papinta and advertisements for Papinta's live show.

96. Mia Generoso, "Meet Taylor Swift's Muse: Dancer and Innovator Loïe Fuller," *Teen World Arts*, July 12, 2024, https://teenworldarts.com/magazine/Loïe-fuller.

97. Ted Merwin, "Loïe Fuller's Influence on F.T. Marinetti's Futurist Dance," *Dance Chronicle* 21, no. 1 (1998): 73–92, 80, http://www.jstor.org/stable/1567999.

98. See Erin Brannigan, "'La Loïe' As Pre-Cinematic Performance—Descriptive Continuity of Movement," *Senses of Cinema* no. 28 (2003), https://www.sensesofcinema.com/2003/ feature-articles/la_loie/; Tom Gunning, "Loïe Fuller and the Art of Motion," in *Camera Obscura, Camera Lucida*, eds. R. Allen and M. Turvey (Amsterdam University Press, 2003), 75–89, 78; McCarren, *Dancing Machines*; Sally Sommer, "Loïe Fuller," *The Drama Review*

19, no. 1: Post-Modern Dance Issue (March 1975): 53–67, 54. Sommer, for example, writes that "[c]entral to Fuller's performance was a moving image made animate by the projection of coloured light and slides" (Sommer, "Loïe Fuller," 53–67, 54). Both Tom Gunning and Noam Elcott also remark on Fuller's use of a darkened theater—a novel practice at the time—which served to enhance the magical effects of her lighting and can be compared to cinematic spectatorship conventions emerging with the Lumiere brothers. See Noam Elcott, *Artificial Darkness* (University of Chicago Press, 2016). Tom Gunning has also linked Fuller's performances with his category of early cinema, the "cinema of attractions" (see Tom Gunning, "The Cinema of Attractions: Early Film, Its Spectator and the Avant-Garde," *Wide Angle* 8, no. 3 (1986): 63–70).

99.   Sommer, "Loïe Fuller," 53–67, 61.

100. Felicia McCarren intentionally uses air quotes around "Loïe Fuller" every time she mentions the Lumiere Brothers' film which features Fuller's imitator, but is credited to Fuller. See McCarren, *Dancing Machines*.

101. For example, in his analysis of the Annabelle Serpentine films made by Thomas Edison, and performed by a dancer named Annabelle Moore, Gunning writes: "the Serpentine was most definitely associated with a single (although widely imitated) dancer who most likely invented it, cobbling together several related practices—and it most certainly made her name famous worldwide: Loïe Fuller." See Gunning, "Art of Motion," 75–89, 78. Rhonda Garelick similarly writes that the Serpentine was "an art form [Fuller] had invented in the United States." See Rhonda K. Garelick, *Electric Salome: Loïe Fuller's Performance of Modernism* (Princeton University Press, 2009), 1.

102. "Nautch" is a British term coined from the Hindu/Urdu word *nachna*, meaning to dance.

103. Loïe Fuller, *Fifteen Years of a Dancer's Life: With Some Account of her Distinguished Friends* (Small, Maynard & Company, 1913), 53.

104. Fuller, *Fifteen Years of a Dancer's Life*, 54.

105. Rhonda Garelick, "Loïe Fuller and the Serpentine," *The Public Domain Review*, November 5, 2019, https://publicdomainreview.org/essay/Loïe-fuller-and-the-serpentine.

106. Stéphane Mallarmé Qtd. in Frank Kermode, "Poet and Dancer Before Diaghilev," *Salmagundi* no. 33/34, DANCE (Spring–Summer 1976): 23–47, 155.

107. Deborah Jowitt, *Time and the Dancing Image* (University of California Press, 1989), 39.

108. Jowitt, *Time and the Dancing Image*, 59.

109. Jowitt, *Time and the Dancing Image*, 43.

110. Jowitt, *Time and the Dancing Image*, 60.

111. On the other hand, Rhonda Garelick argues that Fuller's "refusal" of her body, and "preference for mechanics" and scientific tools, makes her an outlier in the context of American modern dance, which often "portrayed the human body moving in accordance with natural forces, allowing gravity, breath and the dancer's own physical weight to play a visible role onstage." See Garelick, *Electric Salome*, 186.

112. Portanova, *Moving Without a Body*, 23.

113. Portanova, *Moving Without a Body*, 23.

114. Stéphane Mallarmé and Evlyn Gould, "Ballets," *Performing Arts Journal* 15, no. 1 (1993): 106–110.

115. Amy Koritz, *Gendering Bodies/Performing Art: Dance and Literature in Early Twentieth Century British Culture* (The University of Michigan Press, 1995).

116. Merwin, "Loïe Fuller's Influence on F. T. Marinetti's Futurist Dance," 73–92, 87.

117. For feminist interpretations of Loïe Fuller's work, see also Erin Brannigan, *Dancefilm: Choreography and the Moving Image* (Oxford University Press, 2011); Elizabeth Coffman, "Women in Motion: Loïe Fuller and the "Interpenetration" of Art and Science," *Camera Obscura* 17, no. 1 (2002): 72–105; Gunning, "Art of Motion," 75–89; and Dana Mills, "The Dancing Woman Is the Woman Who Dances into the Future: Rancière, Dance, Politics," *Philosophy & Rhetoric* 49, no. 4 (2016): 482–499.

118. Karen Beckman, *Vanishing Women: Magic, Film and Feminism* (Duke University Press, 2003), 5.

119. Anna Sutton, "Infinite Light: The Dance of Loïe Fuller," *The Australian Ballet*, March 23, 2012, https://australianballet.com.au/behind-ballet/infinite-light-the-dance-of-Loïe-fuller.

120. Garelick, "Loïe Fuller and the Serpentine."

121. Tom Gunning calls her "rather pudgy," Ted Merwin mentions Fuller's "stocky body" (qtd in Sommer, "Loïe Fuller," 82), Felicia McCarren writes of her "heavy body not aiming to seduce its public" (62), and Rhonda Garelick describes her as "unglamorous" and "with little natural

grace," noting that Marie Curie's daughter Eve spoke of Fuller's "shapeless figure" (Garelick, "Loïe Fuller and the Serpentine," n.p.). One reviewer of Fuller's show remarked that the audience must insist "upon seeing her pretty piquant face before they can believe that the lovely apparition is really a woman." All of the above quotes come from Sommer, "Loïe Fuller," 53–67.

122. Jean Cocteau, *Souvenirs* (Editions Flammarion, 1935), 5.

123. Garelick, *Electric Salome*, 8.

124. Kraut, *Choreographing Copyright*, 43. See also *Fuller v. Bemis*, 50 F. 926 (C.C.S.D.N.Y. 1892).

125. Kraut, *Choreographing Copyright*, 43. Notably, as Kraut points out, laws around dance changed in the mid-twentieth century, where choreography alone (regardless of whether it contained a dramatic narrative) was eligible for copyright.

126. Kraut, *Choreographing Copyright*, 54.

127. Kraut, *Choreographing Copyright*, 57.

128. Jessica Brit Ingle has analyzed the similarities between the body poses in Fuller's "cabinet cards" and those of Indian nautch dancers, both of which feature the subject holding their skirt with arms outstretched. See Jessica Brit Ingle, "La Loïe" Fuller's Cabinet Cards as Transcultural Celebrity Propaganda," *Texas Graduate Liberal Studies Symposium* (Southern Methodist University, 2018).

129. Fuller, *Fifteen Years of a Dancer's Life*, 28.

130. Kraut, *Choreographing Copyright*, 4.

131. See Zhaoming Quian, *Orientalism and Modernism: The Legacy of China in Pound and Williams* (Duke University Press, 1995) and Yutian Wong, *Choreographing Asian America*, (Wesleyan University Press, 2010).

132. Anne Anlin Cheng, *Ornamentalism* (Oxford University Press, 2018), xii.

133. Cheng, *Ornamentalism*, 17.

134. Cheng, *Ornamentalism*, 17.

135. Fuller, *Fifteen Years of a Dancer's Life*, 40–41.

136. Fuller, *Fifteen Years of a Dancer's Life*, 33.

137. Fuller, *Fifteen Years of a Dancer's Life*, 37.

138. Upon viewing Fuller's *Serpentine* performed live, American modern dancer Isadora Duncan described the aura of the piece as follows: "Before our very eyes she turned to many-coloured shining orchids, to a wavering, flowing sea-flower, and at length to a spiral-like lily, all the magic of Merlin, the sorcery of light, colour, flowing form . . . She transformed herself into a thousand colourful images before the eyes of her audience. Unbelievable. Not to be repeated or described." A section of the same quote introduces this chapter. Duncan qtd. in Brannigan, "'La Loïe' As Pre-Cinematic Performance."

139. Benjamin, "The Work of Art," 3.

140. Benjamin, "The Work of Art," 3–4.

141. Benjamin, "The Work of Art," 4.

142. Kraut, *Choreographing Copyright*, 6.

143. Andre Lepecki, *Singularities: Dance in the Age of Performance* (Routledge, 2016), 15.

144. Kraut, *Choreographing Copyright*, xiii.

145. Kraut, *Choreographing Copyright*, 64.

146. Kraut, *Choreographing Copyright*, 55.

147. This photograph, from the Jerome Robbins Dance Division at the NYPL, depicts Papinta, "posing in a voluminous costume in a 'Serpentine' dance": https://digitalcollections.nypl.org/items/8d7f18e1-dd14-c275-e040-e00a18065814 but the date of capture is approximate (1890–1909) and therefore is unhelpful in determining whether the photo was taken before or after Fuller's "invention" of the dance.

148. M. L. Fuller, "Garment for Dancers," No. 518347. Patented April 17, 1894, https://patents.google.com/patent/US518347A/en.

149. "Fuller vs. Bemis," Circuit Court, S.D. New York, 18 June 1892, "Copyright—'Dramatic Composition'—Stage Dance," https://babel.hathitrust.org/cgi/pt?id=uc1.b3556462&view=1up&seq=968&skin=2021.

150. Kraut, *Choreographing Copyright*, 15.

151. Foster, *Valuing Dance* (Oxford University Press, 2019), 54.

152. Mark Seltzer, *Bodies and Machines* (Routledge, 1992), 143.

153. Fuller, *Fifteen Years of a Dancer's Life*, 270.

154. John Martin, "Metakinesis" in *What Is Dance?: Readings in Theory and Criticism*, eds. Marshall Cohen and Roger Copeland (Oxford University Press, 1983), 22–24, 22.

155. Ann Cooper Albright, *Traces of Light: Absence and Presence in the Work of Loïe Fuller* (Wesleyan University Press, 2007), 2.

156. Ibid.

157. Derrida, "Semiology and Grammatology," 15–36. See also Laurent Milesi, "Derrida and Posthumanism (I): From Sign to Trace," in *Geneaology of Critical Posthumanism*, September 14, 2020, https://criticalposthumanism.net/derrida-and-posthumanism-i-from-sign-to-trace/#_ftn8.

158. Jody Sperling is known for her reconstructions of Fuller's dances, videos of which can be seen online at https://www.youtube.com/watch?v=TQTQ-_kw8pg.

159. Jody Sperling, "Loïe Fuller and the Magic Lantern," Delivered at Dancing in the Millennium Conference, Washington, DC, 2000.

160. McCarren, *Dancing Machines*, 50.

161. Fuller, *Fifteen Years of a Dancer's Life*.

162. From my research, it seems Fuller was never captured on film. This is a consensus shared by scholars such as Felicia McCarren and Lara Karpenko, who writes that the only film which possibly features Fuller is the 1906 film available through the New York Public Library. I agree with Karpenko's eventual assessment, however, that the NYPL film features an imitator and is mislabeled, because "(i) the dancer's face appears different than photographs of Fuller taken from the same time and (ii) the dancer's style appears a bit slow and overly stationary and seems to contradict contemporary descriptions of Fuller's dancing." See Lara Karpenko, "'The Inanimate Becomes Animate': Loïe Fuller, Speculative Feminist Aesthetics, and Posthuman Embodiment," *Nineteenth-Century Contexts* 41, no. 5 (2019): 565–584, 581. There is also a 16 mm film (*Pathé Freres*) supposedly of Fuller dancing the Serpentine, held in collection at the Museum of Modern Art. Once again, the dancer does not seem to resemble Fuller (she is taller and slimmer than Fuller was). This film is referenced by Wendy Haslem in her book *From Melies to New Media: Spectral Projections* (Intellect Books Ltd., 2019), but the only documentation I could find is a video of the video, posted by a gallery visitor: https://www.youtube.com/watch?v=dD2-YEGmfWg.

163. This visibility of the *body* in these various films contrasts with written accounts of Fuller's performance, where her "hidden body," as described by Felicia McCarren for example, is completely eclipsed by her costume, "giving itself over to the representation of something beyond it" (McCarren, *Dancing Machines*, 62).

164. Haslem, *From Melies to New Media*, 68–69.

165. Arnesh Koul, "Understanding YouTube's Algorithm in 2019," *Best Practices*, April 2, 2019, Colorado State University, https://social.colostate.edu/strategy/youtube-algorithm/, accessed June 22, 2021.

166. Gunning, "Art of Motion," 77–78.

167. Gunning, "Cinema of Attractions," 64.

168. Gunning, "Cinema of Attractions," 66.

169. Teresa Rizzo, "YouTube: The New Cinema of Attractions," *Scan Journal* 5, no. 1 (2008): 11–21, 17.

170. Rizzo, "YouTube," 18.

171. I portray Fuller as the author of a set of techniques here rather than a genius inventor extraordinaire, to show how she can never claim full ownership over the Serpentine, even if her exploration of the technical apparatus of the Serpentine was meticulous. Similarly, Roland Barthes's argument in his seminal essay, "The Death of the Author," is that we must make a "countertheological" move away from the tyranny of the author as a genius creator of a text who prescribes an "ultimate meaning" (54). Barthes argues that we should instead privilege the multifaced interpretations readers (or, e.g., the audience of a dance) bring to that text, regardless of what an author intended. See Roland Barthes, "The Death of the Author," in *The Rustle of Language*, trans. Richard Howard (Hill and Wang, 1986), 49–55.

Chapter 2

172. Heinrich von Kleist and Thomas G. Neumiller, "On the Marionette Theatre," *The Drama Review: TDR* 16, no. 3, the "Puppet" issue (1972): 22–26, 22.

173. Von Kleist and Neumiller, "On the Marionette Theatre," 22.

174. Von Kleist and Neumiller, "On the Marionette Theatre," 22.

175. Von Kleist and Neumiller, "On the Marionette Theatre," 23.

176. Kleist's friend's musings on the center of gravity as the location of soul in the puppet, as well as his excitement at the virtuosity of the puppets, who can float and skim the ground, and whose limbs follow their central force, is predictive of the preoccupations of digital animators today. I am thinking in particular of video game designers who use "ragdoll physics," a procedural animation technique meant to simulate the movement of a character when killed. In ragdoll physics, the characters' bodies are understood as a series of rigid bones or a skeletal structure that can collapse to the ground realistically—much like the marionettes in Kleist's essay.

177. This quote comes from another version of Kleist's essay, "On the Marionette Theatre," reprinted alongside Roman Paska's essay, "The Inanimate Incarnate," in Michel Feher, Ramona Naddaff, and Nadia Tazi, eds. *Fragments for a History of the Human Body*, vol. 1 (Zone Books, 1989), 410–428. Despite the biblical associations with the idea of innocence lost, Kleist is not exactly invoking a Christian God or morality as concepts. Seventeen years before Kleist wrote his essay on marionettes, Friedrich Schiller's 1793 essay *Über Anmut und Würde* (On Grace and Dignity) used Kantian philosophy to explain human beauty in terms of a melding of Grace (*Anmut*) and Dignity (*Würde*). Schiller's influence is felt in Kleist's writing (and the two spent time together in Weimar). Whereas Schiller built on Kant's duty-based morality, connecting aesthetic concepts such as grace to moral ideas of dignity and soul, Kleist explored aesthetic categories as not necessarily attached to morality at all. This is typical of Kleist's philosophy and fiction writing; his characters are often morally ambiguous, and in "The Marionette Theatre," Kleist writes of the pure, unselfconscious grace of the dancing puppets as aesthetically superior to the artificial, socially constructed, conscious action (and morality) of humans.

178. Paska, "The Inanimate Incarnate," 419. Here, Kleist and his friend speak briefly about the concept of "infinite consciousness": Kleist says that "grace . . . reappears when knowledge has passed through the infinite, so that it appears purest simultaneously in the human body that has either *none at all* or else *infinite* consciousness—that is, in the puppet or in the god" (420) (emphasis mine). Whereas the ordinary adult dancer "lacks grace" due to an overdetermined awareness of their body and the perception of others that can make their movement affected, puppets do not think before they move, which feels to the onlooker like pure instinct or "innocence"—something graceful and holy, according to Kleist. The puppet is both spiritual, superhuman or god-like, *and* terrestrial or material (the soul is in the movement of their limbs, which suggests a material center of gravity). To be clear, the elevation of a puppet (or any object) to the status of a god would be an absurd idea to most pre-nineteenth-century Western thinkers, and Kleist's thinking in this essay demonstrates a related conflict between German Romanticism and Enlightenment-era thought. The rise of industrialism in the eighteenth and nineteenth centuries was generally met with critique by Romantic thinkers and artists like Kleist, who tended to idealize agrarian lifestyles and mystical forces and who denounced capitalism along with the automation and exploitation associated with human labor in the industrial revolution—phenomena which the dancing puppet embodies. Yet in his essay, Kleist esteems the puppet as the pinnacle of grace and soul, precisely because it is an object without free will. Kleist ends his essay with an anecdote about a bear who, chained to a post and trained meticulously to fence, spars with Kleist and beats him every time. This story again underscores the paradox at the center of Kleist's ideology. He uses the bear to point to the supremacy of an organic world pre-lost innocence, and yet his essay does not romanticize the animal so much as the puppet: a trained, nonorganic body without self-consciousness. The bear in Kleist's concluding anecdote, disturbingly puppet-like, has rehearsed fencing so much that it has become instinctual. It is the rehearsal of this technique that makes the bear like a trained dancer, and it is the bear's unquestioning animal nature that allows it to joust with perceived confidence and grace. The sad image of the bear is one of a body chained to a puppet master, and the puppet master in this case is none other than technique itself.

179. Susan Foster Leigh, "Dancing Bodies," in *Meaning in Motion: New Cultural Studies of Dance*, ed. Jane C. Desmond (Duke University Press, 1997), 237.

180. This idea, of the material human body as an impediment to the expressive capacity of dance, will be familiar to formally trained dancers who often feel this "discrepancy between what they want to do and what they can do" (Leigh, "Dancing Bodies," 237). As Susan Foster Leigh explains, in dance technique and choreography, there is often a "prevailing experience" of "loss, of failing to regulate a miragelike substance"—"one never has confidence in the body's reliability" (237).

181. Jessica de Brier, "Seen, Known, Danced and Spoken: Heinrich von Kleist and the Limits of Being Human," *Pastelegram*, no. 10, Primitive Games, 2015, https://pastelegram.org/e/176.

182. McCarren, *Dancing Machines*, 3.

183. See Jacques Lacan, *The Four Fundamental Concepts of Psychoanalysis: The Seminar of Jacques Lacan*, Book XI, ed. Jacques-Alain Miller, trans. Alan Sheridan (W.W. Norton & Co), 1981. For Lacan, the gaze is different than the "look" because it refers to the sense that the object we are gazing at is looking back at us out of its own volition. This is what makes the dancing machine uncanny, or discomforting: it meets our gaze with its own agency.

184. Sigmund Freud, *The Uncanny*, eds. David McLintock and Hugh Haughton (Penguin Books, 2003), 8.

185. Even though "The Sandman" is a work of literature, it is a story so obsessed with the gaze that it seems to act as a precursor to cinema. Hoffmann's story features countless telescopes and other vision technologies, spying, and voyeurism that lead to obsession, not to mention the audience at the ball where Olympia is debuted, or the childhood trauma Nathanael sustains around the threatened loss of his eyes. *Metropolis* and *Ex Machina*, being films, are also self-referential in the way they present dance to a layered gaze.

186. Here, I am referring to the Greek myth of a male sculptor named Pygmalion from Cyprus, who, discouraged by his experiences with women in the real world, created his ideal woman out of ivory stone and named her Galatea. Aphrodite later brought Galatea to life and Pygmalion married his creation. The myth has been influential to writers, artists, technologists, and corporations as a metaphor for the engineering of life in a feminine form. I have written about this phenomenon elsewhere (see Hilary Bergen, "'I'd Blush if I Could': Digital Assistants, Disembodied Cyborgs and the Problem of Gender," *Word & Text* 6 (Proto-posthumanisms) (2016): 95–113). For another overview of the way the Pygmalion story has influenced the development of machinic, cyborgian, and AI women, see Lelia Erscoi, Annelies V. Kleinherenbrink, and Olivia Guest, "Pygmalion Displacement: When Humanising AI Dehumanises Women," *SocArXiv*, February 11, 2023, doi:10.31235/osf.io/jqxb6.

187. Kang, *Sublime Dreams*, 184.

188. Kang, *Sublime Dreams*, 184.

189. Relatedly, Friedrich Kittler begins his book *Discourse Networks* by analyzing the sigh ("*ach!*") in German poetry. He writes: "If this is not the sigh of a nameless self—no self appears in the sentence—it is certainly not the sigh of any known author. What moves through the cadence of old German Knittel-verse is a pure soul" and is, Kittler argues, "pre-language." Olympia's "ah" produces the appearance of soul where there is none and, as Kittler explains, produces both soul and "woman" as "mechanical effect[s] of discourse." Friedrich A. Kittler, *Discourse Networks 1800/1900*, 3, 42.

190. E. T. A. Hoffmann, *Der Sandmann (The Sandman)*, trans. John Oxenford. Berliner bilinguale Ausgabe, 2. Auflage. German/English bilingual edition (CreateSpace Independent Pub., 2015), 14–15. Olympia's "angelic" gaze here can be interpreted in the context of Kleist's "in-finite consciousness" mentioned above, where the puppet, by virtue of not having conscious-ness, exhibits a neutrality or lack of self-consciousness that makes her god-like. Writing just seven years after Kleist (a fellow German Romanticist) published his essay on marionettes, Hoffmann was undoubtedly influenced by Kleist's thinking.

191. Hoffmann, *The Sandman*, 26.

192. Hoffmann, *The Sandman*, 27.

193. Hoffmann, *The Sandman*, 29.

194. I realize I am using DeFrantz a little out of context here, as he is writing about the performance of James Brown and Black vernacular dance, but his comment communicates something key in the passage of dance *anima* as facilitated by the gaze of the audience—a detail that is useful in analyzing Hoffmann's portrayal of the dance scene in his story. I will pick up on DeFrantz's analysis of scrutiny and wonder in Chapters 3 and 4, where I address race more explicitly.

195. Hoffmann, *The Sandman*, 27.

196. Hoffmann, *The Sandman*, 27.

197. Laura Mulvey, "Visual Pleasure and Narrative Cinema," *Screen* 16, no. 3 (1975): 6–18, 9.

198. Freud, *The Uncanny*, 7.

199. Hoffmann, *The Sandman*, 8.

200. See Bianca Westerman, "The Biomorphic Automata of the 18th Century: Mechanical Artworks as Objects of Technical Fascination and Epistemological Exhibition," *Figurationen* 17, no. 2 (2016): 123–137.

201. Kang, *Sublime Dreams*, 229.
202. Kang, *Sublime Dreams*, 53.
203. For more, see Gary Hatfield, "The Passions of the Soul and Descartes's Machine Psychology," *Studies in History and Philosophy of Science Part A* 38, no. 1 (2007): 1–35; Anik Waldow, "Activating the Mind: Descartes' Dreams and the Awakening of the Human Animal Machine," *Philosophy and Phenomenological Research* 94, no. 2 (2017): 299–325; Dalia Judovitz, "Virtual Bodies: Anatomy, Technology, and the Inhuman in Descartes," *Paroles Gelées* 16, no. 1 (1998): 21–41.
204. Hoffmann, *The Sandman*, 31–32.
205. Hoffmann, *The Sandman*, 32.
206. See Adelheid Voskuhl, "Producing Objects, Producing Texts: Accounts of Android Automata in Late Eighteenth-Century Europe," *Studies in History and Philosophy of Science* 38, no. 2 (2007): 422–444.
207. Characters such as Hadaly, the machine-woman from Auguste Villiers de l'Isle-Adam's French symbolist sci-fi novel, *L'Ève Future* (1886), follow in the vein of Olympia's representation, but notably, Hadaly does not dance.
208. *Maschinenmensch* is the German term for Lang's fictional robot, alternately called "Futura" in von Harbou's novel and "Maria" in Fritz Lang's film adaptation.
209. Andreas Huyssen, "The Vamp and the Machine: Technology and Sexuality in Fritz Lang's Metropolis," *New German Critique* 24–25 (1981): 221–237.
210. Benjamin, "Work of Art," 37.
211. *Ex Machina*, directed by Alex Garland (A24, 2015).
212. The name Ava may be meant to evoke *Ada*, for Ada Lovelace, the English writer and mathematician (and daughter of Romantic poet Lord Byron), who is known for her work on Charles Babbage's early computer prototypes. It was Lovelace who recognized that the computer could do more than just calculate, and her explorations with algorithmic interaction meant that Lovelace is often understood as the first computer programmer. This subtle reference links Ava (the machine under command of the computer programmer Caleb) to Ada (the computer programmer with control), thereby giving Ava some power, and flipping the dynamic with Caleb, via intertext.
213. This pattern also speaks to a trope in cinema and video games called "born sexy yesterday," whereby the female creation is naïve and child-like but also deliberately portrayed in a sexual light. Yorgos Lanthimos's 2023 film *Poor Things*—another story that features a dancing machine in a spellbinding public dance scene—subverts this trope through the character of Bella Baxter, a Frankenstinian monster whose fetus's brain has been transplanted into her head, causing her to be reborn as a baby upon revivification. Bella moves quickly from naivety to sexualized subject, and importantly grows her own insatiable sense of sexual desire that refuses to be contained by the men who have created and want to control her.
214. Huyssen, "The Vamp and the Machine," 223.
215. Cheng, *Ornamentalism*, 144.
216. Jennifer Piejko, "William Forsythe's Choreographic Objects," *Gagosian Le Bourget*, Paris, December 19, 2017.
217. Garland seems fascinated by the potential of dance to straddle the realms of violence and consent. I did not have space to discuss it at length in this chapter, but in another of Garland's films, *Annihilation* (Netflix, 2018), Mizuno plays a character called "Humanoid"—an alien presence who is also a mysterious force of nature that can take on characteristics of humans it interacts with by cloning. In a silver latex suit that covers her completely, making her faceless, Mizuno dances a haunting duet with Natalie Portman's character at the end of the film. What begins as a violent, physical struggle turns into something intimate, like contact improvisation, as Portman's character realizes she needs to relinquish control and move gently and attentively to calm her alien duet partner. Mizuno uses dance to mimic Portman's movements imperfectly, humanly, and tenderness develops between the two of them. The dance *anima* generated by this duet is tangible as it registers in each of their bodies, bringing them together into relation.
218. Huyssen, "The Vamp and the Machine," 81.
219. Hoffmann, *The Sandman*, 242.
220. Hoffmann, *The Sandman*, 243.
221. Hoffmann, *The Sandman*, 243.

222. Cheng, *Ornamentalism*, 14. Cheng explains further: "To attend to ornamentalism is to ask how racial personhood can be assembled not through organic flesh but instead through synthetic inventions and designs, not through corporeal embodiment but rather through attachments that are metonymic and hence superficial, detachable and migratory" (19). I am viewing dance *anima* as one such "detachable and migratory" attachment. However, dance is not just ornament; it is embodied as well.

223. Sandra Huber, *Witchy Methodologies: Bewitchment, Shapeshifting, and Communication with More-than-human Kin*, PhD Dissertation, Humanities, Concordia University, 2022, 48.

224. Katharina Loew, *Special Effects and German Silent Film: Techno-Romantic Cinema*. Film Culture in Transition (Amsterdam University Press, 2021), 219.

225. Papapetros, "Movements of the Soul," 188.

226. While this is not a high number of followers for a pop star (for reference, a celebrity like Rihanna has 149 million followers on Instagram), it is an unprecedented amount for a digital influencer.

227. Miquela's singing voice, like her dancing, is outsourced and modular, and could be the topic of its own chapter. Her persona as a singer/dancer aligns her with Japanese pop star hologram Hatsune Miku, who I write about in my Preface.

228. Comments from an Instagram post on @lilmiquela's account, August 18, 2018.

229. See Kang, *Sublime Dreams*.

230. Daisy Jones, "Why We Follow Lil Miquela, The Model With 900K Followers & No Soul," *Refinery29*, April 10, 2018, https://www.refinery29.com/en-us/miquela-sousa-fake-instagram.

231. Emilia Petrarca, "Sorry, Lil Miquela Could Make *How Much* This Year?" *The Cut*, November 2, 2020, https://www.google.com/search?q=brud%2C+lil+miquela%2C+10+million&oq=brud%2C+lil+miquela%2C+10+million&gs_lcrp=EgZjaHJvbWUyBggAEEUYOTIHCAEQIRigAdIBCDU3MTJqMG0qAIAsAIB&sourceid=chrome&ie=UTF-8 (accessed July 9, 2025). See also Jonathan Shieber, "The Makers of the Virtual Influencer, Lil Miquela, Snag Real Money from Silicon Valley," *Tech Crunch*, April 24, 2018, https://techcrunch.com/2018/04/23/the-makers-of-the-virtual-influencer-lil-miquela-snag-real-money-from-silicon-valley/.

232. Heather Warren-Crow describes Eve's face as a "now infamous image that digitally combines faces of different races to create a composite subject of a networked economy as a symbol of an America with an allegedly increasing acceptance of diversity" (18). Like Eve, Miquela's freckled, brown face is the face (the digital mask, really) of a networked economy (America) that accepts diversity, as long as it is "on brand," or in service of capital. See Warren-Crow, *Girlhood and the Plastic Image* (University of Chicago Press, 2014).

233. For more on Afrofuturism, see for example Kodwo Eshun, *More Brilliant Than the Sun: Adventures in Sonic Fiction* (London: Quartet Books, 1998), Alexander G. Weheliye, *Habeas Viscus: Racializing Assemblages, Biopolitics, and Black Feminist Theories of the Human* (Duke University Press, 2014), and Ytasha L. Womack, *Afrofuturism: The World of Black Sci-Fi and Fantasy Culture* (Lawrence Hill Books, 2013).

234. Cheng, *Ornamentalism*, 4.

235. Cheng, *Ornamentalism*, 13.

236. Nora Khan, "Lil Miquela Shows us the Future of Fame," *Garage*, September 7, 2018, https://garage.vice.com/en_us/article/wjkbex/lil-miquela-interview.

237. The podcasters interview writer Mercedes Gonzales-Bazan, who suggests that Miquela's waning relevance is likely due to the fact she is a Gen Z stereotype created by an older Millennial programmer, and that while digital influencers and models became quite popular to suit the purposes of the pandemic, when all sorts of commercial entertainment migrated online, our post-pandemic era of capitalism casts Miquela in a different (dated) light. See Grace Tatter, Ben Brock Johnson, and Emily Jankowski, "RIP Lil Miquela," Podcast, *WBUR*, April 12, 2024, https://www.wbur.org/endlessthread/2024/04/12/lil-miquela.

238. Donna Haraway, "A Cyborg Manifesto: Science, Technology and Socialist-Feminism in the Late Twentieth Century," *Simians, Cyborgs and Women: The Reinvention of Nature* (Routledge, 1991), 149–181, 151.

239. "Go Borderless: MSI QD-OLED Monitors Take You Beyond the Limits," MSI Gaming, promotional video, May 2024, https://www.youtube.com/watch?v=q9fezzSb_7g.

240. See Richard Hetherington and Rachel McRae, "Make-Believing Animated Films Featuring Digital Humans: A Qualitative Inquiry Using Online Sources," *Animation: An Interdisciplinary Journal* 12, no. 2 (2017): 156–173.

241. It is worth noting that at the time of this book's publication, just five years after the music video for "Hard Feelings" was released, AI animation generators have become extremely ubiquitous. Today, the question of whether a character has been animated with mocap, therefore bearing the "trace" of a real human moving through time and space, does not really matter. In a world of deep fakes and synthetic gesture, Lil Miquela's "realness" can be seen, more than ever, as a moot point.

242. Cheng, *Ornamentalism*, 143.

243. Warren-Crow, *Girlhood and the Plastic Image*, xiv.

244. Warren-Crow, *Girlhood and the Plastic Image*, 42.

245. Warren-Crow, *Girlhood and the Plastic Image*, 42.

Chapter 3

246. Moombahton is an electronic dance music genre derived from house music and reggaeton. "Evolution of Moombahton," Recording Arts, January 29, 2020, https://recordingarts.com/record/evolution-of-house-music/moombahton/.

247. Susanne K. Langer, "The Dynamic Image," in *Feeling and Form: A Theory of Art* (Charles Scribner's Sons, 1953), 78–79.

248. Langer, "The Dynamic Image," 78–79.

249. Langer, "The Dynamic Image," 78–79 (emphasis mine).

250. Deborah Levitt, *The Animatic Apparatus: Animation, Vitality, and the Futures of the Image* (Zero Books, 2018), 118, 128.

251. Levitt, *The Animatic Apparatus*, 128.

252. Sergei Eisenstein, *Eisenstein on Disney* (Seagull Books, 1986), 6; Sergei Eisenstein, *Eisenstein on Disney*, ed. Jay Leyda (Methuen, 1988), 27.

253. Quoted in Maureen Furniss, *Art in Motion: Animation Aesthetics* (John Libbey, 1998), 5.

254. I have reached out to Method Studios multiple times to interview someone from their team about the creation of this video in the ten years since it was released. They have not responded, and there is very little information to be found about how the video was made. I cannot therefore verify that mocap was used here, but a tweet by Major Lazer from 2016 reading "MOTION CAPTURE BY @METHOD STUDIOS" confirms the use of mocap (https://x.com/majorlazer/status/743488264716197888) and commenters on Reddit speculate that the video could have been made with mocap and/or Adobe Mixamo, with rendering using Eevee (https://www.reddit.com/r/blender/comments/jdecw3/about_5_years_ago_i_was_shocked_by_major_lazers/).

255. Levitt, *The Animatic Apparatus*, 1.

256. Alain Badiou, *Handbook of Inaesthetics*, trans. Alberto Toscano (Stanford University Press, 2004), 57.

257. Badiou, *Handbook of Inaesthetics*, 58.

258. Carolyn Lanchner, *Sophie Taeuber-Arp*. Museum of Modern Art, 1981, 11.

259. Mark Franko, *Danced Abstraction: Rudolf con Laban. In Inventing Abstraction, 1910–1925: How a Radical Idea Changed Modern Art*, ed. Leah Dickerman (The Museum of Modern Art, 2012), 293.

260. Flora L. Brandl, "On a Curious Chance Resemblance: Rudolf von Laban's Kinetography and the Geometric Abstractions of Sophie Taeuber-Arp," *Arts* 9, no. 1 (2020): 15.

261. Moritz Wedell, "Notation," in *Routledge Handbook of Interdisciplinary Research Methods*, 1st edition, ed. Celia Lury et al. (Routledge, 2018), 117.

262. Wedell, "Notation," 117.

263. Brandl, "Geometric Abstractions of Sophie Taeuber-Arp," 8.

264. Brandl, "Geometric Abstractions of Sophie Taeuber-Arp," 16.

265. Ryan Pierson, *Figure and Force in Animation Aesthetics* (Oxford University Press, 2020), 116.

266. Pierson, *Figure and Force*, 121.

267. Pierson, *Figure and Force*, 116.

268. Panpan Yang, "Rotoscoping Body: Secret Dancers, Animated Realism and Temporal Critique," *Spectator* 36, no. 1 (2016): 33–42.

269. Yang, "Secret Dancers," 34.

270. Pierson, *Figure and Force*, 121.

271. See Jordan Schonig, *The Shape of Motion: Cinema and the Aesthetics of Movement* (Oxford University Press, 2021).

272. Another way to think of this might be through Roland Barthes's concept of "the grain of the voice." In his essay of the same title, Barthes writes that the grain is the "materiality of the body," the "body in the voice as it sings, the hand as it writes, the limb as it performs." Calloway's motion signature is not just about dance moves like his proto version of the moonwalk; it is also about the particular, *material*, way *his* body moves through space, and the lingering evidence of that material body in his extracted gesture. See Roland Barthes, "The Grain of the Voice," in *Image-Music-Text*, trans. Stephen Heath (Hill & Wang, 1978), 182, 188.

273. Tanine Allison, "Blackface, *Happy Feet*: The Politics of Race in Motion Capture and Animation," in *Special Effects: New Histories/Theories/Contexts* eds. Dan North, Bob Rehak, and Michael S. Duffy (BFI/Palgrave, 2015), 114–126, 119.

274. "Rotoshopping" is an updated process of rotoscoping using computer software. See Allison, The Politics of Race in Motion Capture and Animation," 114–126, 119.

275. Pierson, *Figure and Force*, 121.

276. Pierson, *Figure and Force*, 123.

277. Pierson, *Figure and Force*, 123.

278. Pierson, *Figure and Force*, 124.

279. Pierson, *Figure and Force*, 124.

280. Susan Kozel, *Closer: Performance, Technologies, Phenomenology* (Leonardo, 2008), 220.

281. Mocap does not just make nonhuman entities more human-like; it can also cause humans to become gesturally estranged from their bodies. For example, Terry Notary, a dancer and gymnast who often provides his movements via mocap to enliven animated characters, explains that when he plays nonhuman characters like "apes, birds, dogs, the Hulk, goblins, [and] aliens," he tries to imagine how the character might want to move, even if the character is something inanimate like "crumpled tinfoil or a feather (Kristyn Brady, "Meet the Motion Capture Star Who Brings Hollywood's Creatures to Life Terry Notary," *Dance Magazine*, 2019, https://www.dancemagazine.com/motion-capture/.)

282. In my own (limited) experience with mocap, I have been struck by how slow and static the experience can be. Placing the markers on the right parts of the dancer's body (and making sure they don't fall off) is crucial, mathematical, and painstaking. Add to that the imperative to stay within the demarcated grid while you move so the camera can read your data points. The experience feels almost antithetical to dance, just from a position of kinetics.

283. See "Voices of VR: #1195: Exploring Non-Normative Avatars with Disabled Dancers in "Figural Bodies" Research Project," *Voices of VR*, April 3, 2023, https://voicesofvr.com/1195-exploring-non-normative-avatars-with-disabled-dancers-in-figural-bodies-research-project/.

284. Allison Muri, "Of Shit and the Soul: Tropes of Cybernetic Disembodiment in Contemporary Culture," *Body & Society* 9, no. 3 (2003): 73–92, 73.

285. Arthur Kroker and Michael A. Weinstein, *Data Trash: The Theory of the Virtual Class* (St. Martin's Press, 1994), 20.

286. Roy Ascott, "Gesamtdatenwerk: Connectivity, Transformation and Transcendence," in *Ars Electronica: Facing the Future. A Survey of Two Decades*, ed. Timothy Druckrey (MIT Press, 1999), 86–89, 86.

287. Michael Heim, *The Metaphysics of Virtual Reality* (Oxford University Press, 1993) 100–101.

288. Susan Bordo, *Unbearable Weight: Feminism, Western Culture and the Body* (University of California Press, 1995), 217, 215.

289. Patricia Waugh, "Writing the Body: Modernism and Postmodernism," in *The Body and the Arts*, ed. Corinne Saunders et al. (Palgrave MacMillan, 2009), 131–147, 138.

290. It should be noted as well that most of the songs performed by the penguins in the movie are sonically classifiable within Black genres of R&B, hip hop, and soul. The audio components of the penguins' identities are therefore already coded Black before we consider the function of tap dance in the film.

291. Allison, "The Politics of Race in Motion Capture and Animation," 114–126, 115. I am grateful to Tanine Allison for her presentation at the 2016 SLSA conference, and her subsequent email correspondence, which introduced me to *Happy Feet* as a salient example of this type of erasure.

292. Allison, "The Politics of Race," 116. See also Joanna Bouldin, "Cadaver of the Real: Animation, Rotoscoping and the Politics of the Body," *Animation Journal* 12 (2004): 23.

293. Pamela Krayenbuhl, *White Screens, Black Dance: Race and Masculinity in the United States at Midcentury* (Oxford University Press, 2025).

294. Gottschild, *Africanist Presence*, 1–2.

295. Gottschild, *Africanist Presence*, 23.

296. T. Brown and B. Copano, *Soul Thieves: The Appropriation and Misrepresentation of African American Popular Culture* (Palgrave MacMillan, 2014), 7.

297. Danielle Goldman, *I Want to Be Ready: Improvised Dance as a Practice of Freedom* (University of Michigan Press, 2010), 131.

298. Goldman, *I Want to be Ready*, 131. For more on abstraction, race and contemporary dance, see Miguel Gutierrez, "Does Abstraction Belong to White People?: Thinking About the Politics of Race in Contemporary Dance," BOMB Magazine, 7 November 2018. https://bombmagazine. org/articles/2018/11/07/miguel-gutierrez-1/.

299. Yet when that blank canvas of the "neutral" digital body is animated, it ceases to be blank; it becomes imbued with a liveliness (or *anima*) whose "affective qualities," Sianne Ngai proposes, often bear "racial connotations." She writes: "the ostensibly positive qualities of liveliness, effusiveness, spontaneity, and zeal become affects harnessed to a disturbing racial epistemology, such that these emotional qualities—all variants of what we might call animatedness—are made to function as bodily, hence self-evident, signs of the raced subject's naturalness or authenticity." Here, Ngai is proposing that *all* forms of affective animatedness carry a semiotics of racialization, regardless of whether the movement was mocapped or hand-drawn, and regardless of whether there is an organic referent body. This is distinct from my argument that the dance labor of Black dancers serves a particularly ensouling purpose in extractive animation methods, but Ngai's observations here are worth considering as well, given the semiotic function of dance as a kind of vitality (via movement) in the animated body. In keeping with exploitative histories of nonwhite labor, we could consider that the vitality Ngai identifies in the form of the zany may be conceived as racialized *in order to* condone or even celebrate its containment and exploitation. See Sianne Ngai, "A Foul Lump Started Making Promises in My Voice: Race, Affect, and the Animated Subject," *American Literature* 74, no. 3 (2002): 572–573.

300. Cunningham collaborated with Kaiser and Eshkar in 1998 and 1999 on the critically acclaimed pieces *Hand-drawn Spaces* and *Biped*, both involving motion capture.

301. Goldman, *I Want to Be Ready*, 120. Goldman's book critiques the "utopian project" of contact improvisation and other dance forms that appeal to freedom, within "1970s postmodern dance" (117).

302. Goldman, *I Want to Be Ready*, 113.

303. Goldman, *I Want to Be Ready*, 122.

304. Goldman, *I Want to Be Ready*, 125.

305. Thanks to Sydney Skybetter, who notes these passing comments by Eshkar in a talk on Ghostcatching. See Skybetter, "Ghost Notation," *Jacobs Pillow Dance Interactive*, November 2018, https://danceinteractive.jacobspillow.org/themes-essays/men-in-dance/ghost-notation/.

306. *Ghostcatching* actively engages with what American critical race theorist Fred Moten calls "fugitivity," a category in which freedom and "unfreedom" co-exist as a result of a refusal to be reduced by objectification. For Moten, Blackness and fugitivity are particularly linked, and the concept is of course bound up in histories of slavery, and the weight of that history for Black Americans in particular as both personal and communal. He writes: "The moment in which you enter into the knowledge of slavery, of yourself as a slave, is the moment you begin to think about freedom" and its "overdetermined" structures (76). This, Moten clarifies, is also the "moment at which you become a fugitive" (76). (See Fred Moten, *Black and Blur* (Duke University Press, 2017), 76). Fugitivity, for Moten, is a mode of resistance or rebellion, "a desire for and a spirit of escape and transgression of the proper and the proposed." Likewise, I see dance *anima* (and more specifically, Jones' dance *anima* in *Ghostcatching*) as a concept that can elucidate not only the dancer's desire but the desire of dance, as a thing or force in itself, to escape and transgress the apparatuses that wish to contain it and make it legible. (See Fred Moten, *The Universal Machine* (Duke University Press, 2018), 131.)

307. Marcia Siegel, *At the Vanishing Point: A Critic Looks at Dance* (Saturday Review Press, 1972), 10.

308. Tiffany Barber, "Ghostcatching and After Ghostcatching, Dances in the Dark," *Dance Research Journal* 47, no.1 (2015): 44–67, 48.

309. Jones qtd. in Goldman, *I Want to be Ready*, 120.

310. Goldman, *I Want to be Ready*, 113.

311. Paul Gilroy, *Against Race: Political Imagining Beyond the Color Line* (Harvard University Press, 2000), 47, 43.

312. This is the scene Pierson describes as "figural performance" (as opposed to "embodied performance") referenced earlier.

313. Douglas Rosenberg, *Screendance: Inscribing the Ephemeral Image* (Oxford University Press, 2012), 54.

314. Rosenberg, *Screendance*, 54.

315. Sianne Ngai, *Ugly Feelings* (Harvard University Press, 2005), 101.

316. Also of note here is Koko the Clown's cartoon sheet-costume, which looks suspiciously like a KKK hood, and then, by strange contrast, the character's minstrelesque lips and eyes. These visual elements have not been analyzed often, but this convergence of of white supremacist imagery and racist caricature on the body of a character powered by the dancing and singing of a charistmatic, talented Black man might be seen as an attempt to contain and control that power (*anima*).

317. This tendency would match the trend of white patrons attending events at Black jazz clubs during the Harlem Renaissance. See Christopher P. Lehman, *The Coloured Cartoon: Black Representation in American Animated Short Films, 1907–1954* (University of Massachusetts Press, 2007) 31.

318. Heather Warren-Crow, "After Ghostcatching," *Screen Bodies* 2, no. 1 (2017): 22–44, 32.

319. Nate Sloan, "Constructing Cab Calloway," *The Journal of Musicology* 35, no. 3 (2019): 370–400, 393–395. Sloan explains that Calloway's white audience "provided [him] with an opportunity to execute a feat of vocal excellence, channeling the uplifting sound of Negro spirituals and establishing his credentials as a standard bearer of New Negro values," but Calloway's slippery identity prevented him from satisfying the desires of both white and Black patrons (398). In responding to this opportunity with humor, light satire, and a refusal to be pigeonholed, "Calloway resisted a monolithic racial identity, forging an anti-essentialist persona that could be mobilized in different ways by different audiences" (398). Calloway's alter-ego in performance therefore "becomes another mask [. . . that can] maximize the singer's reach. Whether embodying the Hi-De-Ho Man or the Harlemaestro, the crooner or the choir singer, Calloway's shifting persona reflects the plasticity of identity" of Harlem in the 1930s.

320. See also Brynn Shiovitz, *Behind the Screen: Tap Dance, Race and Invisibility During Hollywood's Golden Age* (Oxford University Press, 2023). Shiovitz writes about what she calls the "protean" guise—or the strategic appearance of shape-shifting through changes in facial expression, vocal quality, costuming, and so on—within the practice of covert minstrelsy. The protean guise is further accessed via animation technology, where "artists can easily detach one element of a cartoon's body or voice, make it disappear, re-attach it to another part of the body, or even create a completely new form." Shiovitz argues that "such protean transformations allow the racial imaginary to run wild thus creating new stereotypes and upholding old" (*Behind the Screen*, 18).

321. This is also what Austin Lillywhite describes as "an over-mechanized whiteness turning to blackness as a sort of salt of the earth in order to request a reanimating sustenance," or sustaining energy that carries reminders of slavery. See Austin Lillywhite, "Is Posthumanism a Primitivism? Networks, Fetishes, and Race." *Diacritics* 46, no. 3 (2018): 100–119, 111. https://dx.doi.org/10.1353/dia.2018.0018.

322. Ngai, *Ugly Feelings*, 99.

323. From "In the Wake: A Salon in Honor of Christina Sharpe" (Featuring Christina Sharpe, Hazel Carby, Kaiama Glover, Saidiya Hartman, Arthur Jafa, and Alex Weheliye), *Barnard Center for Research on Women*, February 2, 2017. Accessed June 2, 2024. YouTube, https://www.youtube.com/watch?v=DGE9oiZr3VM. See also Tina Marie Campt, "Black Visuality and the Practice of Refusal," *Women & Performance: A Journal of Feminist Theory* 29, no. 1 (2019): 79–87. doi:10.1080/0740770X.2019.1573625.

324. Alondra Nelson, ed. "Introduction: Future Texts," in *Social Text* 20, no. 2 (Summer 2002): Special Issue: "Afrofuturism." 1–15, 1. https://muse.jhu.edu/issue/1883. In her introduction to this special issue on Afrofuturism, Nelson writes that "the founding fiction of the digital age" is the idea "that race (and gender) distinctions would be eliminated with technology" (1). Dance *anima*, which may be extracted but not eliminated, is one of many examples of how embodied identity perseveres (and is capitalized on) in the digital age.

Chapter 4

325. Harald Kleinschmidt, "The Military and Dancing: Changing Norms and Behaviour, 15th to 18th Century," *Ethnologia Europaea* 25, no. 2 (1995), 165.
326. Guibert's *General Essay on Tactics*, Translated and annotated by Jonathan Abel, *History of Warfare*, Vol. 137, Eds. Kelly DeVries, John France, Paul Johnston, Michael S. Neiberg and Frederick Schneid (Brill Books, 2021), 62.
327. A Reddit thread that was posted shortly after the video was released, for example, contains a conversation between two commenters about whether the video has been augmented with CGI-based animation. Commenter *LaVieEstBizarre* argues that at companies like Boston Dynamics, they "have a CGI to real robot pipeline where they turn the CGI into an offline trajectory optimisation problem and follow it online using a Model Predictive Controller." Commenter *robothrowaway2020* responds: "The line gets blurry when you're looking at physics constrained animation, and blurrier when you talk about robots. After all, industrial robots are hand programmed with trajectories and we don't consider that CGI. Animation also uses some techniques you might find in robotics such as inverse kinematics or dynamics. Sometimes, CGI is entirely procedural. In this case what was done was a mixture of different techniques, some familiar to CG animators and some less so. Some of it was procedural. Some was hand animated. Some was a mixture of motion capture and other techniques" (https://www.reddit.com/r/engineering/comments/kmkc47/boston_dynamics_do_you_love_me/). The fact that these videos inaugurated such speculation about how the spectacle was achieved points to the impressive nature of the robots' performance—dance is doing exactly what it is supposed to do in this case.
328. Sydney Skybetter, "Clock, Fall: Choreorobotics and Near Futures of Choreographic Practice," Keynote talk, Harvard University, April 18, 2024, https://www.skybetter.org/clockfall.
329. There is a cinematic history of robots who are characterized as "loveable," including Pixar's WALL-E (2008), C3PO and R2D2 from the original *Star Wars* movies (1977–1983), and the titular character from *The Iron Giant* (1999).
330. Notably, a more recent version of Atlas, released on April 18, 2024, is shown in a video *not dancing* but contorting its body into shapes and positions impossible for a human, with a head that swivels 360 degrees and legs that bend backwards. The result is a nightmarish body with a clearer association to weaponry or threat. The absence of dance in this video may represent a shift towards an acceptance of their machines' weaponized function on Boston Dynamic's part.
331. Actually, to be more accurate, Atlas has a white body and limbs, but its hands, feet, and head are black, so if we understand Atlas to be wearing white clothing, perhaps its body is coded Black after all. Another shiny white robot who "performs Blackness" is Apptronik's humanoid robot, Apollo. At the 2024 South by Southwest Festival, Apollo, who is designed for future space missions, performed a dance "derived from movement training data extracted from YouTube videos by Czech / Nigerian choreographer, Yemi A.D" (Skybetter, "Clock, Fall").
332. Like the stereotype of the "happy darky" from Harriet Beecher Stowe's 1852 novel *Uncle Tom's Cabin*, Atlas is content and subservient (as proven by his song and dance), despite his enslavement.
333. Skybetter, "Clock, Fall," 2024.
334. Skybetter, "Clock, Fall," 2024.
335. Skybetter, "Clock, Fall," 2024.
336. Gottschild, *Digging the Africanist Presence*, 15–16.
337. Gottschild, *Digging the Africanist Presence*, 8–9.
338. Jessica Rajko expands upon the idea of race as "additive" in Jessica Rajko, "Techno-Liberalism's Body: Dance(r) Labour in Computing Research and Race as Always Already Additive," BCS Learning and Development Ltd, *Proceedings of Politics of the Machines—Rogue Research*, 2021, 23–31.
339. Brian Roberts, *Blackface Nation: Race, Reform, and Identity in American Popular Music, 1812–1925* (University of Chicago Press, 2017), 20. For more on vitalist racism, see Jackson Lears, *Rebirth of a Nation: The Making of Modern America, 1877–1920* (Harper Perennial, 2009).
340. Rajko, "Techno-Liberalism's Body," 29.
341. Sydney Skybetter, Personal communication, May 2024.

342. Lepecki, "Choreography as Apparatus of Capture," 86.

343. Giorgio Agamben, *"What Is an Apparatus?" and Other Essays* (Stanford University Press, 2009), 14.

344. It's worth noting that, in an erasure common to dance, Monica Thomas's name was not originally released as choreographer by Boston Dynamics; it was only after dance scholar Jessica Rajko and roboticist Amy LaViers pointed out the omission on Twitter that Thomas's name became attached to the project (Rajko, "Techno-Liberalism's Body").

345. Calvin Hennick, "All Together Now," *Boston Dynamics blog*, June 29, 2021, https://blog.bos tondynamics.com/all-together-now (accessed June 4, 2022).

346. Hennick, "All Together Now."

347. Alessia Minaeva, Chris Grun, and Oleg Pariser, "Dance Biometrics," https://www.f6s.com/ dancebiometrics (accessed July 10, 2022).

348. Minaeva et al., "Dance Biometrics."

349. Dancers are often expected to work for free, without legal contracts or any kind of health or employment insurance. A fitting example of this is American dancer Taja Riley's activism, which exposes the double target of exploitation that are dancers of color. Riley exposed the 2022 Superbowl as a proponent of such behavior when the half-time show organizers asked countless dancers—specified as "African American movers"—to perform in "exchange for exposure," or in other words, for free. In a phone conversation with me, Riley explained that challenging these harmful practices can be uncomfortable because of an ingrained belief that dancers' primary role should be to bring joy to audiences. As Riley puts it, it's hard to ask the question, "how are you going to value me in the form of dollars?" "Taja Riley in Interview with Hilary Bergen," February 7, 2022, Zoom.

350. McCarren, *Dancing Machines*, 17.

351. McCarren, *Dancing Machines*, 9.

352. Cheng, *Ornamentalism*, 4–5. For an in-depth analysis of Baker's persona and performances as they relate to race, the early machine age, and modernism, see also Cheng's *Second Skin: Josephine Baker & The Modern Surface* (Oxford University Press, 2011).

353. Sianne Ngai, *Our Aesthetic Categories: Zany, Cute, Interesting* (Verso Books, 2012), 30.

354. For more on Chaplin and Taylorism, see Owen Hatherley's *The Chaplin Machine* (Pluto Press, 2016), which examines the convergence of Hollywood slapstick, the "scientific management" of Frederick Taylor and Henry Ford, and the Soviet avant-garde.

355. Crucial to note that for Ford, dance was integral to the maintenance of and assimilation to whiteness—and to the protection of, as *Dearborn Independent* author Harvey Rexford writes, "the mental, moral, and physical vigour of the Anglo-Saxon race." Katherine Brucher details the ideological and practical function of contra dance training for Ford, who saw the contra form as an "instrument for social righteousness" that was "racially American" and believed dance training could complement his workers training in physical labor. See Katherine Brucher, "Assembly Lines and Contra Dance Lines: The Ford Motor Company Music Department and Leisure Reform," *Journal of the Society for American Music* 10, no. 4 (2016): 487, https://www. cambridge.org/core/journals/journal-of-the-society-for-american-music/article/assembly-lines-and-contra-dance-lines-the-ford-motor-company-music-department-and-leisure-ref orm/F91300432F272FBC9206CDF18814867D#fn27.

356. McCarren, *Dancing Machines*, 29.

357. Rosenberg, *Screendance*, 37.

358. American theorist Fred Moten writes that Muybridge's work "exhibits a scientism that moves in the direction of an ever-greater accuracy that is itself the effect of an ever-greater deanimation of the body," a "near-pathological deanimation" (73). This quest for scientific accuracy works alongside the stopping of the body—a state of stasis—to further, as Moten calls it, "a certain photographic naturalism that seeks to reflect and to attach itself to a law of development or movement—the mechanics of a more-than-personal history" (73). In other words, Muybridge's studies attempt to standardize and generalize natural "truths" about bodies, irrespective of their histories, personal, and otherwise. Muybridge breaks movement down into its component parts in order to better understand it but, Moten argues, loses emotional, personal, and cultural resonances in the process, viewing the body in motion as merely a machine whose analysis can benefit scientific progress and efficiency of labor. Moten, *Black and Blur*, 73.

359. Wolfgang Ernst, *Chronopoetics: The Temporal Being and Operativity of Technological Media* (Rowman & Littlefield, 2016), 48.

360. Elizabeth Stephens, "Cultures of Hyper-Productivity and the Quantification of Work," *SSN Seminar: Deakin Science and Society Network*, November 17, 2020, YouTube, https://www.youtube.com/watch?v=T89i5HBT0L0.

361. Stephens, "Cultures of Hyper-Productivity."

362. Stephens, "Cultures of Hyper-Productivity."

363. Rick Poyner, "Exposure: Motion Efficiency Study by Frank Gilbreth," *Design Observer*, April 12, 2016, https://designobserver.com/feature/exposure-motion-efficiency-study-by-frank-gilbreth/39272.

364. Poyner, "Exposure: Motion Efficiency."

365. Alain Badiou, "Dance as a Metaphor for Thought," *Handbook of Inaesthetics*, trans. Alberto Toscano (Stanford University Press, 2004), 59.

366. "Spot's on It," Boston Dynamics, YouTube, June 29, 2021, https://www.youtube.com/watch?v=7atZfX85nd4.

367. Hennick, "All Together Now."

368. Darren Wershler notes the importance of imagination in such assemblages that include humans (choreographer, robotics engineer, camera operator, YouTube viewer), but not necessarily as primary agents. As he writes in the afterword to Nick Thurston's book, "the point is not that the mechanism is empty, like some kind of neutral reproducer. The point is that it is a mechanism that already includes a spot for you, . . . whether that spot is in front of it as a player, inside it as the operator, behind it as the spectator being shown its misleading components, [or] from afar as the critic describing and demystifying it by virtue of your criticism" (Darren Wershler, "Afterword," Nick Thurston, *Of the Subcontract: Or Principles of Poetic Right* (Information as Material, 2013), 135).

369. On the Boston Dynamics blog, Monica Thomas describes how choreographing robots holds a series of different challenges from choreographing human dancers. For one, "Spot has twice as many legs as a human dancer," Thomas explains. "When I try to replay the choreography on my own body, my knees bend the wrong way, even if I put myself on all fours," she says. "I have less knowledge about what things even could look like, and so I have a lot more flexibility about what it does look like." (See Hennick, "All Together Now.")

370. Brynn Shiovitz notes that Berkeley selected dancers for his choreographies based on whether they adhered to a rigid standard of white beauty (from the peroxide of their blonde hair to the slenderness of their ankles—body parts often focused on in his use of close-ups), but his fetishization of the female form paled in comparison with Berkeley's obsession with the camera—the true star of his films. See Shiovitz, *Behind the Screen*, 111.

371. Shiovitz, *Behind the Screen*, 11. Here, Shiovitz goes on to argue that Berkeley's use of spectacle in fact distracts from the ways in which his choreographies present women's bodies as commodity objects to be admired and consumed—a strategy she sees as intentional, to quell rising anxieties about "the growing economic and social power of women" in 1930s US (112).

372. Jean Baudrillard, *Simulacra and Simulation*, trans. Sheila Faria Glaser, *The Body, in Theory* (University of Michigan Press, 1994), 97.

373. Baudrillard, *Simulacra and Simulation*, 97.

374. McCarren, *Dancing Machines*, 142.

375. Siegfried Kracauer, *The Mass Ornament: Weimar Essays* (Harvard University Press, 1995), 78.

376. Kracauer, *The Mass Ornament*, 76.

377. See Steve Giles, "Cracking the Cultural Code: Methodological Reflections on Kracauer's 'The Mass Ornament,'" *Radical Philosopy* 99 (January/February 2000), 31–39; Joan Ockman, "Between Ornament and Monument: Siegfried Kracauer and the Architectural Implications of the Mass Ornament," Thesis, Wissenschaftliche Zeitschrift der Bauhaus-Universitat Weimar (2003), 75–91; Leif Tystad, "Cracks in the Ornament: Spectatorial Relationships and Labors of Looking in *Gold Diggers of 1933*," *Film Matters* 12, no. 3 (2021): 129–139; Rachel Walls, "Imperfect Machines: Animation, Dance, Anxiety," 35th Annual Society for Animations Studies Conference: Animating Change, University of New South Wales, Sydney, Australia, (1 July 2024).

378. Shiovitz, *Behind the Screen*, 91. In Shiovitz's full quote, she remarks on the way Berkeley's presentation of orderly bodies articulates to representations of race in the early Code era. She writes: "unlike the wild and 'hot' presentations of Black dancers on the 1930's screen, it was the camera's duty to organize these White bodies into patterns and formations that gave off a sense of order and productivity. Not only was it important for Hollywood to offer stability during

this era, but it was also tactical to place the tight geometry of these White bodies alongside the more unruly actions of these films' differently-raced performers" (91).

379. This is partially inspired by McCarren's description of "the force or energy mobilized in labour power" as *"puissance du travail"* (McCarren, *Dancing Machines*, 17).

380. Canadian Oxford Dictionary.

381. Pasi Valiaho, "Marey's Gun: Apparatuses of Capture and the Operational Image," *Researching Cinema and Media Technologies—Their Development, Use, and Impact.* (Amsterdam University Press, 2014), 169–176, 171.

382. Valiaho, "Marey's Gun," 171.

383. Valiaho, "Marey's Gun," 172–173.

384. Badiou, "Dance as a Metaphor for Thought," 67.

385. Badiou, "Dance as a Metaphor for Thought," 67.

386. Badiou, "Dance as a Metaphor for Thought," 67.

387. Badiou, "Dance as a Metaphor for Thought," 67.

388. Hilary Bergen, "Posthuman Dance: Body Heart and Haptic Intimacy in ORA," *Culture Machine* 17 (2018): Thermal Objects, https://culturemachine.net/vol-17-thermal-objects/.

389. "About the Spot Robot," *Boston Dynamics Support*, https://support.bostondynamics.com/s/article/About-the-Spot-robot.

390. Lev Manovich writes about the shift from optical to digital capture in his work on database as symbolic form in *The Language of New Media*.

391. Badiou, "Dance as a Metaphor for Thought," 59.

392. Badiou, "Dance as a Metaphor for Thought," 59.

393. Erin Brannigan's clever response (in *Performance Philosophy*) to Badiou's framing of dance as an instrument to be used by philosophy has "dance" answer back to Badiou's assertions. See Erin Brannigan, "Talking Back: What Dance Might Make of Badiou's Philosophical Project," *Performance Philosophy* 4, no. 2 (2018): 354–373, 365.

394. Badiou, "Dance as a Metaphor for Thought," 59.

395. Wiliam Hardy McNeill, *Keeping Together in Time: Dance and Drill in Human History* (Harvard University Press: 1995), 4.

396. Harald Kleinschmidt, "The Military and Dancing: Changing Norms and Behaviour, 15th to 18th Century," *Ethnologia Europaea* 25, no. 2 (1995): 163.

397. Kleinschmidt, "The Military and Dancing," 164.

398. Kleinschmidt, "The Military and Dancing," 164.

399. Kleinschmidt, "The Military and Dancing," 165.

400. Kleinschmidt, "The Military and Dancing," 168.

401. James Vincent, "The French Army Is Testing Boston Dynamics' Robot Dog Spot in Combat Scenarios," *The Verge*, April 7, 2021, https://www.theverge.com/2021/4/7/22371590/boston-dynamics-spot-robot-military-exercises-french-army.

402. Vincent, "The French Army Is Testing Boston Dynamics' Robot Dog."

403. David Hambling, "U.S. Marines Test Robot Dog Armed with a Rocket Launcher," *Forbes*, November 1, 2023, https://www.forbes.com/sites/davidhambling/2023/11/01/us-marines-test-robot-dog-armed-with-a-rocket-launcher/?sh=660cb0b76d27.

404. "Israel Military Company Purchases Robot Dogs for Use in Gaza War," *The Middle East Monitor*, December 14, 2023, https://www.middleeastmonitor.com/20231214-israel-milit ary-company-purchases-robot-dogs-for-use-in-gaza-war/.

405. S. Ryan, "The First Robot Genocide: Israel Experimenting with Dystopian Militarized Robot Dogs in Ongoing Extermination Campaign," *The Kansas City Defender*, March 5, 2024, https://kansascitydefender.com/world/ai-genocide-gaza-urgent-call-action-against-tech-tyranny/.

406. Skybetter, "Clock, Fall," 2024. Skybetter also references a Tweet by US Representative Alexandria Ocasio Cortez stating that "robotic surveillance ground drones are [currently] being deployed for testing on low-income communities of color with under-resourced schools" (February 25, 2021), thus illustrating the shameless use of expensive military technology in underfunded areas of the US.

407. Skybetter, "Clock, Fall," 2024. For more on the history of surveillance technologies and anti-blackness, see Simone Browne, *Dark Matters: on the Surveillance of Blackness* (Duke University Press, 2015) and Ruha Benjamin, *Race After Technology: Abolitionist Tools for the New Jim* Code (Wiley, 2019).

408. There are also more recent videos of soldiers and military personnel kicking, pushing, and generally acting as obstacles in the way of the new "Big Dog" model robot, based on earlier Spot prototypes. This abuse is intended as a mode of testing (and proving) the robot's ability to get back on its feet and carry on with the task, regardless of how many times it is pushed over.

409. Alison Reed and Amanda Phillips, "Additive Race: Colorblind discourses of Realism in Performance Capture Technologies," *Digital Creativity* 24, no. 2 (2013): 130–144, 1.

410. Rajko, "Techno-Liberalism Body," 27.

411. Cheng, *Ornamentalism*, 7.

412. Alexander G. Weheliye, "'*Feenin*': Posthuman Voices in Contemporary Black Popular Music," *Social Text* 20, no. 2 (2002): 21–47, 28.

413. Weheliye, *Feenin'*, 28. In *Blackness and Value: Seeing Double* (Cambridge University Press, 2009), Lindon Barret further analyzes this association between Blackness and embodiment through the auditory register. He names the "*signing voice*" as that which represents the "literacy of the white Enlightenment subject"—"full humanity, whiteness and disembodiment"—whereas he writes that the "*singing voice* metonymically enacts blackness, embodiment and subhumanity."

414. See Manning, *Modern Dance, Negro Dance*.

415. Weheliye, *Feenin'*, 28.

416. Saidiya V. Hartman, *Lose Your Mother: A Journey Along the Atlantic Slave Route* (MacMillan, 2007), 6.

Conclusion

417. Lynneth J. Miller, "Divine Punishment or Disease? Medieval and Early Modern Approaches to the 1518 Strasbourg Dancing Plague," *Dance Research* 35, no. 2 (2017): 149–164, 149.

418. John Waller, "A Forgotten Plague: Making Sense of Dancing Media," *The Lancet* 373, no. 9664 (2009): 624–625.

419. Hans Christian Anderson, "The Red Shoes," in *New Fairy Tales*, First Volume (C. A. Reitzel, 1845).

420. *The Red Shoes*, dir. Michael Powell and Emeric Pressburger (Eagle Lion Films, 1948).

421. "The Red Shoes," Studio Album, Kate Bush (Abbey Road, 1993).

422. Liam J. Donaldson, Julie Cavanaugh, and J. Rankin, "The Dancing Plague: A Public Health Conundrum," *Public Health* 111, no. 4 (1997): 201–204.

423. Liam J. Donaldson et al., "A Public Health Conundrum," 201.

424. John Waller, *The Dancing Plague: The Strange, True Story of an Extraordinary Illness* (Source Books, 2009).

425. Michel Foucault, "Panopticism," from *Discipline & Punish: The Birth of the Prison, Race/Ethnicity: Multidisciplinary Global Contexts* 2, no. 1 (2008): 1–12, 1.

426. *New York Times* headlines like "Will Social Distancing Bring Us Back to Our Bodies?," "How We Use Our Bodies to Navigate a Pandemic," and Carina del Valle Schorske's "Dancing Through New York in a Summer of Joy and Grief" show us that thinking about the pandemic through dance is not a new idea, *yet* I cannot help but feel there is a connection to be made between the content of my book and the world historical event during which it was produced: the pandemic forced a shift from individual concerns to those of the (choreographed) group, and highlighted human bodies as fundamentally porous and affecting to one another.

427. Andre Lepecki, "On Choreography," *Performance Research: A Journal of the Performing Arts* 13 (2008): 1–6.

428. Legacy Russell, *Glitch Feminism* (Verso Books, 2020), 56.

429. Wood begins by externalizing subjecthood, putting "self" in the third person in the poem's first line, which also draws from natural images of branches and blooming, suggesting a constant regeneration, and indefatigable return. These verdant growths are juxtaposed with the "glorious machine" of the body, Galoup's body, most likely, which has had "made" and in which "joy clangs free." That body is also produced (is "wholly of") the room, the dance floor, the "generous, generous music." In drawing our attention to Galoup's body as something that is made by assemblage, Wood configures his dance as the product of a collective agency that works on it and compels it to move, rather than as something springing up naturally from

within. She ties minor gestures (Galoup's spasming vein, which Denis's camera lingers on before cutting to the dance floor appears to be dancing to "The Rhythm of the Night" as the song bleeds across both frames) to the more dramatic moves ("the gazing, moving and lunging") that transpires on the dance floor. In Chapter 2, I wrote about Heinrich von Kleist's friend, who described dancing marionettes as ensouled by the force of gravity. In her poem, Wood references pulleys and an animated center, drawing on the imagery of the marionette to evoke a body that holds a bashing force, or *anima*, established equally by "repetition" and "command." In this, Wood's poetic interpretation conjures very much the mood of Denis's film's ending and the ethos of *Dance Anima*.

430. Sigmund Freud, *Civilization and Its Discontents*, trans. James Strachey (Norton, 1961), 12, 15.
431. Tavia Nyong'o, "I Feel Love: Disco and its Discontents," *Criticism* 50, no. 1 (2008): 101–112, 105.
432. The Japanese dance form butoh is one that acknowledges the influence of death in its very philosophy. Damiano Fina's Master's thesis, "Grief, Dance, Eternity: Rethinking Death Through Philosophy," a moving meditation on dancing in the wake of the death of one's mother, cites key practitioners of butoh to prove this, writing: "For Tatsumi Hijikata the butō dance is a dead body desperately holding itself up (Fraleigh & Nakamura, 2006). For Kazuo Ohno, the body in butō is the universe dancing on the border between life and death (Ohno, 2004). For Tatsumi Hijikata, during the dance we shake hands with the dead, who send us encouragement from beyond our bodies" (10). Damiano Fina, "Grief, Dance, Eternity: Rethinking Death Through Philosophy," Master's Thesis, Department of General Psychology and Department of Philosophy, Sociology, Pedagogy and Applied Psychology Master in Death Studies & the End of Life for the Intervention of Support and the Accompanying, University of Padova, 2023.
433. Goldman, *I Want to Be Ready*, 5.
434. Goldman, *I Want to Be Ready*, 3.
435. Jacques Derrida, *Writing and Difference* (University of Chicago Press, 1978), 12.
436. Derrida, *Writing and Difference*, 12.
437. Damiano Fina, "Grief, Dance, Eternity," 13. Fina cites Italian philosopher Emanuele Severino here, on death as a navigation between being and nothingness.
438. Thomas DeFrantz and Philipa Rothfield, eds., *Choreography and Corporeality: Relay in Motion* (Palgrave MacMillan, 2016), 213.
439. DeFrantz and Rothfield, *Choreography and Corporeality*, 217.

Index